I0820898

THE ROCK & ROLL HALL OF FAME

ALSO BY CRAIG J. INCIARDI

Play It Loud: Instruments of Rock and Roll (coauthor)
The Metropolitan Museum of Art, New York

THE ROCK & ROLL HALL OF FAME

THE OUTRAGEOUS, DEFINITIVE, AND UNTOLD HISTORY

CRAIG J. INCIARDI

DIVERSION
BOOKS

Diversion Books
A division of Diversion Publishing Corp.
www.diversionbooks.com

For more information, email info@diversionbooks.com.

Hardcover ISBN: 979-8-89515-048-1
e-ISBN: 979-8-89515-049-8
First Diversion Books Edition: September 2025

Cover design by Jonathan Sainsbury / 6x9 Design
Interior design by Neuwirth & Associates, Inc.
Printed in the United States of America

1 3 5 7 9 10 8 6 4 2

For Joan, our daughters, Alessandra and Anastasia,
and my mother, Anne

CONTENTS

Hey hey, my my
Rock and roll can never die
—NEIL YOUNG

CHAPTER ONE

THE PRINCE OF DARKNESS

Ozzy Osbourne had been on my radar for a couple of years. Black Sabbath were pioneers of heavy metal, forming in 1968—in fact, they were largely responsible for creating the heavy metal genre. Ozzy's howling voice along with the band's doomsday riffs and catchy songwriting made Sabbath one of the most influential bands in rock.

It was June 1996, and as the Rock & Roll Hall of Fame's curator, I had methodically called Ozzy's office in Los Angeles twice a year to persuade him to meet and discuss representing his life and music at the museum. Making inroads with artists has always required a great deal of persistence. It's a balancing act: The trick is to be persistent but not annoying. No easy feat, but my calendar had been reminding me to call Ozzy's people two weeks after New Year's Day and then again in the summertime.

So I checked in again with his Los Angeles assistant—who, after many years, had grown to recognize my nasal voice on the other end of the line. By this point, we had a nice, casual rapport.

To my surprise, Ozzy's office called back to say that Ozzy and his wife, Sharon, would be happy to receive me at their home in the English countryside. I typically made two trips to England each year—parachuting into a region and packing in a bunch of meetings over a few days. During these semiannual sweeps, I crisscrossed the country, connecting with artists, families, record company execs, and collectors.

I built this semiannual trip around my meeting with Ozzy and was able to get a lot of work done in London and the surrounding area. It was just more than a year after the Hall of Fame's opening, and there was still a mad rush to nail down as many collections as possible. I met with Led Zeppelin's infamous manager, Peter Grant; visited with the family of pianist Ian Stewart, a founding member of the Rolling Stones; and traveled to acquire the giant photo backdrop from the Stones' 1969 Hyde Park memorial concert for Brian Jones.

Over the years, I spent hundreds of hours in London's iconic black cabs, going to meetings and hauling instruments and other artifacts to our shippers in Hackney (who also worked for the British Royal Family). It was one long, glorious Easter egg hunt.

Sharon sent for a chauffeur-driven Rolls-Royce to pick me up from my hotel in Mayfair and take me to the Osbournes' residence in Buckinghamshire, about twenty miles outside of London. The Osbournes lived in the so-called gin-and-Jag belt, which was chock-full of bucolic towns and enormous estates that provided celebrities and the aristocracy with a great deal of privacy. As the Rolls approached the house, we passed through an imposing gatehouse, and I could see a large estate at the end of a long, tree-lined driveway. It was an enormous redbrick mansion complete with two Dutch-style gabled attics—a Grade II-listed property called Welders House built in 1899. The building and its accompanying tennis courts aptly summed up the archetype of the English gentleman rock star.

Welders House had been a "lunatic asylum" and later (after a proper name change) served as a mental hospital—a "Home of Rest"—for nurses who had suffered post-traumatic stress during World War I. Knowing Ozzy's reputation, it wasn't ironic that he was living in this house. Naturally, I was aware of the legendary incident when Ozzy bit the heads off two live doves at a record label meeting in the early 1980s. (Several people at that meeting screamed, vomited, and ran out of the room.) That was followed by the even more grisly episode at a Des Moines concert, when Ozzy unknowingly bit the head off a live bat onstage. What nice mental images to have as my car rolled up the driveway.

As I stepped out of the car, I saw a figure in the courtyard dressed in all black—

And holding a rifle.

It was John Michael "Ozzy" Osbourne, the Prince of Darkness himself. He turned toward me with the most marvelous, shit-eating grin; but as it turns out, the weapon he was holding was just a BB gun. Ozzy was pretending to shoot birds to try to get a rise out of me. "Good fucking morning," he said warmly. "How ah yah?" Ozzy led me into the house. Sharon was standing at the door and couldn't have been more charming. She had been managing Ozzy for years—and saving him from ruin—and would soon become a famous television celebrity. She had met Ozzy through her father, Don Arden, who had managed Black Sabbath, Small Faces, Electric Light Orchestra, and other acts.

They gave me a tour of the house—a magnificent place with many large rooms for entertaining. The dining room was decorated with nearly two dozen gold records on the walls. In front of me was the high school dropout from Birmingham who grew up in poverty, worked at a slaughterhouse and a mortuary, and went to jail; now, he owned one of the most exquisite private residences in England. That's one of the beauties of rock 'n' roll: A true rebel living in a mansion who made the jump in one generation. Not the typical English way to do things. Ozzy had tattoos decades before it was mainstream, and when he met Queen Elizabeth, he did his best to be respectable. "When I went up to the Queen,

I tried to keep my hand in my pocket," he recalled. "I was afraid she would faint when she saw the tattoo on my hand [that spelled out O-Z-Z-Y on his fingers]. She said, 'I understand you're quite the wild one.'"

On the grand staircase, I met their daughter Kelly and son Jack, who were young children at the time. We sat down in one of their beautifully furnished drawing rooms, and I was offered tea. Very proper and all. There were large bay windows that were swung wide open and overlooked formal grounds, flower gardens, and rolling lawns. The main features of the grounds were a magnificent rose garden and a replica of the famous Bethesda Fountain in New York City's Central Park.

Butterflies flew into the room from outside.

We spoke about the Rock & Roll Hall of Fame, which had opened the previous year. I told them I wanted to document and preserve Ozzy's important legacy, and Ozzy told me he had many interesting objects that could be exhibited. He removed the cross he was wearing around his neck and handed it to me. "My father made this cross," he said proudly. "He was a toolmaker." It was beautifully crafted, and Ozzy explained that his dad had also made crosses for the other members of Black Sabbath. "They were meant to protect us when we were out in the world." I explained that we were collecting for a heavy metal exhibit that would include objects from many of the most important metal artists: Metallica, Iron Maiden, Judas Priest, and others.

"I recently met with Delores Rhoads"—the mother of the deceased guitarist Randy Rhoads—I informed Ozzy. "She is loaning us Randy's Flying V"—an iconic Gibson electric guitar decorated with polka dots. Rhoads was Ozzy's close friend and the lead guitarist in his hugely successful post-Sabbath band. He died in a plane crash in 1982 when the pilot recklessly swooped down toward the band's tour bus, which was transporting Ozzy, Sharon, and the rest of the band.

The incident was certainly one of the most bizarre and tragic misadventures in rock history, one I distinctly remember hearing about when I was in high school. I thought mentioning Randy Rhodes would have impressed Ozzy.

I was clearly mistaken.

As soon as the words came out of my mouth, his mood changed. Even though Rhoads had died fifteen years earlier, just my mention of his name deeply upset Ozzy. I tried to steer the subject back to the Hall of Fame, but Ozzy was getting more and more upset. He began crying. And while his Birmingham accent was difficult enough for a Yank like me to decipher, it wasn't hard to understand when he shouted, "I miss him so much!"

I had stepped on a land mine.

Sharon tried to calm Ozzy down. I sat there frozen. Suddenly, Ozzy jumped up from the sofa and made a running leap out of those giant windows, landing in the garden next to a four-wheeled ATV—clearly stationed there for a quick escape. I looked down and saw Ozzy rev up the engine and then tear furiously through the gardens, disappearing into the distance. Meeting adjourned.

On the way back to London, I couldn't stop thinking about this crazy episode, seemingly ripped straight from the script of *This Is Spinal Tap*. Ultimately, though, it was no laughing matter: In 2003, Ozzy almost died after he crashed his Yamaha Banshee 350 ATV on the grounds at Welders House. He cracked a vertebra in his neck, broke eight ribs, and burst several blood vessels. He underwent emergency surgery at a nearby hospital and, thankfully, recovered. A few years later, Ozzy auctioned off all his motorcycles and four-wheelers. You just can't make this shit up.

I've been told many times in my career that I had the ultimate dream job. I wouldn't disagree. For more than thirty years, I was paid to travel the world to hang out with rock stars—in their lavish homes, recording studios, trashed hotel rooms, Rolls-Royces and sports cars, and backstage while crowds clapped and stomped their feet. This job afforded me access to rock's most iconic artists—musicians who undeniably changed history and culture. My gig? I was a founding curator of the Rock & Roll Hall of Fame, and it was my job to scavenge through attics, warehouses, and drafty barns, rescuing treasures that might otherwise be sold, tossed in a landfill, or, in some cases, eaten by rats.

It was three whirlwind decades of meeting extraordinary people and soaking up the very essence of rock 'n' roll. I still pinch myself that I made a successful career of it all. Being in the catbird seat for the creation of a national treasure was a privilege and a calling; I had the opportunity to uncover and preserve rock's important history, and to give the art form and its creators the long overdue respect they craved and deserved. Along the way, I collected stories, lots and lots of stories. And while there are a few things that, for various reasons, I can't tell you—buckle up!

CHAPTER TWO

THE SULTAN AND HIS GANG

I began working at the Rock & Roll Hall of Fame in 1991, but the organization had been around for several years before I joined the team. The Rock Hall's creation unfolded with enough jaunty plot twists for a Hollywood screenplay. It happened on a whim, completely by chance, with just the right confluence of events and people—much like rock 'n' roll itself. "Inadvertence, accident, happenstance, and serendipity." That's how the Rock & Roll Hall of Fame's cofounder Jann Wenner described the combined forces that brought the institution into existence.

Remove a key component and you get something completely different.

It all began in 1983 when Black Tie Network producer Bruce Brandwen conceived of a pay-per-view television program—called *The Rock & Roll Hall of Fame*—that would include an awards ceremony and performances. The following year, he hired Bob Dylan's big-time attorney David Braun, who had deep contacts in the music business and was game to help make something happen. Brandwen and Braun walked into legendary Atlantic Records music mogul Ahmet Ertegun's office at Seventy-Five Rockefeller Plaza with an ace in the hole: A shrewd twenty-six-year-old woman named Suzan Evans, who was working on the new enterprise with them.

"I was hired in the spring of 1983 as Executive Director," said Evans. "But in order for his award show to work, [Brandwen] needed to form a legitimate Hall of Fame."

Before working with Brandwen, Evans had spent her first eighteen months after law school unhappily working as a bankruptcy litigator at a well-known boutique firm in New York. She was contemplating taking a leave of absence to consider her options. At that time, Evans recalled, a friend of hers who was an entertainment attorney representing Black Tie Network asked "if I would consider working for one of her clients who needed someone to establish a 'Rock and Roll Hall of Fame organization' so that he could produce a television show around it." The idea intrigued Evans, who had spent time in Los Angeles as a journalism student working at *Soap Opera Magazine* and rubbing shoulders with actors like Robin Williams, Billy Crystal, and Richard Lewis. Evans left the law practice to work for Black Tie Network at the company's office in an old Manhattan firehouse on Twenty-Eighth Street.

Brandwen had the expertise necessary to produce a television show, but he needed someone like Ertegun to get the rock stars to show up and give the event some authenticity. It wasn't easy at first—Ertegun had initially declined to participate.

Though Ertegun was still trying to decide whether he wanted to be involved at all, and if so, in what capacity, he and Evans met several times weekly over the course of a month to discuss ideas for the Hall of Fame. They developed an excellent rapport, which turned out to be fortuitous.

"I was new to the music industry and didn't know many people," Evans said.

That changed quickly.

"I was pretty persistent, and he finally agreed to be chairman and to take the leadership role in forming the hall."

As soon as Ertegun agreed to become chairman that summer of 1983, he moved Evans into the headquarters of Atlantic Records, just two doors down the hall from his office, and the two strategized about who should be invited to join the board of directors and the nominating committee. "We wanted influential leaders in the music industry and hoped to have a board composed of the heads of all the major labels, top executives, attorneys—and those who would today be called 'influencers,'" Evans explained.

Even before Ertegun's involvement, the nominating committee was taking shape during meetings that spring at the firehouse. It included the legendary record producer John Hammond—who signed Bob Dylan, Pete Seeger, Aretha Franklin, Bruce Springsteen, and Leonard Cohen—popular radio show host and DJ Norm N. Nite, and artist Lesley Gore, among others. "Gore became involved with the project at the request of her cousin, who worked at Black Tie," recalled Evans. "She lent her name at the very beginning, before I came aboard, so her name was listed with mine on the incorporation documents."

It bothered Ertegun that while he would be donating his time and energy to this project, a television producer would be reaping the rewards as a business venture. That soon changed. "When he agreed to be chairman, it was with the understanding that the organization must be run as a nonprofit—and that it not be televised—in order to earn the respect of the artists," said Evans.

At the 2005 induction ceremony, Ertegun recalled in his opening remarks, "It's been twenty-five years since Suzan Evans walked into my office with a group of people asking me to form the Rock & Roll Hall of Fame. I chased them out of my office, but I eventually relented. I relented when I thought of the tremendous pleasure I've had listening to the various kinds of music subsumed under the general heading of rock 'n' roll and of the many great musicians and singers that performed it and the fabulous people who inspired it."

Ahmet's position as founder and chairman of the Hall of Fame was a role that could have been conceived by Hollywood's Central Casting. Born in Turkey into a privileged family during the last days of the Ottoman Empire, class, gentility, and impeccable style seemed to be almost a birthright. Ertegun spent his teen years in Washington, DC, living in the Turkish embassy, where his father was the ambassador to the United States. Later, with a chauffeured limousine, he and his brother Nesuhi embedded themselves in the 1940s jazz community, hosting concerts and amassing an enormous record collection.

Ertegun cofounded Atlantic in 1947 with a $10,000 loan from a Turkish dentist, and he was there at the dawn of rock 'n' roll working closely with on-the-rise artists like LaVern Baker, Ray Charles, Professor Longhair, Ruth Brown, Big Joe Turner—and later with juggernauts like Cream, the Rolling Stones, and Led Zeppelin.

As a record executive, Ertegun was an anomaly. Many music men came from working class backgrounds and had thick Brooklyn accents. Ertegun, on the other hand, spoke six languages, and his friends included Mick Jagger, Eric Clapton, Henry Kissinger, Oscar de la Renta, and Jackie Onassis. Dapper and wickedly irreverent, he was always out late—but always arrived at the office the next day looking fresh in a crisp shirt and bespoke Savile Row suit.

As it turns out, Ertegun was very fortunate to have been approached first about the Hall of Fame—and to have instantly bonded with Suzan Evans. David Braun could have easily connected Brandwen and Evans with someone else—someone such as Clive Davis, who would have most certainly created something far more commercial and less oriented to the roots of rock 'n' roll. Or Braun could have done nothing at all. "There were a lot of organizations that started in the hopes of honoring artists," said Evans, "and they didn't go anywhere." There was, of course, no guarantee of success, but Ertegun's participation and leadership encouraged participation from the entire industry. He had a magic touch.

Ertegun wanted a prestigious board composed of influential leaders in the music industry. He gave Evans a list of suggestions, and then she would meet with candidates, giving presentations of her and Ertegun's vision. Ertegun's participation spoke volumes. "Of course, because of Ahmet's involvement, everyone wanted to be a part of it," said Evans.

Label heads were a high priority for Ertegun; he needed the music industry's buy-in from the outset. "One of Ahmet's first ideas was to enlist Seymour Stein, then the President of Sire Records," Evans remembered. The mercurial Stein, who started working at *Billboard* as a teenager, was already renowned in the music business for having signed Talking Heads, the Pretenders, Depeche Mode, the Ramones, and Madonna.

"Ahmet said, 'We need to have that kid who runs Sire Records,'" Evans recalled. "I walked into Seymour's office, and there was Madonna on the phone, sitting at somebody's desk, wearing her black bra and red lipstick." This is 1983. "I saw the quote 'kid' Seymour sitting behind his desk—at that time, he was probably forty-one years old. To Ahmet, who was sixty, he *was* a kid." Stein, who was in awe of Ertegun, immediately signed on.

Initially, Ertegun thought he should invite Jann Wenner, the editor and publisher of *Rolling Stone*, to serve on the nominating committee, but then decided he should include him on the board as well. "That was a stroke of genius because Jann was such an energetic and brilliant force," said Evans. "He was instrumental in the Hall of Fame's success."

Evans also wanted a successful and highly respected music attorney on the board since they were good conduits to artists and labels and great networkers in general. "David Braun told me there were two choices, and then described the personalities of the top two music attorneys in New York," said Evans. "When he described one as an affable, out-going, aggressive—yet well-liked—extrovert who knows everyone and who could get anyone to take his phone calls, I said, 'He's the one I want.' His name? Allen Grubman"—none other than the legendary music-business dealmaker.

On April 30, 1983, the Rock and Roll Hall of Fame Foundation was officially formed. Six people—Ertegun, Wenner, Stein, Evans, Grubman, and Ertegun's long-time assistant and vice president of Atlantic Records, Noreen Woods—were the initial core group, meeting often to brainstorm and develop goals and guidelines for the Hall of Fame. Ertegun organized a lunch at Pearl's Chinese Restaurant in Midtown as an introductory meeting—the first time everyone sat in a room together to hear his concept and ideas for the hall. "Those early meetings were fun—we laughed so much as our camaraderie developed that Ahmet used to compare us to the *Saturday Night Live* cast," recalled Evans. In between all of the jokes and guffaws, the group crafted a well-thought-out plan with no precedent. "We managed to put together a mandate and rules flexible enough to sustain over all these years."

As they started to organize the first few induction ceremonies, the core board grew to include Elektra Records' Bob Krasnow, attorney Ben Needell (who was a voice of reason and common sense), Bruce Springsteen's manager and producer Jon Landau, and, as more time passed, basically the entire leadership of the music industry. "It was one of the first times in the history of the industry when all of these competitors worked together on a labor of love," Evans recalled. (One of the only other industry-wide efforts before the Rock Hall was the T.J. Martell Foundation, but that was largely a fundraising effort for leukemia and, later, AIDS research.) The Hall of Fame was truly a collaborative endeavor.

Even though the team worked well together, they were certainly not all friends. Everyone had a big ego, everyone was wealthy, and there was always competition when signing new artists. When Atlantic and Elektra were courting Metallica, Bob told band members Lars Ulrich and James Hetfield that Atlantic was a piece of shit. Both labels were under Steve Ross's ownership, and they weren't allowed to compete against each other. Krasnow assumed that he would be fired for badmouthing Ertegun, so he called Steve Ross. According to Krasnow, Ross said, "I'm not getting involved." Krasnow signed Metallica.

"Ahmet agreed that the Rock & Roll Hall of Fame was long overdue," said Evans. He also felt passionately that it was essential to recognize the contributions of rock's forefathers: country, gospel, R&B, and the blues. Ertegun also strongly believed that the Hall of Fame needed to be done as a true not-for-profit, so that the artists would respect it as a legitimate and worthy organization. His intuition proved to be correct.

Ertegun assembled the board from his many friendships and business relationships, some of which went back to the 1950s, and these record producers, managers, agents, and label heads all gave the nascent organization much-needed legitimacy "for the purposes of recognizing the artists, composers, and producers who were responsible for making this music the most popular of all time—not only in America, the land of its birth, but all over the world," Ertegun said. (The non-profit Rock and Roll Hall of Fame Foundation had already signed an agreement with Bruce Brandwen's Black Tie Network to deliver a television show within five years.)

Ertegun added influential historians and musicologists with expertise representing all genres of rock 'n' roll to the nominating committee. The original committee included: Ertegun himself, Wenner, Stein, Bob Krasnow, journalist Robert Hilburn, *Rolling Stone* writer Kurt Loder, Ertegun's former Atlantic Records partner Jerry Wexler, Bob Porter, John Hammond, disc jockey and author Norm M. Nite, Atlantic artist Nile Rodgers, and Ertegun's brother, Nesuhi. While the nominating committee members had a deep knowledge of music and had witnessed history up close, it could also be described as an echo chamber of like-minded people—and they were all men.

Jerry Wexler—a legend in the music business best-known for producing everyone from Aretha Franklin and Ray Charles to Dire Straits—called Suzan Evans the day before the first nominating committee meeting at the office of Atlantic Records. "Although he had agreed to serve on the committee, he told me that he wasn't sure he could bring himself to attend the meeting at Atlantic, explaining that he hadn't spoken to Ertegun in many years since they split up, and wasn't sure he would feel comfortable walking into Atlantic's offices again," said Evans. "It was a long conversation, and I kept reassuring him that he would feel very welcomed and comfortable—and that because he was so highly respected in the industry, it was crucial to have his input and participation." He finally agreed to attend. The next day, as soon as Jerry entered the boardroom, Ertegun gave him a big hug. "Jerry's apprehension just vanished," said Evans. Wexler thought it was an exciting meeting, and he became an influential and active member of the nominating committee for many years.

The committee made a slate of forty-one nominees, which was presented to the Rock Hall's brand-new voting committee, comprising two hundred music historians, journalists, and industry insiders. Each of the artists in the inaugural class had to have released their first recording no later than 1960.

Jann Wenner said, "The first meetings about who would be the first ten inductees had been filled with reminiscences and stories of how our lives had been blessed and shaped by them—making those decisions was an act of love as much as scholarship. Who were truly the founding fathers? Which early executives were significant? We chose Sam Phillips, who owned Sun Records, and Alan Freed, the DJ who coined the phrase *rock 'n' roll*, loved it, played it, and brought it to the world."

Meanwhile, Ertegun had meetings and informal visits every day with both influential artists and—as we'll soon see—politicians. "He would bring many of them down the hall to my office to introduce me," recalled Evans. "And he often joked, 'Maybe Suzan will induct you one day!' I remember Mick Jagger responding in a theatrical voice, 'Maybe I can be induced!'"

There was a flood of creative juices flowing in those days amid Atlantic's very talented A&R department. As someone without a music background, Evans learned and absorbed a lot from Ahmet, who would allow her to sit in his office as he listened to artists' tapes at deafening volumes, assessing the quality of the recordings.

Very soon, though, Wenner stepped up and became a driving force to propel the Hall of Fame forward. He and Ertegun grandly reinvented the concept: Instead of a mere one-off TV special, they envisioned a museum in a small townhouse, a library, and an archive, and a lavish annual induction ceremony to properly honor the artists and raise money for this museum they envisioned, as well as for an endowment. "We thought that we would probably buy a brownstone somewhere in Manhattan and have a Hall of Fame with small exhibits and artifacts," said Evans.

They understood that the musicians they were setting out to honor had created an extraordinary art form that changed culture and history and broke down barriers, and they should be given the respect and accolades they deserved. "In many cases, the artists who planted the seeds of rock 'n' roll have received little recognition for their efforts," said Ertegun.

But while Wenner was eager to take the lead, he was mindful of Ahmet, whom he worshipped. Wenner was hitting his stride in his forties, and *Rolling Stone* was reaching new peaks. The publication had been part of the cultural zeitgeist since the late 1960s and had been gaining more cultural currency with each passing year. Wenner had a brand-new Gulfstream jet to whisk him around to meetings while Ertegun had the finesse and the deft touch to bring people on board, and the two of them—through smarts and sheer force of personality—made a great team with overlapping skill sets. Their love for rock 'n' roll was palpable, and they were confident that all of their sweat equity would soon pay off.

While the team was ramping up for the first induction ceremony, New York oldies disc jockey Norm N. Nite approached Ertegun with an outrageous idea: to build the Rock Hall's museum in Cleveland. Yes, *Cleveland*. Nite, who had cut his radio teeth in the city, brought a contingent—and had $25 million ready from backers in Ohio. "We were blown away," said Evans. "We weren't expecting much, but the mayor of Cleveland, the governor of Ohio, and a well-known US congresswoman participated; their presentation was quite impressive. Noreen Woods passed me a note at the meeting that read, 'Pack your bags. I think you're moving to Cleveland!'"

"We said, you know what? This is really interesting that a major city would be interested in raising money to build a Hall of Fame," said Evans.

Then things went sideways.

Stakeholders in Cleveland were hoping to lock up a deal and build the museum without any competition. It would be a clandestine operation, right under the noses of mayors and governors from across the country.

But then word traveled fast. The Hall of Fame announced the first induction ceremony, and the press release stated that they were in talks with Cleveland to build a museum. Radio coverage and petitions followed, and when the news landed on the desks of politicians in other cities, Ertegun's phone started ringing off the hook as he fielded offers from coast to coast—all of it a complete and utter surprise to everyone involved. "The board's opinion was split at first on location," recalled Evans.

Ahmet and his gang got cracking. In addition to Cleveland, according to Wenner, "We began visiting cities that had expressed interest in having a Hall of Fame: Philadelphia, Chicago, Memphis.... New York had shown almost no interest; they had more than enough museums, and the city was emerging from massive debt. The concept of a museum was barely on the radar." Wenner preferred Philadelphia. "They offered us a Greek-columned building on the University of Pennsylvania's campus," he said.

On October 4, 1985, Wenner, Grubman, Evans, Stein, Ben Needell, and others from the Hall of Fame's New York delegation boarded a chartered jet to Cleveland, where Mayor George Voinovich was waiting for them on the tarmac. At a red-carpet press conference, he and Ertegun spoke to a gaggle of journalists. Ertegun was presented with a key to the city and a petition signed by more than 750,000 people who wanted the Hall of Fame built in Cleveland.

Cleveland—reviled at the time as the "Mistake on the Lake" (an unfair nickname, to be sure, but still)—was a bitter pill for the board to swallow, though they recognized it as the most sensible and pragmatic choice. There was a bunch of money already on the table. "No one on the board really wanted to be in Cleveland, once a dynamic big city—now best known for the Cuyahoga River catching on fire from its industrial waste," said Wenner.

They had a bird in hand, and after Wenner and Ertegun concurred it was the best move, Stein, Grubman, and the others agreed. "The city obviously wanted us and offered us $25 million to build it," said Wenner. The offer was quickly increased to $35 million. "Ahmet told us at the time he thought it would in the end cost $100 million, which it did."

While groundbreaking on the construction of the Rock & Roll Hall of Fame was still years away, on Thursday, January 23, 1986, New York City's Waldorf Astoria was electric as 1,200 artists, their families, music industry insiders, and other guests arrived for the first-ever induction ceremony. Ertegun had envisioned an elegant affair. "Ahmet thought that the artists would really enjoy having it black-tie so it would reflect the specialness of the evening," said Evans. The ceremony was held in the hotel's gilded ballroom, which, in the past, had hosted Prince Rainier III of Monaco and Grace Kelly's engagement party, an event for Queen Elizabeth II, and a birthday gala for President Kennedy. "I thought I'd seen everything, but now we've got rock 'n' roll at the Waldorf," said Quincy Jones.

Though it was not a given that they would show up, every one of the living artists from the inaugural class were in attendance—Fats Domino, Ray Charles, Chuck Berry, James Brown, Jerry Lee Lewis, and the Everly Brothers. The one exception was Little Richard, who was recovering from injuries sustained in a car accident.

"We didn't know how the evening was going to go," recalled Evans. "Remember: Nobody knew what the Rock & Roll Hall of Fame was yet, so we all worked hard to get all the artists to show up and participate."

The families of Elvis Presley, Buddy Holly, and Sam Cooke were there, too. Buy-in from the artists was outstanding from the outset, which was a testament to Ertegun. He was the most-respected record man on the planet, and he had the juice to get everyone to turn out.

Ertegun stepped up to the podium to introduce the inaugural dinner: "Rock and roll has generally not been taken as seriously as popular art, but it is a direct outgrowth of American musical traditions, especially Black traditions, and because the artists who planted the seeds have received little recognition, those of us who know where this music came from have an obligation to acknowledge and honor them."

There were vetted photographers and press, but no need for personal bodyguards. There was hired security for the evening, but there were so many possible entrances into the Waldorf that some people simply snuck into the room.

"We were very busy removing people who didn't belong there," said Evans.

Jann Wenner looked back on that first dinner and was struck by the significance of all the honorees attending the ceremony. "I wondered what hardscrabble guys like Little Richard, Chuck Berry, or Jerry Lee Lewis, who had never made big money off their talent, would feel like coming into a formal celebration in this place seeing their image on the wall being honored for their way of life."

The elephant in the room, of course: No women were inducted in the inaugural year. (Roberta Flack, who was there to induct Little Richard, recited a list of female artists that she hoped would be inducted in the future.)

Most of the artists knew each other, having spent days on the road together decades earlier. It was like a giddy high school reunion of men who grew up on the Chitlin' Circuit, were hounded by Jim Crow, and endured the highs and lows of show business. The artists were deeply touched. It was a brand-new organization with no history, but that didn't matter to them.

A few hours before the ceremony, Chuck Berry was sitting in the hotel's coffee shop when Phil and Don Everly walked in. "Give me a hug!" Berry said. They hugged, and he continued, "Man—we came out there together."

"No," said Phil Everly, "we followed you out there. You kicked the door down."

The first artist inducted was Berry. Who better than Keith Richards to present the award to the Father of Rock & Roll? "It's very difficult for me to talk about Chuck Berry," Richards said, "because I've lifted every lick he ever played—this is the gentleman who started it all!" Chuck's response: "Dyno-mite!"

There were other poignant reunions: Keith Richards hung out with Don and Phil Everly for the first time in many years. Their connection was deep. The Rolling Stones had opened for the Everly

Brothers during a UK tour in 1963, and it was then that Don Everly famously showed Keith his open tuning technique, which Richards adopted in the late '60s, reinventing his entire sound and songwriting technique. (In 2018, I interviewed Richards about his guitars and playing style, and he talked in detail about Don and the open tunings that Don had shown him. More on that later.) Richards also reconnected with his idol and friend Jerry Lee Lewis. Keith always hangs photographs of "The Killer" in his dressing room when he's on tour.

A thousand-plus record business execs and their guests all stood on chairs and tables to witness what was essentially a private award ceremony. The jam session was a bit shambolic, but there was still space for great playing. "We were hoping to have a jam session at the end, but we didn't know if that would happen or how it would happen," recalled Evans. Bill Graham was instrumental in making the jam a reality, getting the artists up onstage. "It worked," recalled Evans, "and everybody had a great time."

Keith Richards ripped open his tuxedo jacket to reveal a leopard-skin-pattern shirt. Rented instruments from Studio Instrument Rentals (SIR) were handed out to everyone who wanted to play. Chuck Berry sang and got down on his back on the floor, gyrating in a slapstick fashion. He went through "Little Queenie," "Roll Over Beethoven," and "Johnny B. Goode"—a rock 'n' roll hymnal—all penned by Berry. Julian Lennon joined in on vocals. Jerry Lee Lewis was right in the pocket, pounding the piano keys with his signature karate chop moves, and Richards was in top form, dropping in tight, succinct solos in the right places. Jerry Lee's wingmen were Billy Joel and Steve Winwood, who played keyboards on "Gimme Some Lovin'," his 1967 hit with the Spencer Davis Group.

The evening was an unabashed success. "It was the beginning of something huge. No one knew quite how important that first evening was, but the induction ceremony became an annual event that everyone looked forward to—the most cherished evening of the year for the music industry," recalled Ertegun. Both Ertegun and Wenner realized that the Hall of Fame concept was not only brilliant, but valuable, and they felt that they were the best custodians to honor the artists. At the ceremony, it was officially announced that the board had chosen Cleveland as the site to build the museum.

After the jam session was over, Evans remembers changing into comfortable shoes and finishing up her work of closing down the room. As she walked out of the Waldorf, she heard applause and saw Wenner and his wife, Jane, with Ertegun and his wife, Mica. "They were applauding me as I was walking out of the hotel," she recalled. She stayed and had drinks with them and rehashed the evening. "We were so excited that it had gone as well as it did. It exceeded our expectations, and it was a lot of fun."

From the outset, Ertegun made it clear that he wanted the Chinese architect I. M. Pei, one of the most famous architects in the world, to design the museum. His buildings included the Javits Center, the addition to the Louvre in Paris, the East Building of the National Gallery in Washington, and other iconic buildings. No other architects were considered.

There was one problem. Pei knew nothing about rock 'n' roll whatsoever. Suzan Evans recalled, "He called me to say that his daughter asked him why we wanted him to design the museum; she told him that he was an old man who didn't know anything about rock 'n' roll. 'Those are fighting words,' he said to me."

So Ahmet and Jann happily took it upon themselves to give the architect a crash course that could inspire him to design a building that was worthy of the music. "We set out to teach him about rock 'n' roll, sending him books and taking him to concerts," recalled Evans. Ertegun and Wenner and their wives took Pei and his wife, Eileen, on an educational tour to Memphis and New Orleans, along with Evans and Seymour Stein. "It was quite a bonding experience for all of us."

The group toured Graceland and then went on to New Orleans, where they visited Cosmo's Factory and Tipitina's, where Wenner and Ertegun proceeded to get drunk. (The wives were upset.) Of course, Ertegun knew everyone in town, and they rolled out the red carpet.

After returning to New York, Pei, clearly absorbing what he had seen and heard, called Evans and said, "I've got it! Rock and roll is about energy! That's what the building I design will reflect—energy!"

Twenty-two artists were inducted at the second annual induction ceremony held on January 1, 1987: the most ever in one evening. The nominating committee was playing catch-up; there were so many worthy artists, and the board wanted to clear the decks as quickly as possible, knowing that, in the following year, there would be a paradigm shift as the more limited but foundational music of the '50s would be eclipsed by the '60s juggernauts, beginning with the Beatles and Bob Dylan.

Chuck Berry was back again, as was Keith Richards. In the early days, board members would stand on the side of the stage to watch the action. Bruce Springsteen, Roy Orbison, John Fogerty, Jerry Leiber, and Chuck Berry were all up there jamming. Berry looked over and saw Evans on the sidelines. "I don't like attention, and Chuck looked at me and said, 'We're gonna have some fun now.'" Then he scooped Evans up and started swinging her around in her ball gown. "I was mortified," she said. A photograph capturing this moment was taken by famed photographer Ron Galella, and it's one of the most memorable images from the early ceremonies.

That night, the Coasters, Eddie Cochran, Bo Diddley, Marvin Gaye, Bill Haley, B.B. King, Clyde McPhatter, Rick Nelson, Roy

Orbison, Carl Perkins, Smokey Robinson, Big Joe Turner, Muddy Waters, Jackie Wilson, and Aretha Franklin were inducted. With Franklin being the only woman honored, the nominating committee was making it clear that gender diversity wasn't a consideration: Many worthy women, including Tina Turner, Ruth Brown, LaVern Baker, the Supremes, Gladys Knight, Mary Wells, and Esther Phillips, were nominated that year but didn't make the cut. (As of this writing, all but Wells and Phillips have been inducted.)

In just a couple years, the induction ceremony had become a highly respected event. The presenters for each inductee were very carefully selected, and the board had to be certain that whoever was making the presentation was well respected and somehow influenced by that inductee. "So that it was an honor going both ways—for the inductee and for the presenter," said Evans.

Ertegun was adamant that the show should not be televised—a strategy that worked at the beginning. "The fact that we refused to do a television show for many years really built the prestige of the organization," said Evans. "The artists bought into it because they realized what an honor it was—and that it was *not* an excuse for some television show. Years later, it was the artists themselves who came to the board and said the evening should be shared with the public." Ultimately, said Evans, "it was too special to keep private."

The third ceremony, held on January 20, 1988, ushered in 1960s artists including the Beatles, Bob Dylan, the Beach Boys, and the Supremes. An early hallmark of the induction ceremonies, though, has always been drama—discord, rifts, and lawsuits between many of the groups being honored—and this year was no exception: Paul McCartney—mired in a lawsuit with his former bandmates and

Yoko Ono—was a no-show, as was Diana Ross (she had recently had a baby and had fallen out with fellow Supreme Mary Wilson). The Beach Boys had endured endless internal strife—from Brian Wilson's revolving door exits from the band to the tragic death of his brother Dennis Wilson—and were now embroiled in a decades-long legal battle over that usual inter-band problem of who really owns their name and the work they did together. (It wasn't until 2008 that the legal skirmishes were resolved.)

Creative partners from bands were being honored, but not all of them were on speaking terms. "I'd get a call from one saying, 'I won't get up onstage with him, he's crazy,'" recalled Evans. Then, when the night came, everybody kind of rose to the occasion because of the gravitas of the event. "This wasn't like a Grammys, where you're voted for the best album of one year," said Evans. But while the honors at hand seemed to impart a certain degree of civility to the proceedings, there were still plenty of antics.

Elton John and his then-wife, Renate Blauel, along with his songwriting partner Bernie Taupin, were making their way to their table when they realized that George Harrison had given one of their seats to Bob Dylan. Elton went ballistic, abruptly left the scene, and headed back to his hotel suite. At a nearby table, Mick Jagger was seated with Little Richard and his entourage—but alas, the hotel's waiters had been bumping into them again and again while carrying oversized platters of food, so the Jagger–Little Richard crew eventually joined Elton and his crew upstairs in Elton's suite as the ceremony began. The job of herding them all back to the proceedings eventually fell to a Beatle, Ringo Starr, who ran upstairs to collect everyone. Elton John pulled the same thing years later.

Something was also up with Beach Boy Mike Love that night. Accepting honors on the stage, he was—there seems no other way to say it—*unhinged*, and called out Mick Jagger, saying he was "chicken shit" for not coming onstage to perform.

Later in the ceremony, when it was time for Bob Dylan to accept his award, the love started to flow more freely when Dylan said, "I'd like to thank a couple of people who are here tonight who helped me out a great deal coming up: Little Richard, who's sitting over there—I don't think I would have even started out without listening to Little Richard. And Alan Lomax, who is over there somewhere too. I spent many nights in his apartment house visiting and meeting all kinds of folk music people who I never would have come in contact with." It was slightly surreal to see Dylan depart from his typical cryptic and detached demeanor and speak from a place that seemed unapologetically heartfelt and nostalgic.

And then, winding up, Dylan said, "And I want to thank Mike Love for not mentioning me."

Mick Jagger was on hand to induct the Beatles: "We were doing Chuck Berry songs and blues and things, and we thought that we were totally unique animals. And then we heard there was a group from Liverpool, and they had long hair and scruffy clothes—but they had a recording contract. And they had a record on the charts with a bluesy harmonica on it called 'Love Me Do.'" When he heard the combination of all those things, Jagger said, "I was almost sick . . . we were playing a little club in Richmond, and suddenly they were right in front of me. The Fab Four! John, Paul, George, and Ringo—the four-headed monster. They never went anywhere alone at this point, and they all had these beautiful long, black leather trench coats. I could really die for one of those and I thought, *Even if I have to learn to write songs, I'm gonna get this.* We went through some pretty strange times. We had a lot of rivalry in those early years, and a little bit of friction, but we always ended up friends, and I'd like to think we still are because they were some of the greatest times of our lives."

George Harrison and Ringo Starr were on hand, along with Yoko Ono and Sean Lennon. Though Paul McCartney had decided to stay home, he released a statement: "After twenty years, the Beatles still have some business differences which I had hoped would have been settled by now. Unfortunately, they haven't been, so I would feel like a complete hypocrite waving and smiling with them at a fake reunion."

While there were some personal and business differences on display, the 1988 jam is largely regarded as the best of all time. "I guess it took a couple of years for that to really build up and have people looking forward to jamming," said Evans. Onstage for the jam: Jagger, Dylan, Springsteen, Little Richard, Elton, Billy Joel, John Fogerty, and George and Ringo, among others. Dylan singing "Like a Rolling Stone" accompanied by George Harrison and Mick Jagger? Nothing like this had ever occurred before. Both the artists and the assembled audience were gobsmacked by the live superstar jam session—all of it completely unrehearsed. On nights like this, it seemed like anything could happen—somebody new could grab a microphone, and the assembled musicians could turn on a dime. It was pure magic.

Just as things were concluding, Jeff Beck began to play the opening of "Satisfaction"—and when Jagger heard the introductory notes, he took off his jacket, stashed it behind Springsteen's bandmate and then-girlfriend Patti Scialfa, and headed for the stage, clearly thrilled. (It wasn't even a given that Beck was going to play that night—he'd injured one of his fingers.) Jagger sang the first two verses, and then he and Bruce shared the microphone as they traded verses and harmonized. Bruce was already a legend by this point, but he was clearly in awe of Jagger, one of his greatest idols. (Bruce's bands in the 1960s used to cover Stones songs.) Bruce looked like he had gone to heaven and needed to pinch himself; everyone else joyously jumped in (and, of course, knew exactly what to play: every note, every chord, every tempo change).

A little-noticed moment occurred while Neil Young was tucked toward the back of the stage, standing on a riser behind everyone else. He was playing the "Satisfaction" riff, too—but he intentionally modified it, playing it in a double-drop-D tuning like he did when he lifted the same riff for Buffalo Springfield's song "Mr. Soul." Mick turned around for a moment and acknowledged Neil, who was grinning. It was a little gem of a moment that almost nobody in the room noticed: Neil playing a riff that he stole from another guy's song—that he modified for his own tune—and then putting his own version of the riff back into the originator's composition!

At the ceremony, there was also an unveiling of I. M. Pei's design for the future Hall of Fame in Cleveland. "There's no timetable," Ertegun said, "and, frankly, we're not in a rush. We want to make sure we don't make any mistakes."

Those first ceremonies were videotaped only for archival purposes, and after five years, there was still no TV show. As Brandwen recalled, "Grubman kept saying, 'We're going to do it; give us time,' and when the five years expired, with no induction and no television, they said the five years are up—you've lost your rights. Which was not atypical of how the music industry could operate." In 1988, the Black Tie Network filed suit against the Rock and Roll Hall of Fame Foundation, with Brandwen eventually settling out of court. (Board member and attorney Ben Needell later said, "We did take it from [Brandwen]—it was easy." Brandwen called it a "beautifully crafted stall.")

The following year, 1989, it was the Rolling Stones' turn to be enshrined. The band were on hand to accept their awards, and they participated in the jam session even though Jagger and Richards were barely on speaking terms—a testament to the kind of reconciliation that the Hall of Fame encouraged. A few months later, the Stones released their album *Steel Wheels* and embarked on their first world tour since 1982. Pointedly, all members of the Stones, past and present, were inducted, including pianist Ian Stewart, who had been pushed out of the official lineup in 1963. This kind of extra special treatment, though, was not extended across the board to all artists: It was the beginning of an uneven acknowledgment—certain artists received more honors and goodwill, forbearance and understanding; others didn't.

Pete Townshend was onstage to do the honors for the Rolling Stones: "I can't analyze what I feel about the Stones, because I'm really an absolute fan of the Stones and always have been. Their early shows were just shocking, and absolutely riveting, and stunning, and moving. And they changed my life completely. The Beatles were fun, there's no doubt about that—I'm talking about their live shows; I'm not demeaning them in any way. But the Stones were really what made me wake up. At the Beatles shows, there were lots of screaming girls, but the Stones were the first to have a screaming boy." Townshend also roasted the band as if Don Rickles were there, ribbing Bill Wyman about the big book advance he had received, and calling out Keith and Charlie's drug problems and Ron Wood's face and teeth. Then he really took Mick to task, saying, "Mick gave me something too. A really bad case of VD!" The audience erupted in laughter. "Sorry, sorry, sorry! No, no that's wrong—Mick's *CD* had a bad case!" But it was all in good fun. Townshend spoke lovingly about the band's music and Mick and Keith's songwriting partnership.

When it was time for the Stones to pick up their statues, Jagger parried back: "Pete Townshend said that we're all his friends, but I'm not so sure, after that speech, we are all his friends anymore. Next year, Pete, it's a sobering thought: You're going to be in this old hot shoe, so someone else is going to wind you up like that."

The Rock Hall wasn't really an institution yet, but the superstars onstage that evening were honored. They had been to the Grammys, but this was different. In the end, it was the heartfelt speeches from their peers that meant the most to them. Pete told Suzan Evans that he was so moved by the speeches from the Soul Stirrers, who were also inducted that night, that he made a major life decision.

"Pete called me," said Evans, "and said that their speeches encouraged him to go back on the road."

CHAPTER THREE

IN THE BASEMENT AT SOTHEBY'S

While the first Rock & Roll Hall of Fame induction ceremonies were happening, I was making an early career move from Phillips Auction House to Sotheby's. The business of the auction house institution Sotheby's subsisted on the so-called three D's: Death, Debt, and Divorce. And the firm, which sold everything from art and wine to real estate, had an insatiable appetite. Each of the three D's were, of course, commonplace grand-scheme occurrences, so there was always an unending supply of great art and property to sell.

On June 1, 1988, I exited the subway at Seventy-Seventh Street and Lexington Avenue—the same train station I had used during my daily commute to my previous job at Phillips auction house, which was just seven blocks north. But Sotheby's might as well have been on another planet. Phillips's offices were in a converted parking garage; Sotheby's, on the other hand, were in an enormous building that took up half a square block. I remembered a visit during college and had a general idea to expect extremely well-dressed colleagues, so I bought four new summer suits from Paul Stuart's sales rack. At the time, a jacket and tie were still mandatory for men conducting business, and in my field at least, you were expected to look fabulous. When the Sotheby's doorman greeted me that morning and ushered me inside, I felt like a minor-league ballplayer who had been called up to *The Show*.

Sotheby's was inhabited by the "chronically rich"—trust funders, nepo babies, old money, new money. It didn't really matter what you wanted to call them, really: It just meant that many people employed there didn't really need to work, but they wanted to, which was somehow admirable. (After all, it was a great place to possibly meet your future spouse.) This was all new to me. I had no pedigree. I hadn't even heard of Andover, or St. George's, let alone attend a posh boarding school. I was an Italian American kid from Brooklyn who cleaned up pretty good and had no accent whatsoever. All I could do was show up, rely on my wits, and present myself like I knew what I was doing. I received a quick tour of the building: mail room, photography studio, loading dock, the works. In short, Sotheby's was a vast place packed wall-to-wall with paintings, furniture, and almost anything else imaginable.

Just two years earlier, I was on the verge of graduating from Fairfield University with absolutely no plan for the rest of my life. I had double majored in English and communications—a fairly typical liberal arts degree at the time, though one that is now often derided as both impractical and a waste of money. I only knew with conviction what I was *not* going to pursue. Graduate school was out of the question—somehow I just knew deep down that whatever I would be doing wouldn't require an advanced degree. And Wall Street, where so many of my friends and schoolmates were headed, wasn't happening for me either. I simply didn't have the passion for that kind of work.

Joan—then my girlfriend, and the love of my life, now my wife of thirty-six years—had brought me to the Metropolitan Museum of Art, the Museum of Modern Art, the Guggenheim, and a bunch of other museums in the city during weekends and school breaks.

She'd also invited me to audit several of her art history classes, which included a visit to the Old Master paintings department at Sotheby's New York location.

Sotheby's seemed like a museum where everything—paintings, exotic cars, silverware, paper weights, snuff boxes, jewelry, and antique furniture—was for sale. It was also a major revelation for my college-aged self to learn that a legendary and prestigious company like Sotheby's was selling . . . rock 'n' roll memorabilia? Pretty cool, but I didn't think much else of it until a couple years later.

I was interested in the creative side of advertising, and I had enjoyed an internship at an advertising agency in Manhattan during the summer after my junior year. I worked on television commercials and print ads and helped produce some radio spots; I felt comfortable on set, and especially enjoyed the editing and post-production process. And I thought I had lucked out: I was told there would be a plum entry-level job waiting for me at the agency after graduation.

And then one night, something fortuitous happened that would shape my entire career. I was reading magazines with Joan at her beach house off campus, and after finishing an article, she glanced at a page and said, "Hey, check this out—it's right up your alley."

What I saw was mesmerizing: A glitzy, full-page advertisement for Dewar's White Label Scotch featuring a photo of a young guy in a bowtie who worked at Sotheby's auction house as their "Rock & Roll expert and appraiser."

The ad was part of a long-running advertising campaign called "The Dewar's Profile," which featured interesting people—Broadway stars, ballerinas, artists, writers—describing what they do and their interests. (The campaign was created by the Leo Burnett agency in the 1970s and first featured the actor Jerry Orbach.) This "Rock & Roll expert" was Mish Tworkowski. I stared at the ad and said, "I want that job! It would be perfect for me!" Joan offered a cautionary counterpoint: "Sotheby's already has that guy—how many of those jobs do you think exist?" I grinned and tore the page out of the magazine and stashed it away in my notebook.

Upon graduating, I was informed that my promised advertising job had evaporated. Tucked away somewhere is a picture of Joan and me in our caps and gowns that we often joke about: We both looked like sweaty, anxious messes and had that same expression of uncertainty on our faces that all but cried out, "What now?!"

While I was sad that college was ending, I had luckily made arrangements that would cushion the blow: a six month, under-the-radar, rent-controlled apartment in a pre-war doorman building on the East Side of Manhattan—or, less grandly, I was sharing a dank studio facing an alleyway on East Fifty-Eighth Street with a friend from school. I moved in a few days after graduation with one suitcase, my stereo, and a handful of records. The best part: Rent was only $300 per month, and my portion was a paltry $150. I would spend the summertime leisurely looking for a job on Madison Avenue.

Joan had hit the ground running, intent on making a career in New York's vibrant art scene. She landed in the accounting department at Phillips Ltd., a London-based auction house with a New York outpost on East Seventy-Ninth Street. Joan had no interest in accounting, but she figured it was a way into the auction world. Other freshly minted grads were also hired at Phillips as receptionists or assigned to the exhibitions staff, which mostly entailed smiling and handing out catalogues on the sales floor. Joan was assigned to accounts receivable and spent her days calling people who were late paying their bills.

Even though she shared a windowless office with a group of chain-smoking accountants, Joan had a bright outlook. She was on the inside, and there were interesting people coming in and out of her office every day. (There were also incredible benefits, including an eye-popping six weeks' vacation for everyone on staff! Those

Europeans were used to their long holidays, and everyone else benefited too.)

I enrolled in a night class at the School of Visual Arts called "Introduction to Copywriting." The class, taught by two instructors from advertising agencies, was filled with people in their twenties and thirties who wanted to learn the basics and hoped to land a marketing firm job. It was a competitive, intimidating environment, and I found the first assignments challenging. I wasn't pleased with the copy I had written, on top of being frustrated and bored. It finally dawned on me: I didn't want to be in the business of hocking merchandise for the likes of Procter & Gamble or R. J. Reynolds. Frankly, I wasn't good at it. At the conclusion of the class, I thought to myself: *Who wants to sell soap anyway?*

I had no Plan B. Instead, every day, I ritually clipped want ads from the *New York Times*, but most of the classifieds that I clipped were from employment agencies, and they all required a typing test before even reviewing your resume—which was both soul-crushing and, in more practical terms, a deal-breaker, as my typing was adequate at best. I tried to focus on any job that mentioned the word "creative"—but of course, thousands of other recent graduates were doing the same thing.

A month or so later, Joan heard that Phillips was hiring porters and asked me if I was interested. "What's a *porter*?" I asked. She said a porter was a British term for an art handler. "It's somebody who moves furniture, loads trucks, unpacks boxes, and does whatever's needed." Having been woefully unsuccessful so far in landing a job doing anything else, I decided to give it a try.

The foreman in charge of the porter's crew, Gerry, was a smart, funny Irishman who singled out all the porters with college degrees for extra insults. To this day, I have never heard so many vulgarities used in such clever ways. That, combined with his brogue, injected welcomed levity in the day. We laughed a lot, and every day was different. Sometimes our crew of five or six found ourselves working in a sweltering warehouse in Harlem; on other days, I ran a freight elevator for hours. Occasionally, I was sent to an airport to pick up a painting. These were pre-9/11 days, so you could get a security pass and meet somebody at the gate. Crucially, the porters also received tips—this being the one and only job that I ever had that included this happy addition. When one day I received a crisp $100 bill for delivering a small Renoir to an elderly Frenchman at JFK Airport, I was thrilled.

Auction days were exciting. The porters wrapped paintings and small pieces while the auctions were still occurring, and we would watch the auctioneers take bids from people in the audience as a sea of auction paddles bobbed up and down. "Do I have one thousand?" "Do I have fifteen hundred?" "Do I have two thousand?" and on and on. There was electricity in the room. Some dealers would use a secret signal to hide their identity from competing bidders. Once, I was even asked to stand on the stage and hold a painting while the auction moved along. Occasionally, Gerry asked me to clean the ladies' bathroom before an auction. I didn't complain. I was having fun. I had started out working two days per week, and by the end of the summer, I was working full-time.

Hell, sometimes we even took afternoon naps on the job if things got slow. I remember a porter from London who had a clever idea of making a makeshift mattress from a pile of furniture blankets.

Being a porter, though, meant a lot more than moving furniture and being an all-around step-and-fetch. Believe it or not, when you spend hundreds of hours hauling art and antiques around, you can learn quite a bit about them—and Phillips's specialists were more than happy to tell you about an object if you showed interest and asked questions. Many of them were generous with their time and enjoyed the role of mentor. In London, some of the world's top art experts began as porters. It was all about acquiring on-the-job knowledge.

Joan was biding her time in the accounting department, and when she found a free moment, she would sneak upstairs to the paintings department to look at the new consignments and chat with the experts there. Joan made it known that she wanted to move out of accounting and into paintings. She had majored in art history and French, after all.

That September, I went on my first-ever business trip. Phillips had just landed an enormous antique doll collection in Montgomery, Alabama, and I flew down with my friend Dave from college, who had joined me as a porter, to pack up the collection and load it into a truck. We checked into a Holiday Inn and encountered drunk, middle-aged men hosing down girls in bikini bottoms and T-shirts in the lobby, country music blasting, everyone cheering—a wet T-shirt contest. We inhaled a load of ribs at a local BBQ shack and then went to a nearby bar for a drink. The moment we entered, I realized I wasn't appropriately dressed. (I was wearing a pair of plaid Bermuda shorts, a polo shirt, and penny loafers.) A few minutes after we took our first sip of beer, a scruffy guy came over and asked us just what we were doing there. "We're in town doing some work," I said. "We're from New York City." He frowned, looked us up and down, and then said, "It's best you boys leave." We did just that.

Dave and I arrived at an old farmhouse the next morning and spent the day packing about five hundred antique porcelain dolls, many of them with human hair. They were creepy-looking, and their eyes would open and close as if they were real babies. Boxing them up felt like placing them in small coffins. After about ten hours, the truck was packed, and we waved goodbye to the driver, who would arrive at Phillips in a few days.

The biggest industry draw for me wasn't the porcelain dolls (obviously), or the tips, or the paintings—it was the auction process itself. My parents, who collected antiques, had once brought me to an antiques auction in upstate New York when I was a kid, and I never forgot it. I loved the energy that an auction produced, and I now had a number of responsibilities to help generate that energy: I began to catalogue lots for auctions, and I worked on the photo shoots and catalogue layouts we sent to the printers. Phillips had been trying for years to break into New York's competitive auction market where Sotheby's and Christie's were the big players. Sure, we were far behind, but everyone at Phillips was rowing in the same direction, dedicated to making the place a success. Joan and I realized that we were lucky to be there. So many of our friends were stuck in dead-end jobs or hadn't found work yet. We were making new friends and finding our footing in the art world. And, yes, now and again, celebrities would pop in to check out the wares. Yoko Ono and Andy Warhol even dropped in together one afternoon, which was a thrill.

Phillips was an intoxicating place to be. I was learning a whole new vocabulary. Words like *Biedermeier*, *Stickley*, *Daum*, *patina*, *filigree*, *impasto*, and *majolica* were all part of my new common vernacular. I had enrolled in a crash-course apprenticeship in art history, design, and, most importantly, connoisseurship. I was learning how to examine an object with specific intent. Was it repaired? Was it original or a reproduction? Could it be fake? Being a porter put me on track to become a *generalist*—someone in the art world who knows something about everything.

In the New Year, Joan made the great escape to the paintings department. She was in her element, and she was elated. I wanted to follow her path and make a transition to one of the specialist departments, but I didn't know much about art history, and I spoke no foreign languages. (Joan was fluent in French.) I couldn't bullshit my way into an art department. Realistically, the only one option for me was the Collectibles Department, which was a potpourri, the proverbial kitchen sink at auction houses that included toys, dolls, records, costumes, cookie jars, autographs, and whatever couldn't fit in elsewhere.

All incoming phone calls were filtered through a central switchboard before being routed to the appropriate departments—people selling furniture, paintings, jewelry, silver, etc., were all transferred to specialists upstairs. But when the receptionists received a call from a client who had some sort of oddity to sell, they always transferred those calls to my department—Collectibles. Most things amounted to nothing, but occasionally something extraordinary would come our way. One day, I received an old nautical life ring—under normal circumstances, not really something we'd be interested in. But this life ring bore the words RMS *Lusitania*. (The British ocean liner RMS *Lusitania*, launched by the Cunard Line in 1906, was sunk off the coast of Ireland on May 7, 1915, by a German U-boat, killing 1,198 passengers and crew—a major factor in building support in America for entering World War I.) Singular historical objects like this were exciting to see up close and to touch. I realized for the first time that an object could emotionally connect you to history in a visceral way.

In a stroke of great luck, the job I wanted actually came to me: One day I heard through the grapevine that Sotheby's needed a young staffer in the Collectibles Department, and I fit the description. With some solid experience, I had a few good interviews and landed the job. A few months earlier, Joan had taken a position as a corporate art curator at Cantor Fitzgerald in the World Trade Center.

In the pecking order, the collectibles department wasn't a moneymaker, but it did generate tremendous publicity. The masses didn't care about Picasso paintings selling for $20 million—but you're damn right that a lace bra once owned by Marilyn Monroe that sold for $10,000 made worldwide news. My new office was in the bowels of Sotheby's (we didn't need sunlight or windows, which were essential for the examination of fine art), but being located below grade wasn't so bad. I settled into my new office and met the staff in the adjoining Arcade Department, which sold lower-priced items up to about $5,000.

I took a stroll around the building and checked out all the specialist departments. As I walked around, I heard people on the phone doing business in Spanish, French, Russian, Japanese, Chinese, and German. Since New York was five or six hours behind Europe, they made those calls early in the day. I also witnessed the daily brigade of attractive young women arriving at work wearing their standard uniform: a Chanel suit, perfectly blown-out hair, a fancy handbag, and high heels. Some added an additional accessory—a small dog comfortably tucked into a Gucci pet carrier. These were the precursors to the now-ubiquitous "therapy dogs," and this was long before every Hollywood starlet required a canine accoutrement.

I already knew some of the basics of the auction business: writing condition reports, filling out bid slips, etc. But now I was really going to see how the sausage was made. My boss, Dana Hawkes, had given me my first assignment: typing rejection letters to people who had sent photographs of items they wanted to sell. I would be informing them politely that Sotheby's wasn't interested. These letters were known company-wide as "NSV Letters," meaning no sale value. We were gearing up for the next auction, which would take place two weeks later on June 17 and 18, including dolls, toys, mechanical banks—and rock 'n' roll memorabilia.

The next morning, the guy from the Dewar's advertisement walked into the office. Mish Tworkowski in the flesh, looking just as I had remembered: boyish, with blond hair and a beard, and wearing a suit and bowtie. I don't think he realized just how excited I was to meet him. Charming and approachable, he was twenty-eight but could have passed for a high school kid. Mish explained that he would be transitioning out of the collectibles department to head up the coin department, and I would be working with him on the upcoming rock 'n' roll auction.

Mish would be training me so that I could eventually take over as Sotheby's rock 'n' roll expert. I felt like I had won the lottery!

IN THE BASEMENT AT SOTHEBY'S

I realized very quickly just how different Sotheby's was from Phillips. It wasn't just the people working there and the size of the building—the sheer volume of business and the energy level are what made Sotheby's so exceptional. Christie's was their only true competitor, and there was enough business to go around that enabled both houses to do exceptionally well. My new colleagues were mostly well-off and had decades-long relationships with old money families and the newly minted rich. That's what kept the gears moving. Every morning when I arrived at the office, the telephones were already ringing.

Of course, shopping for expensive baubles is something that had been going on for centuries. Staff and clients were often from the same social set, and the biggest evening sales of the season were black-tie events, with men in tuxedos and women in gowns. It all made for a great work environment. Among other perks, there was always time for a proper lunch—the days when you would eat your dreary salad at your desk while surfing the web were still over a decade away. Women sometimes sunbathed on the roof during lunchtime. One pretty summer intern from Dartmouth had just appeared in a *Playboy* feature entitled "Girls of the Ivy League," and a certain paintings expert frequently used the freight elevator for the occasional lunchtime quickie—he'd stack up furniture blankets to make a cushy mattress and piled them into an elevator car, and when the freight elevator operators were taking a mandatory break, he'd stop the car in between floors. I once saw him and a woman looking slightly disheveled exiting the elevator at midday. It was routine to see celebrities in the building who had come in to browse, or to do some serious shopping. Jack Nicholson was often in the building looking for Picassos, and Rod Stewart was a regular, with his eye on pre-Raphaelite paintings. After work, the porters, many of whom were from Jamaica and Trinidad, played cards and sipped whiskey milk punch inside an elaborately constructed clubhouse made from cardboard boxes.

At the beginning of my second week in my new position, Sean Lennon came in to see me. His mother, Yoko Ono, had started auctioning some of her and John Lennon's artwork and furniture and a few of his less important musical instruments at Sotheby's in 1983, inadvertently jumpstarting the entire high-end market of rock 'n' roll memorabilia. But on this day, he wanted to check out the famous Nehru jacket that Jimi Hendrix had worn on the album cover of *Are You Experienced.* Sean was just thirteen years old at the time, and he arrived with his tall governor, Dane Worthington, who accompanied him everywhere. Lennon tried on the jacket, and I was amazed to see that it fit him perfectly. (I didn't really realize until then how extremely thin Hendrix was.)

Speaking of celebrity clothing, whenever we were auctioning such garments, we used models to wear them so they could be photographed for the catalogues. (A live model was always better than a mannequin to bring an old garment to life.) I always called around the building looking for volunteers who would be willing to be photographed. It was great fun: My friend Paul Song volunteered to wear one of Paul McCartney's famous collarless Beatle suits, and Benjamin Doller, now the vice chairman of Sotheby's, indulged me to model one of John Lennon's outfits. I once modeled one of Bill Haley's tuxedo jackets and styled my hair like his.

When word got out that we had landed a mink bikini swimsuit that had been worn by Marilyn Monroe, I didn't need to ask for volunteers—three women on staff simply showed up in the photo studio ready to try it on, but they were all waifs and couldn't fill out the swimsuit. Luckily, a college intern had the right figure.

As I continued my work at Sotheby's, I realized more and more how historical objects could have immense power and meaning to people. When the Metropolitan Museum of Art exhibited the King Tut collection back in 1978, more than 1.27 million visitors saw the show—the second highest attendance record for an exhibition at the Met. In that instance, seeing an object up close emotionally connected you—transported you—and reinforced the notion that King Tut actually lived. After all, his remains from thousands of years ago were right there in front of you. Sometimes the connection was even more visceral. Several times, I saw middle-aged men sniffing one of Marilyn Monroe's old bras. Monroe may have been long gone, but they still wanted a piece of her.

On Friday, December 9, 1988, I was leaving work in the early evening, anticipating Sotheby's upcoming Hollywood Memorabilia auction along with the public exhibition the next morning. I had already put on my coat and was walking out the door when my phone rang. I could have let the caller just leave a message, but at the last minute, I picked up. A woman with a thick Queens accent was on the other end of the line: "I am calling from Donald Trump's office. Mr. Trump would like to meet you tomorrow morning at 8:00 a.m. to see the *Casablanca* piano." I didn't plan to be at the office that early, but I couldn't say no to The Donald.

The future president arrived the next morning promptly at 8:00 a.m., wearing a suit and tie. The piano in question was the actual fifty-eight-key upright green prop piano from the film *Casablanca*, the one from Rick's Café that Sam used to play "As Time Goes By." It had been scaled down to a lower height, as Humphrey Bogart wasn't a tall man. (The producers of the film went to great lengths to make sure that Bogart appeared much taller than Ingrid Bergman, with the costume department fitting him with four-inch wooden platforms strapped to his regular shoes.) Trump looked at the piano and was impressed. He was friendly, asked several questions, and told me he was going to place a bid. In the end, the piano fetched $154,000, and it wasn't from Trump, though he had been the underbidder who had driven the price up. (A successful auction always needs at least two strong bidders.) The buyer ended up putting the piano back up for sale at Sotheby's in 2012, when it sold for a whopping $602,500.

Random people sometimes showed up unannounced with things to sell. The week after my morning meeting with Trump, Patty Hearst dropped in with a friend who wanted to sell a baseball that had been autographed by Babe Ruth. I also met Graham Nash, who was selling his photography collection.

But one of my most thrilling Sotheby's rock 'n' roll experiences was snagging the Buddy Holly estate in 1990 and beating out our main competitor, Christie's, for it. Since his death in 1959, virtually all of Holly's possessions had been well-preserved by his family. Yet nobody outside of Lubbock, Texas, was aware of what the family had, and they had everything. Dana Hawkes and I put together one of the greatest rock 'n' roll estate sales, which included a trove of letters Holly had written to his parents, homework assignments, his high school diploma, and a great deal of his clothing—including many pieces that were worn onstage and in promotional photographs. The highlights of the sale included his iconic eyeglasses (it was actually Holly's distinctive look that gave John Lennon—a huge Buddy Holly fan, who named his new band the Beatles because Holly called his group the Crickets—the confidence to wear eyeglasses in public). The two top lots of the sale were his guitars: a circa-1943 Gibson J-45 wrapped in hand-tooled leather that Holly himself had crafted and the Holy Grail—his iconic Fender Stratocaster with the tobacco sunburst finish. Back then, recording artists didn't have dozens or hundreds of instruments, and Holly owned maybe five. (The others known to exist include his banjo and an acoustic guitar that he used after he moved to New York in 1959.)

The auction was a watershed moment for the burgeoning rock 'n' roll memorabilia market; interest was enormous, coming from many musicians and recording artists. In early June 1990, I received a call from Eric Clapton's manager Roger Forrester. E. C. wanted to view several items from the Holly estate before it went on public exhibition. I knew that Clapton had made an album with the Crickets, and I was a huge fan of Cream; I also understood that Clapton would be recognized—and probably bothered by fans and onlookers—in a public setting, so I naturally obliged him.

The following week, Clapton showed up at my office with a few roadies, and we spent several hours looking through Buddy's belongings. Clapton was at first mostly intrigued by the letters that Buddy had written to his parents while he was on the road; they revealed his very close relationship with them, and with his mother in particular. Holly's public-facing image and personality were very genuine, and based on the letters, you could tell he loved his parents and was certainly a man of his era in the late 1950s. The collection's stash of Holly's high school homework assignments, meanwhile, revealed that he was a dedicated and fastidious student.

Since Eric—we were now on a first-name basis—had been mostly playing Strats for the past twenty years, I naturally assumed he'd be interested in Holly's Fender Strat, but he wasn't. Instead, he asked me, "Would you mind if I tried on Buddy's motorcycle boots?" I was a bit surprised. I said, "Sure, but they are really small—a size nine." Eric sat down, removed his own shoes, and put on Buddy's boots then walked around. He looked very pleased and said, "They fit perfectly!"

Later, as he was leaving, he thanked me and autographed my copy of his self-titled solo album from 1970, inscribing it to me. This was the last time I ever asked anybody for an autograph.

The night before the auction, my colleagues and I had dinner with Holly's widow, Maria Elena Holly, who had a great sense of humor and a vivacious personality. She had been flirting with me all night, and as she prepared to leave the restaurant and return to her hotel, she whispered to me, "I'd like to wake up with your shoes under my bed." I smiled and left with Joan.

When I was ordering the auction, I decided to make the motorcycle boots one of the last lots of the sale, figuring this would give Eric plenty of opportunity to bid on other things from the sale. Bidding interest overall was tremendous; this would be the one and only chance to acquire something from Holly's estate, and there were hundreds of people in the sales room, order bids left with the auctioneer, and nearly a dozen phone bidders.

I was juggling multiple telephone bidders from different time zones—one of them the actor Gary Busey, who had starred in *The Buddy Holly Story* and was committed to walking away with Buddy's famous Gibson acoustic guitar, with Holly's handcrafted leather decoration encasing the instrument. Busey won the guitar—the hammer price was $243,000, which, in retrospect, was a bargain. Clapton didn't show up to the sale, but Roger Forrester was dutifully there, sitting in the front row for the entire auction—and was eventually the winning bidder on Buddy's boots. He delivered them to Eric.

A few months later, we received a Fender Telecaster that Eric had supposedly played in Derek and the Dominos. I was skeptical and decided to call Roger for confirmation. On October 3, 1991, I received a fax from Roger asking for photos he could show Eric. As it turns out, the guitar was legit.

Sometimes I would pick up the phone and found myself speaking to, say, the daughter of a deceased New York Yankees legend who needed money and, somewhat reluctantly, wanted to consign a game-used baseball bat or uniform. On other days, I encountered a steady stream of Beatles autographs. So many of the new titans of Wall Street were branching out beyond the typical things to collect, and pop culture was a potent talisman that connected them with the music of their youth. Lennon, McCartney, Dylan—they were becoming the new Hemingways and Faulkners for the Baby Boomer generation.

Around December 1990, my friend and colleague Paul Song summoned me to his office when I was working late to show me one of the most extraordinary objects I had ever seen. I entered the room and there was Mish Tworkowski and the Coin Department's consultant David Tripp. They asked me to sit down and open my hand, and then one of them placed a small coin in my palm. I stared down at it, quickly noting that it was well worn and very, very old. "What is it?" I asked. "It's a Brutus EID MAR," Paul said—one of the Ides of March coins that Brutus had made in 43 BC to commemorate the murder of Julius Caesar. There are perhaps 150 of them in the world. I was blown away. The coin was from the Nelson Bunker Hunt Collection, which Nelson Bunker and his two brothers were forced to divest after losing more than $1.5 billion speculating in the silver market in the 1980s. It would be sold at Sotheby's in a few months (June 1990). The coin ended up fetching $99,000. To me, it was impossible to process the mere fact that such a thing still existed. Coins like this now sell in the millions.

A few months later, I flew to Tokyo hand-carrying $5 million worth of baseball cards in a small crate for a special traveling exhibit promoting the James Copeland sports memorabilia auction. The plan was to introduce Japanese clients—many of them already baseball fans—to American baseball cards. That trip ended up being an unintended boondoggle, but the Copeland sale was a huge success and a watershed moment for the sports memorabilia business.

You see, Sotheby's was like a museum where everything was for sale—and that meant that serious buyers were able to touch the object, regardless of its value or fragility. When musical instruments were up for auction, they could be touched but not played. When I landed an exceptional consignment, I, too, would call colleagues from other departments to come down and take a look. One day, we received several of the original costumes—beautifully crafted of bright felt fabric—that were worn by the Munchkins, the little people from the 1939 film *The Wizard of Oz*.

As a museum curator, you dream of finding such things because often these objects are lost or thrown away, leaving historians to conjecture about an artist's thought process. Because rock 'n' roll was not considered fine art, it wasn't respected or taken as seriously as other art forms. And while it was extraordinary to learn, say, how much correspondence Vincent van Gogh had with his brother Theo—correspondence that explained so much of the artist's thought process, along with when and where he did his work—there was scant correspondence in the rock 'n' roll era.

An important distinction to note: The term *rock 'n' roll memorabilia* is applied broadly. Sotheby's certainly sold memorabilia—Beatles nodding-head dolls, Monkees lunch boxes, Elvis posters and backstage passes—but that was just one part of a larger picture. A great deal of what was offered was archival material that delved deep into the history of an artist and their life, and it was this material that was of utmost importance to scholars and music historians. I was beginning to realize this after seeing the ephemera and letters from the Buddy Holly collection.

Memorabilia also encompassed material related to an artist's creative process, their stage presence, and their personal lives. We landed a large cache of Jimi Hendrix's personal papers, for example, and they were a window into the last year of his life. Hendrix was at the peak of his powers but was in a financially precarious position—something revealed in correspondence with his attorneys. One extraordinarily revealing letter from Hendrix's attorney Henry Steingarten, dated June 11, 1970, reads:

> Dear Jimi: Regina Jackson, or Diane Carpenter, whichever name you prefer, is contemplating initiating paternity proceedings against you. I met with her lawyer and her on Tuesday in Minneapolis. She told me she had spoken to you about two weeks previous, but you never mentioned this to me. The lawyer has some grand ideas about your setting up a trust for the child to assure her education and support. Under normal circumstances, this would be desirable, but in your present financial condition it is impossible. We will have to work out some kind of weekly or monthly support payment. The baby is having a blood test made in Minneapolis and I will be informed of the laboratory in New York where you are to have your test taken. The bloods will then be matched and will determine whether or not you are the father. Please call me because there are many things to talk about. Sincerely Henry.

Hendrix never got the blood test—though he reportedly met with the woman in New York. The young girl, Tamika James, was born in 1967. Hendrix didn't acknowledge fathering the child. Of course, if Hendrix *had* taken the blood test and it matched, Tamika would have inherited Hendrix's entire estate. In 1972, though, a judge ruled that the alleged daughter would not share in his estate, which went entirely to Hendrix's father. This letter, though only one page, opened an extraordinary window into what Hendrix's life was like in his last few months—personal turmoil, his financial situation precarious, and his drug use problematic. A few months later, he was dead.

The Hendrix cache also included extensive architectural plans and correspondence related to the construction of Electric Lady

Studios, which Hendrix was building on Eighth Street in Manhattan's Greenwich Village. Construction costs were enormous: There were curved walls, multiple mixing consoles, and elaborately painted murals, and after Hendrix closed on the property, the contractors discovered that there was an active stream flowing right under the building's foundation.

It was at this point when I realized that the memorabilia business was far more than just that. It could reveal little-known histories and uncover secrets that made the business I found myself part of more akin to archaeology.

The Hendrix auction generated huge interest worldwide. Paul Allen, the cofounder of Microsoft, was hovering, along with many A-list musicians who had been friends with Hendrix or admired him. My colleague Debbie Hatch, who worked in Special Client Services—a very discreet and insulated department at Sotheby's that handled the company's most important customers—introduced me to Seymour Stein, who was keenly interested in the Hendrix sale. I didn't know who Seymour was at the time, but I was well aware of Sire Records, the company that he cofounded and headed up. Seymour stopped by my office on December 12 to discuss the Hendrix manuscripts with the intent of acquiring a piece for the future collection of the Rock & Roll Hall of Fame.

Hatch explained to me that Seymour was one of those insane collectors who, after locking eyes on something he coveted, had no restraint. It helped that he had a great eye for quality, along with the resources to vacuum up anything that he fancied.

We discussed several pieces, including Hendrix's handwritten setlist from the Woodstock festival, an astonishing artifact (and a marvel merely that it still existed), and the lyrics to "Crosstown Traffic." But we agreed that the crumpled-up original lyrics to "Purple Haze"—an early draft, when the song was still titled "Purple Haze, Jesus Saves"—was the best choice. The pre-auction estimate was $8,000–$12,000. The lyric draft was almost completely different from the recorded version, but the phrasing and rhyme scheme perfectly matched the melody of the song. It was breathtaking to handle and mind-boggling to think that Hendrix had apparently tossed the paper into the trash. (Luckily, it was rescued by an employee who worked for Hendrix's manager Michael Jeffery.)

The auction took place on December 17, 1990. I arranged to be on the phone with Seymour and bid on his behalf, and I was able to give him a sense of the action in the sales room. Ultimately, Seymour was the successful bidder on behalf of the Rock & Roll Hall of Fame, with the "Purple Haze" manuscript selling for a very reasonable $14,000.

I decided to hand-deliver the lyrics to Seymour at his office at Seventy-Five Rockefeller Plaza. The place was littered with Art Deco antiques and paintings, and near the door was a statue of the RCA mascot, the famous "Nipper" dog. Seymour was a lot of fun to watch, and he had a devious sense of humor. He examined the manuscript and said, "You know, Jann Wenner was very annoyed that I went ahead and bought these lyrics without consulting the [Rock & Roll Hall of Fame's] board." Although this was understandable, Seymour had made a shrewd purchase with great foresight. (Ultimately, Wenner realized it was the right move.)

We got to talking, and I pumped Seymour about my favorite bands he'd signed, particularly the Smiths, who had broken up four years earlier.

Seymour told me he would do almost anything to close a deal. "When I signed the Smiths," he said, "I had to buy Johnny Marr a special guitar." I knew the exact guitar he was talking about: a 1960 Gibson ES-355, similar to Chuck Berry's main guitar. Seymour knew absolutely nothing about musical instruments, he told me, but he certainly knew where you could buy them. He brought Johnny Marr to what was known as Manhattan's Music Row—a stretch of midtown, which was packed with instrument shops of all kinds, from guitars to accordions. In an interview, Marr later explained, "Seymour took me down to 'We Buy Guitars' on Forty-Eighth Street. . . . I took it back to the Iroquois Hotel and wrote 'Heaven Knows I'm Miserable Now' and 'Girl Afraid,' immediately." Marr's rhythm-lead guitar style was unique and unmistakable, utilizing unusual chord sequences and arpeggios, and this Gibson semi-hollow body was just what he needed. Seymour also told Marr about guitar shopping with Brian Jones on the very same street. I walked away from his office impressed with the way he could make things happen.

By early March 1991, we had another collection of Jimi Hendrix manuscripts coming up for sale. The first auction had done so phenomenally well that the interest in the next auction was even more immense. People who thought that they had missed out were happy to have another chance at a second tranche of material. Monika Dannemann, one of Hendrix's girlfriends, made an appointment to see me to examine the manuscripts. Monika was with Hendrix on his final night on earth; the ambulance picked him up from her London flat and transported him to the hospital where he died. She was from a very prominent German banking family, and his death had totally consumed her remaining years until her eventual suicide in 1996. She examined the manuscripts and told me that she had Jimi's last black Strat. After that meeting, she wrote to me occasionally, asking for photographs of other Hendrix artifacts.

In fact, girlfriends and former groupies were a whole category of consigners in Sotheby's rock sales. They would periodically drop in to consign something, usually letters or clothing. One woman came in with a four-line poem Jim Morrison had written for her. Another woman came in with one of Jimi Hendrix's hats. One day, a well-dressed Italian woman in her early forties who was looking at Impressionist paintings with her husband in one of Sotheby's upstairs galleries slipped downstairs to quickly show me a red paisley scarf that Brian Jones had given her. "I spent a weekend with him in '66," she said, showing me a snapshot of them together, with Jones wearing the scarf. When I told her that the scarf was probably worth around $4,000, she simply laughed and stuffed it back into her Hermès handbag.

Incredible manuscripts were coming in with more frequency. One of the best I had ever seen arrived via one of Jim Morrison's close friends—a six-page manuscript that Morrison had written a few days after hearing about the death of Brian Jones. Morrison had self-published the poem, creating a limited edition of approximately one hundred, but nobody had ever seen the actual manuscript. I unpacked the pages, which were on lined yellow note paper, written in Morrison's distinctive handwriting:

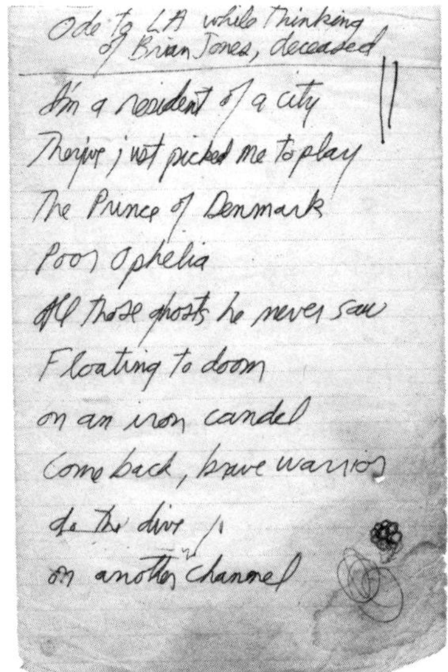

Ode to LA while Thinking
of Brian Jones, deceased

I'm a resident of a city
They've just picked me to play
The Prince of Denmark
Poor Ophelia
All those ghosts he never saw
Floating to doom
on an iron candle
Come back, brave warrior
do the dive
on another channel

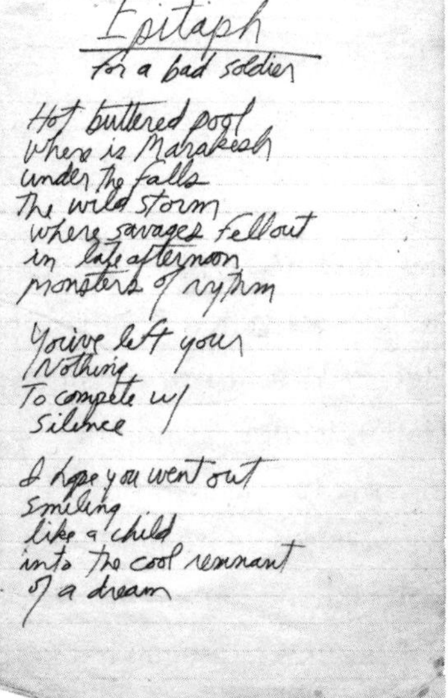

Epitaph
for a bad soldier

Hot buttered pool
Where is Marakesh
under the falls
The wild storm
where savages fell out
in late afternoon
monsters of rythm

You've left your
Nothing
To compete w/
Silence

I hope you went out
Smiling
like a child
into the cool remnant
of a dream

Two pages from Jim Morrison's 1969 manuscript, "Ode to L.A. While Thinking of Brian Jones, Deceased," written after the Rolling Stones guitarist's death by drowning. Morrison died two years later on the exact same day. CREDIT: Gottahaverockandroll.com

Morrison passed out copies of the poem in pamphlet form at concerts in 1969. The poem was dedicated to his beloved Los Angeles, and to Jones, a kindred spirit. It was both ironic and disturbing that Morrison would die two years later to the day—July 3, 1971—and, like Jones, was found submerged underwater.

Another Doors item was being sold for charity: a brand-new Casio keyboard donated by the band's keyboardist, Ray Manzarek. He had autographed the instrument, upon which he had played the first minute of "Riders on the Storm" and then saved it to the keyboard's built-in memory so it could be played back.

It was a great piece, and I occasionally listened to it while cataloging the sale—until the day before the auction, when I accidentally erased Manzarek's recording. I screamed after realizing what had occurred, but thankfully Manzarek was a very good sport. I shipped the keyboard back to him in Beverly Hills, he rerecorded his keyboard part, and eventually it made its way to the winning bidder.

In March 1991, Seymour Stein asked me to come over to his office for a chat. When I walked in, he simply blurted out, matter-of-factly: "Would you consider moving to Cleveland to work for the Hall of Fame?" I said nothing. Seymour explained that things were moving forward with the museum. I was intrigued, but I had just read an article in *Spin* describing the endeavor as "The Rock and Roll Hall of Shame." I told Seymour that I was aware the induction ceremonies had been happening for a few years, and I knew there was still no date to break ground in Cleveland. He assured me that a site had already been secured and that financing was well underway.

"The search is on for the position of Chief Curator," he told me.

We left his office together, taking the elevator to the lobby. As we exited, Seymour hit the buttons for nearly every floor, lighting the panel up like a Christmas tree. He laughed and said, "You should throw your hat into the ring."

Truth is, before that meeting, I was already beginning to question whether I wanted to spend my entire career in the auction world. I loved my job at Sotheby's; it was an exciting and glamorous place to work, and I had learned quite a lot in a very short period. The relationships I was making were invaluable. But I realized that my opportunities to rise were very limited. Collectibles wasn't a profit center. The real success was in the money-making departments like Impressionist paintings, contemporary paintings, and modern art. Those auctions were grossing hundreds of millions of dollars.

The opportunity to be part of something brand new; something so ambitious, so grand, and so outrageous—a museum about rock 'n' roll—was just too hard to ignore. I went home and spoke with Joan, who was very supportive. At the same time, I was thinking about what Mick Jagger said when the Rolling Stones were inducted into the Hall of Fame: "Now that Jann finished his house in East Hampton and Ahmet finished his house in Turkey, I hope they can get down to building the phantom temple of rock in Cleveland."

But it was everything else that Mick had said that evening when the Stones were inducted that convinced me to interview for the job. Not usually one to be nostalgic or sentimental, Jagger had delivered a heartfelt speech about his bandmates and the music that he loved: "You know it's slightly ironic that tonight we're all going to see us on our best behavior, but we're being rewarded for twenty-five years of bad behavior, and it's also a bit amusing on the side but actually slightly sappy, I suppose, and I must say I'm very proud to work with this group of musicians for twenty-five years. . . . I'm very proud of the songs that Keith and I have written over the last twenty-five years. I'd like to pay tribute to two people who can't be here tonight: One,

Ian Stewart, a great friend, a great blues pianist whose bold but invaluable musical advice kept us on a steady bluesy course for most of the time. And to Brian Jones, whose individuality and musicianship often took us off the bluesy course with often marvelous results."

Those words struck me—and not only because the Stones were my all-time favorite band. I was a true believer in rock 'n' roll—in the power of music and how it could change culture, history, and your life. Ultimately, it was the music itself that pushed me toward the Rock & Roll Hall of Fame.

A month or so later, I walked into the boardroom at Atlantic Records and sat in the one empty seat at the head of the table. I was among approximately ten candidates interviewing for the job. Around the table were titans of the music business: Seymour, Ahmet, Bob Krasnow, Jon Landau, Jerry Wexler, Allen Grubman, A&M Records' Michael Leon, Suzan Evans, and a few others. The questions from them came in rapid-fire succession: "Who do you know? Can you spot a forgery? What do the members of Led Zeppelin have in their personal collections? What about Yoko? What does the Hard Rock have?" And so on. I think I read the room pretty well, and I could tell they liked me.

I went to see Jann Wenner the following morning at the old *Rolling Stone* offices on Fifth Avenue across from Bergdorf Goodman. I found it interesting that he hadn't been at the previous meeting. In front of his desk was one of Pete Townshend's famous shattered Gibson SGs encased in Lucite. Townshend had smashed it during a photo session with Annie Leibovitz. Jann was equal parts charming and intense. I could see he had a short attention span, so I spoke as quickly and succinctly as possible. His questions were similar to those of the other board members, but then he asked follow-up questions, drilling down. He wanted specificity. Luckily for me, I happened to have a good answer to most of his questions.

I didn't get the job. Bruce Conforth, a forty-year-old Indiana University professor with great credentials and a doctorate in musicology, did. Suzan Evans told me that I had impressed the board, but they just thought I didn't have nearly enough experience to head up such a large undertaking. I didn't dispute that assessment. In any case, I was happy enough to remain at Sotheby's because we had several big auctions coming up. But there was no getting around the fact that I was disappointed; it would have been an extraordinary opportunity.

I tried to expand my portfolio at Sotheby's beyond rock 'n' roll, Hollywood, and sports memorabilia, setting my sights on exotic cars, then an emerging department for our New York office. I loved cars, and I would get the odd phone call here and there about one or another, but usually I just referred the matter on to our London office. The only call of great interest that I received was from a car collector who had part of the transmission of James Dean's Porsche Spyder that he was driving when he died. (Parts from that car ended up being salvaged and sold to other Porsche collectors who needed parts for their own cars.)

Then, in October of 1991, I was out to dinner with Seymour at his favorite Italian restaurant, Coco Pazzo, a fancy white-tablecloth spot off Madison Avenue on the Upper East Side. Among his guests were Jerry Blavat, the (allegedly) mobbed-up Philadelphia radio disc jockey a.k.a. "The Geator with the Heater, The Boss with the Hot Sauce," who was friends with Frank Sinatra and many 1950s rock 'n' roll legends. Suzan Evans was there, too. Seymour held court, and at the end of the evening, he serenaded the table with obscure doo-wop songs. And finally he told me: "The Hall of Fame needs additional help building the collection, and the board has decided to create a position for you."

Well, I was already over the moon, leaning back in my chair to take it all in, when Suzan told me: "There's more good news—the job is here in New York."

When word got out that I was leaving Sotheby's, a bunch of my clients called to congratulate me. The collector Jan Edward Bridge, who had purchased Buddy Holly's high school diploma in the auction we ran, told me that he would be donating it to the Rock & Roll Hall of Fame in my honor. I was off to a good start, and I facilitated the gift before my first day at my new job.

One item in the bank already!

CHAPTER FOUR

THE BOILER ROOM

In 1991, I arrived at the Rock and Roll Hall of Fame Foundation's office on West Fifty-Second Street with some books, a few auction catalogues, and my Rolodex. It was December 18, Keith Richards's birthday—something I considered a good omen. I didn't know it yet, but this was where I would spend the next thirty-one years working. The shared office space—just me and Suzan Evans—was located amid *Rolling Stone*'s brand-new headquarters in Rockefeller Center. With Jann Wenner being cochairman of the Rock Hall, it made sense that his pet project was down the hallway.

The Hall of Fame had just signed a $5.3 million contract with architect I. M. Pei, who called the event "one of the happiest days of my life." I was happy, too: I was on the ground floor of something extraordinary, and I never took it for granted. Of course, it made great sense for the Hall of Fame to have a curator working in New York—a big chunk of the music business was based in the city, and there were also a lot of artists and collectors who lived in the city—but I felt beyond lucky that it was me. Also, while Sotheby's had been located in a quiet, residential neighborhood, my new office was in the heart of Midtown. It was an exciting new place to be, and the record companies were all nearby. Seventy-Five Rockefeller Plaza, where Atlantic, Elektra, and Sire were all located, abutted our building, and there was a single fire door down a nondescript hallway where you could access it. Below street level there were tunnels and corridors that the Rockefellers had built during the 1930s for shops and convenient passage between buildings. Out my window I could see across the street to CBS's Black Rock building, where Columbia Records and Epic Records were also based.

There seemed to be infinite possibilities to whatever we might be building: in-depth exhibits about the Chicago blues; the American proto-punk scene of Television, the Sonics, and the New York Dolls; the Stones, for God's sake!; Tina Turner; or, of course, the Holy Grail: a full-fledged Beatles exhibit digging into their mountainous archives and storage vaults.

I had been subscribing to *Rolling Stone* since I was a kid in Miami, and it was a thrill to meet the writers I had been reading for years. Having my office at *Rolling Stone* had other advantages, too: There was a great library with a reference librarian, and Jann was generous with his time. But the environment couldn't have been more different from Sotheby's. The writers were a scruffy lot: Their T-shirts, jeans, and sneakers would have been in gross violation of the Sotheby's dress code. There were no more Saville Row suits, nor Chanel—only Jann Wenner and the accountants wore suits. There was a windowless office around the corner from mine, as well as a closet, where staffers got high. Down the hall, there was also a designated room where account executives from the advertising sales team retreated to smoke cigars. (You could still smoke cigarettes anywhere back then.)

On my third day, someone shouted that Hunter S. Thompson had just entered the *Rolling Stone* offices. He flew past my desk, making a beeline for Jann's office. I saw Hunter yank a big fire extinguisher off the wall as he stormed in, and there was a loud commotion as he sprayed the entire space. Jann ran out, very pissed off and coughing up a lung. As it turned out, the fire extinguisher had done its job: It removed most of the oxygen from the room.

Hunter, Jann, and *Rolling Stone*'s National Affairs Editor William Greider were heading down to Little Rock, Arkansas, to interview Bill Clinton, then riding high on the campaign trail. The Hall of Fame, meanwhile, was gearing up for its seventh induction ceremony—in a feat of great timing, shortly after my start date.

Jann asked me to check out the storage vault that the Hall of Fame had rented to store their collections. Sounded like a good idea; I'd need to see what had already been acquired to give me some direction. It still wasn't clear just when the museum was going to open. Financing was still not completely in place—something I knew when I took the job, but I was confident that the money would eventually come through with so many people in New York and Cleveland having invested so much of their sweat equity in this project.

The vault was in the Galleria Building on East Fifty-Seventh Street, and to gain entry to it, I had to enter a special codeword—BOYS—that had been given to me by Suzan Evans. The guard led me down a long hallway to an iron door. The anticipation was killing me. Finally, the door swung open, revealing . . . a shallow closet containing a couple of film cannisters, a few Betamax tapes, a single manila file folder, and one guitar. That was it—the entire collection of the Rock & Roll Hall of Fame: *a closet full of nothing.*

I should have broken out into a cold sweat, but I just laughed out loud and opened the guitar case. Inside was the Gibson Les Paul that Les Paul himself had donated when he was inducted in 1987. It was a reissue—no great shakes—but at least it came from one of the giants of the music business. Paul was like the Thomas Edison of rock 'n' roll: He held many patents, invented multitrack recording, and was there when the solid-body electric guitar was invented, along with his friendly competitor and colleague Leo Fender.

I opened up the file folder to find a few sheets of lined paper, and instantly recognized Jimi Hendrix's early handwritten lyrics to "Purple Haze."

But that was it. I thought to myself, *Holy shit—there is a lot more work ahead than I anticipated.* And the clock was already ticking. I. M. Pei was designing the building, a giant 125,000-square-foot glass pyramid, and it was incomprehensible how we were going to build a collection, create exhibits, and literally fill a museum in just a few years.

If anyone was going to inspire everyone to step up to the challenge, it would be Ahmet Ertegun. It's hard to overstate Ahmet's contributions to rock 'n' roll and popular music. Lesser known, though, was what a great raconteur he was. At an early Hall of Fame–related dinner, he performed an elaborate routine for our amusement about how to succeed in the music business, standing up from the table and walking around hunched over like a caveman. "If you're very lucky," he said, "you will bump into a genius—and that genius will make you rich." The room erupted into laughter. Ahmet, of course, discovered and nurtured several generations' worth of talent, changing the course of art and commerce while building an independent record label from scratch. At its core, though, his work came down to finding talented artists and giving them what was needed to succeed.

Over the next few months, I sent out more than two hundred letters to artists, managers, and record companies, trying to set up meetings to explain what the Rock & Roll Hall of Fame was about and how we could preserve the legacies of these important artists. Sometimes I'd get a reply through the fax machine, one of those rolled-up pieces of paper that soon turned yellow. Jann sent out a bunch of letters of introduction for me and made a few calls on my behalf to connect me with people, but it was very slow going. I felt like I was stuck in the boiler room in David Mamet's *Glengarry Glen Ross*, desperate to make a sale.

In those early days, the Rock Hall only meant one thing: the induction ceremony. The idea of a museum? Well, it was hard to get people's attention focused on it. People were still joking about Mick Jagger calling the project the "phantom hall of rock—in Cleveland."

I decided to check in with Roger Forrester, Eric Clapton's manager. We always had an excellent rapport when I was at Sotheby's, so why not build on that relationship? Cream would soon be eligible for induction, and the timing seemed right to reconnect. Clapton had an amazing collection of guitars—hundreds of them—and I knew that if I could get just one, it could help when approaching other important guitarists. And so one day, I faxed Roger a letter, just as I did at Sotheby's; Roger would either fax me back or call me the next day.

This time? Radio silence. It was another reminder that I was no longer at Sotheby's. I was at a nonprofit now, asking artists for a lot more than a mere favor: I was asking them to donate some of their most historic and cherished objects. And because of my previous work at Sotheby's, I had contributed to the increased value in these objects. The artists knew what they had. My sales pitch, at its core, was that we would preserve their legacy in perpetuity. That pitch was powerful and clearly meant something, but not all artists understood or appreciated the museum's solemn mission. Some were more entranced by the mighty dollar.

Dialing the phone, meanwhile, was like playing a roulette wheel: You never knew when something good would happen.

Eventually I got a lucky break and managed to get ahold of Keith Moon's mother, Kit, who lived in London. We spoke for more than an hour. I could tell she was a lovely lady, and she was so proud of her son, the iconic drummer for the Who. She told me that she missed Keith very much and that she had preserved her son's bedroom and left it just as it was when he first moved out in the early 1960s. She described it as a shrine and mini museum dedicated to Keith. By the end of the call, I still hadn't acquired anything for the collection, but it was a start—and any time I needed motivation, I just thought about that empty storage vault.

Margaret Everly, the mother of Don and Phil Everly, had similarly preserved Phil's bedroom from the early 1960s—her sons were on the road most of the time and had no need for their own places, so when they were back in Nashville, they stayed at the family homestead. Margaret showed me Phil's room—the walls and ceiling were all painted black, and she had their matching stage clothing and many of their instruments. She had loaned a vast collection to the museum.

CHAPTER FIVE

THE LAST JAM SESSION

The seventh induction ceremony was upon us, and I was excited to be inside. The Waldorf ballroom was jam-packed with rock stars, with no bodyguards in sight. It was January 15, 1992, and as a mere civilian fan of rock 'n' roll, I had never experienced anything quite like it. Mingling about were Jimmy Page, Jeff Beck, the Edge, Keith Richards, Neil Young, Johnny Cash, Steve Cropper, Sam Moore, the Isley Brothers, Carlos Santana, Jimi Hendrix's drummer Mitch Mitchell and bassist Noel Redding, and Booker T. & the M.G.'s.

The people-watching was fascinating: Steve Ross—the former parking lot king who had decades earlier acquired Atlantic Records, Sire Records, Warner Bros Records, Elektra Records, and other labels—had just died. Ross's label heads made up the nucleus of the Hall of Fame's board, and they were all in attendance: Ahmet, Seymour, Bob Krasnow, Doug Morris from Atlantic, and Mo Ostin from Warner Bros. The heads of Columbia, Arista, Capitol, EMI, and Island were there, too.

The night's inductees included Bobby "Blue" Bland, Booker T. & the M.G.'s, Johnny Cash, the Jimi Hendrix Experience, the Isley Brothers, Sam & Dave, Elmore James, Professor Longhair, Leo Fender, Bill Graham, Doc Pomus, and the Yardbirds.

As usual, the ceremony was not broadcast on television, though a video crew was there to capture the proceedings for archival purposes. With the intimacy of the ballroom and the free-flowing booze, the inductees were comfortable and unguarded, leading to passionate, profanity-filled speeches, completely unlike canned, garden-variety awards ceremonies. Periodically, I saw security escorting out people who had snuck into the ceremony.

The night was by far the longest induction ceremony in the organization's history, not concluding until after 1:00 a.m. Phil Spector gave a meandering speech honoring the songwriter Doc Pomus, who had recently died. He also announced from the stage that his son Philip Jr. had died. Eventually, Ahmet and others tried to give Spector the hook, but they couldn't get him to leave the podium. It was simultaneously hilarious and excruciating.

When the Yardbirds were inducted, Jeff Beck was the last band member to speak. "I have done other music after the Yardbirds," he said. "Anyway, somebody told me I should be proud tonight. But I'm not, because they kicked me out—they did. Fuck them."

Jimmy Page, who was standing next to Beck, laughed hysterically. This wasn't the first time that grievances were voiced from the stage, but it was the first time I saw firsthand how the ceremony could bring out raw emotion.

As the induction part of the ceremony concluded, roadies handed out rented instruments. Starting up the jam session was the ultimate crowd-warmer, Booker T.'s classic instrumental "Green Onions." Johnny Cash played "Big River" with the Edge, and Jeff Beck led a rollicking version of "Soul Man." Jimmy Page jammed with the Isley Brothers on "Shout." It was a thrill to witness; pure joy.

Earlier, when Johnny Cash accepted his induction, he'd said: "Little Richard and I were talking. He said God is watching over things tonight. And I feel that, Richard. I thank you for reminding me of that. I asked June [Carter Cash, his wife], 'What should I say when I get up there?' and she said, 'Just ask God to guide you, and it'll be all right.' I find that works, not only tonight but every day of my life."

Later, as I watched Johnny Cash jam on "Purple Haze," I felt like I had gained access to a secret society—not as a member yet; I was just someone lucky enough to be there. At the same time, much like the previous jam sessions, there were too many people playing, and the sound was cacophonous.

The evening's standout performance was Neil Young fronting an all-star band of guitar gods playing Bob Dylan's "All Along the Watchtower." Young, who was clad in black leather, was backed up by none other than Keith Richards, Jimmy Page, Carlos Santana, the Edge, Steve Cropper, Jeff Beck, and Johnny Cash. He seemingly flicked a switch and delivered a bravura performance: For whatever reason, his sound was uncluttered, perhaps due to the song's simple rhythm and chord changes. It was an astonishing, on-the-fly performance: no plan, no rehearsal, no soundcheck. I stood at the side of the stage and marveled.

The jam was exhilarating, but also loose and, yeah, sometimes messy—everything was, as usual, done on the fly, and that was the beauty of it. Genuine improvisation. Paul Shaffer was the magician that kept everything together as best as possible. I didn't know it then, but this would be the very last of the impromptu jam sessions; the last time that unpredictable magic would happen.

Robbie Robertson, who attended and performed, complained to Jann afterwards. "Robbie called me the next day," Jann later wrote, "not to tell me how much fun he had had, but how sloppy the show was."

Jann simply told Robbie to stop bitching and asked him if he wanted to help work on the next year's show. Similarly, Suzan Evans said, "Jon Landau told me that Bruce Springsteen said the jams were 'becoming non-musical.'"

Bruce and Robbie's criticisms were heeded, and Jann had been itching to change things up. So Jann sprung into action to ensure that things would be different the next year.

CHAPTER SIX

YOU GOTTA ROLL WITH IT

One of the great benefits of working with Jann Wenner was that he had a phone number and an address for *everyone*. From their two hubcap-sized Rolodexes, his two assistants constantly fed me contact information for artists and family members that I wouldn't have otherwise been able to reach. But in return, Jann wanted constant progress reports. Better than anyone else, he knew there were looming deadlines. And while Jann was very demanding and only wanted your best work, he was always reasonable; we had a great working relationship from day one.

After a few months, Jann told me to give Art Garfunkel a call. "He'll like you," he said.

I had been a huge fan of Simon & Garfunkel since childhood, and I felt a deep connection to their songs. When I called Garfunkel at home to introduce myself, I could hear over the telephone line that soft, gentle voice I was so familiar with. He invited me to come by the next day to his penthouse on the Upper East Side in one of those white-glove buildings where the elevator opened right into the apartment. As the uniformed elevator operator manually slid open the gate, Art was standing there smoking a joint. "Craig, this going to be a fun day," he said.

Art led me up a spiral staircase to his study, where he pointed out about a dozen boxes of material for me to examine—and then left me to my own devices, telling me he'd be back in a few hours to see if there was anything of interest.

Before Simon & Garfunkel had signed to Columbia Records in 1963, they had been a duo in the 1950s called Tom & Jerry. (Art's stage name was Tom Graph because he loved mathematics, and amid the boxes Art showed me to were photographs of Tom & Jerry—Artie and Paul—with flat-top haircuts.) Their songs, like "Hey, Schoolgirl," sounded very much like their idols the Everly Brothers; the Queens boys were learning to harmonize and write songs. I found something fascinating, though, in the papers that day: Art had charted the rise of the Tom & Jerry songs on the Billboard charts, plotting the songs on graph paper from his geometry class, in handwriting so meticulous that it looked like it was produced by a typewriter. I came back the following week to continue looking and found signed contracts and letters that Paul Simon had written to Art from summer camp discussing girls, camp life, and music.

Garfunkel popped upstairs now and again to check on my progress. On the wall next to us was a giant map of the United States, with pins in various locations and lines drawn in between, similar to the way he had graphed the charting of those early Tom & Jerry songs. When I asked him about the map, he replied that he was walking across America, bit by bit. "Every few months," he said, "I fly back and resume my walk from the last spot." Art explained that walking gave him time to see the country and think about life. He stayed in hotels and inns along the way as he walked on foot. As he spoke about the experience, I could sense there was something spiritual about his journey. We connected quickly, and it was apparent that Art was comfortable letting me see the way he lived. He was sensitive and warm, and I continued to plow through the boxes.

I spent my first few months with the Rock Hall mostly bottom-feeding, but working with Art Garfunkel was definitely not included in that category. I had landed a few collections of gold records, sales awards, and some mediocre promotional posters, but there were some bright spots, too: Jann had generously donated *Rolling Stone*'s album library. And while I thought that the news that Jann had made a substantial gift would be noticed and would spur others to be similarly generous, I was clearly mistaken.

Jann also assigned me the job of editing next year's induction program—an exciting project that gave me more access to the inductees. It also kept me busy, as there were only so many museum-collection prospects at this juncture. I had been an English major in college, had written a couple of record reviews in school, and had edited my high school newspaper—one of the few in the country that published weekly—so I felt up to the task.

Being based in New York had so many advantages; besides all of the artists in town for concert appearances or meetings, the Hall of Fame's power structure was there. Gradually, I gained more access to the artists—though that didn't always mean that I was able to convince them to work with us at the Hall of Fame. I met Bo Diddley backstage at a show in Central Park and received an unpleasant reception as Bo reminded me that he wasn't inducted in 1986 in the first class of inductees that included Elvis, Chuck Berry, and Little Richard. I didn't know my Hall of Fame history very well back then, and it didn't occur to me that this was a slight. I told Bo about the progress we were making, and that we hoped to break ground on our building the following year. I asked him if he would be willing to donate one of his iconic square guitars for the future museum. "I got stuff for *sale*," he told me. True to his word, Bo never donated anything to the Hall of Fame—but he did sell quite a few of his distinctive rectangular guitars to collectors.

By the spring, I was making slow progress with the collection, and I went back to the storage vault to drop off a few more record-sales awards that I received from a defunct distributor on Long Island. They looked like horrible bowling trophies from the '70s, but they were better than nothing. I glanced at the "Purple Haze" lyrics and noticed there were now two other sheets of lined paper in the folder. The handwriting looked familiar. I started to read:

> The first time that I heard Bob Dylan. I was in the car with my mother, and we were listening to, I think, WMCA, and on came that snare shot that sounded like somebody kicked open the door to your mind from "Like a Rolling Stone." And my mother, who was no stiff with rock 'n' roll—she liked the music, she listened—she sat there for a minute, she looked at me and she said, "That guy can't sing." But I knew she was wrong. I sat there. I didn't say nothing but I knew that I was listening to the toughest voice that I had ever heard. It was lean and it sounded somehow simultaneously young and old, and I ran out and I bought the single. I played it. Then I went out and I got *Highway 61* and it was all I played for weeks. I looked at the cover with Bob with that satin blue jacket and that Triumph motorcycle shirt. Bob's voice somehow thrilled and scared me. It made me feel kind of irresponsibly innocent. And it still does, but it reached down and touched what little worldliness I think a fifteen-year-old kid in high school in New Jersey had in him at the time . . .

I continued to read the manuscript, and then focused on the actual handwriting. I studied the curves and loops of each letter, and to my shock and amazement, I realized it was Bruce Springsteen's handwriting, which I had seen many times at Sotheby's. I was holding Bruce's speech he had written to induct Bob Dylan.

The speech was something extraordinary. The induction had taken place in the ballroom back in 1988. I thought: *Holy shit. Somebody took this off the lectern and stashed it away for the museum.* The speech was one of those singular objects, not unlike the "Purple Haze" manuscript—a true one-of-a-kind. There were no copies. Bruce was a brilliant speaker, and this was the speech that he had written for Dylan, one his greatest idols.

I practically ran back to the office to inform Jann about my big discovery. When I delivered the news, Jann said, "That speech is mine. Could you bring it over to my office?" For a second, I thought he was joking, but he wasn't. I left his office feeling deflated. *How could this be?* A few days later, I decided to conveniently forget about his request. It never came up again.

I started honing my sales pitch to managers, artists, and their families. Jann wrote more letters of introduction and made phone calls connecting me with people. I hadn't realized how difficult my job would be. I knew it would be challenging—but there was no building to talk up, no date for groundbreaking in Cleveland . . . and not everyone in the music business was sold on the idea of even putting the museum in Cleveland! Elektra's Bob Krasnow was adamant that the board should change course, pull out of Cleveland, and build in Lower Manhattan. I had heard the endless jokes about the "Mistake on the Lake." Cleveland had secured the site of the future museum back in 1986, but they had yet to raise the promised funds. Jann and the board gave them an ultimatum: Show us the money, or we're pulling out.

"They were always trying to come up with ideas to show there was progress going on," Jann said, "but they were all public relations ideas." He saw through the bullshit.

And sometimes I felt like *I* was shoveling bullshit. The nature of my new job was profoundly different from working at Sotheby's, or at Phillips for that matter. For one thing, the phone never rang. Most of the music business didn't know what we were doing—didn't know our goals or what we were seeking. In 1992, the music business still resembled its old self: We were still years away from the digital revolution, when Napster and iTunes upended the business, and there were still record shops selling CDs packaged in long boxes. Property flooded into Sotheby's; the auction house had been open since 1744 and had branches all over the world. I was just a guy sitting at a desk in Midtown dialing a telephone.

I had realized when I accepted my position that the deadlines and goals for opening a new museum would be daunting. I mean, for God's sake: Collecting, curating, and mounting dozens of exhibits for a vast new museum—one designed by a world class architect—was a very heavy lift. We really were starting from scratch, and probably the only reason I didn't panic was due to stupidity.

In those early days, the Rock & Roll Hall of Fame meant one thing and one thing only: the annual induction ceremony at the Waldorf Astoria. The idea that a museum was going to be built, and that we would be collecting from the artists and record labels, was on nobody's radar. It was hard to convey the seriousness and ambition of our mission, though of course I would have shouted from the rooftops if presented with the opportunity. The only thing that I didn't do was hire a guy wearing a sandwich board to stand on Fifty-Second Street in front of Columbia Records' building, handing out leaflets.

Trying to explain to somebody in England that I was calling from the "Rock & Roll Hall of Fame" was like pounding sand, even though the induction ceremonies had been taking place for the past eight years. I had a goal of calling at least fifteen people each week. Sometimes the phone number was missing a digit, or the call went to voicemail, and then there were the gatekeepers at the management offices. It was always a relief when someone picked up the phone and gave me a few minutes of their time. I kept thinking about that damn storage vault—the vision of that near-empty closet was enough to put me in a cold sweat.

Meanwhile, I had embarked on an enormously ambitious project of contacting the writers who had conducted what *Rolling Stone* called "The *Rolling Stone* Interviews." These were the long-form interviews that the magazine became famous for in the 1970s, many of which were landmarks in journalism. The subjects included John Lennon, Mick Jagger, David Bowie, Tom Wolfe, and Bob Dylan. The goal was to acquire the audio tapes. (Most of these interviews were recorded on cassette tapes and transcribed by the writers.) Jann had conducted some of these interviews, including some of the most historic ones with Bob Dylan, Jimi Hendrix, and John Lennon. There was gold on these tapes, and it was our hope that we could utilize the audio in some way at the museum. Jann sent each of the writers a letter explaining the project and giving them a heads-up that I would be contacting them. I wrote to filmmaker and former *Rolling Stone* writer Cameron Crowe, to Jerry Hopkins, and to Ben Fong-Torres, among others. And down the hallway in the magazine's offices, I popped in to see writers David Fricke, Jim Henke, and Anthony DeCurtis—all of whom I had been reading since I was in high school. In the end, though, Jerry Hopkins and Ben Fong-Torres were among the only writers who cooperated.

I went to see Ahmet as much as possible to update him on my progress. He wore these amazing English suits and shirts from Turnbull & Asser, along with these amazing crocodile shoes. One afternoon, he surprised me. "I've got something interesting for the museum," he said. Sitting on his desk was an old shoebox. "All of this is from Big Joe Turner," he said as he handed it to me. Inside were three passports, along with some handbills, old press clippings, and other assorted documents. This was a real find. In the short time that I had been working, we had collected nothing of significance from an important bluesman. Big Joe Turner was an icon and had recorded for Atlantic Records, and in his later years, when Turner was in bad health, Ahmet had helped him out and paid a lot of his medical bills. When I was leaving, Ahmet asked me to meet with his old friend Bobby Robinson, an independent record company owner who had produced and managed blues legend Elmore James, who had just been inducted into the Hall of Fame. He had also produced Gladys Knight & the Pips and King Curtis, among other artists. He wrote down his phone number and said, simply, "Give him a call."

I went up to Harlem to see Bobby the following week. He was impressed with our recent acquisition of the Big Joe Turner collection. Bobby took me to lunch at Sylvia's, the legendary soul food restaurant, where he introduced me to Congressman Charles Rangel. Robinson was grandfatherly and humble, despite his success. He was particularly proud that Elmore James had been inducted into the Hall of Fame—at the ceremony, it was Bobby who collected the award on the family's behalf. He also owned one of Harlem's most famous record shops. In the 1970s, he had had the incredible foresight to sign several of the very first hip-hop acts, including Doug E. Fresh, Treacherous Three, and Spoonie Gee. He was always open to new ideas and sounds, and I was astounded that he was able to pivot from working with artists like Elmore James to then nurture the birth of hip-hop. I made sure to keep in touch with Bobby. He eventually donated one of James's guitars, which was splattered with white paint. When I asked him about the paint, Robinson told me that James had to resort to painting houses to earn extra cash long after his career was established.

In fits and starts, I was making more progress. Next, I met with LaVern Baker, who had been one of Atlantic's first big stars. She was elegant and charming and had been inducted into the Hall of Fame two years earlier. She donated a small but significant collection. As I began spending more and more time nurturing relationships with these artists, I finally realized the time it might take to make the kind of progress that was expected of me.

In December 1993, Jann Wenner hired Jim Henke—who had worked for him as *Rolling Stone*'s music editor—to replace Bruce Conforth as chief curator at the Rock Hall. Henke had most recently been working at Elektra for Bob Krasnow, was originally from Cleveland, and had worked at the local paper *The Plain Dealer*. Henke's roots in Cleveland were helpful, but it was his many years at *Rolling Stone* that made him an excellent choice for the job. Even though Henke and Wenner were close in age, he considered Jann a father figure, and their working relationship was relatively smooth.

In Cleveland, Henke worked out of offices that the Hall of Fame was renting at Tower City, a large commercial and retail complex that was owned by the Ratner real estate family from Cleveland and New York. Albert Ratner, the patriarch of the family, was a big supporter of putting the Hall of Fame in Cleveland, and if there was one board member in that city who could take credit for having the building constructed and getting the job done, it was him.

There were challenges building on Lake Erie. Turner Construction, which had been tasked with building I. M. Pei's creation, had to essentially build a basin to prevent the lake from encroaching on the construction site, compounded by Cleveland's brutal winters and lake-effect weather that delayed the pouring of the foundation. It was so cold that vast acreage had to be tented and heaters had to be brought in so the concrete could cure properly.

Jann charged Jim with ramping up the collecting process. The clock, of course, was ticking, and Henke quickly hired a team of consultants—largely people whom he knew from *Rolling Stone*, along with other writers.

Rock and roll, of course, didn't just spring to life in the mid-1950s. The music came together organically, combining gospel, the blues, folk, rockabilly, and country music. As we began envisioning the museum in greater detail, we devised exhibits that highlighted all the artists from these different genres. Even some knowledgeable rock fans didn't know the complete origin story of rock 'n' roll's development, so this was a great opportunity for us to present an accurate representation of how this art form evolved. The plan was to mount an individual exhibit for each of these genres—something that would require an extraordinary research and collecting. Stitching it all together, we commissioned a film called *Mystery Train*, which brilliantly showed how all of these disparate genres came together. The film was just more than ten minutes, but it was a great primer for a new museum about popular music.

We also planned exhibits featuring individual artists, including Elvis, Chuck Berry, the Beatles, and the Rolling Stones. In addition, we decided that since geography had always been a factor in rock 'n' roll, we should feature exhibits on specific cities: London, Liverpool, Seattle, Motown, Los Angeles, and San Francisco. And along with identifying and explaining objects, we created wish lists for the kind of stories we wanted to tell—and then went out to hunt down artifacts to tell these stories.

All of this, though, was mere prelude to the actual Hall of Fame. The concept envisioned by the Burdick Group, who had been charged with building the interiors and designing the exhibits, was that the higher you went into the pyramid, the more quiet and reverential the experience became—and at the apex, you'd be surrounded by the signatures of all the inducted artists and feel like you were in a cathedral or temple. There would also be exhibits about censorship in rock 'n' roll, obsessive fans, interactive databases that showed visitors how one artist influenced the next, and an exhibit about one-hit wonders.

At Jim Henke's welcome meeting, many of the same people whom I had met during my first interview with the hall were there to congratulate him. Since I already knew him—he was one of the writers I had approached the previous year to acquire his vast collection of interview tapes—I said, "Welcome to the team." Like most of the other fifty or so writers I had contacted earlier, Henke didn't donate his tapes. Now we were colleagues, and he would very soon realize just how difficult it would be convincing people to part with their cherished possessions. I reminded him about his tapes and promised him I wouldn't be giving up.

CHAPTER SEVEN

INDUCTIONS REVAMPED

Los Angeles's music-biz machers were acutely aware that the Rock & Roll Hall of Fame was a New York thing, and they desperately wanted in on the action. All that prestige and exclusivity? Hell, it needed to be shared.

Ahmet and Jann got the message.

Many record labels, of course, were based in Los Angeles, so it was time to have the inductions on their own turf. "Fifty percent of the music industry was in LA," Suzan Evans noted. "We thought it would be the right thing to do."

And it garnered a lot of participation from people who otherwise might not have come to New York.

The reinvention of the event into a less spontaneous, more organized affair was handled by Jann and his kitchen cabinet of Robbie Robertson and Jon Landau. They planned for better film packages, suggested songs to be performed, and put a stop to the ragged, shambolic jam sessions. Going forward, all artists being inducted would rehearse properly and perform a mini set.

"We brought in Joel Gallen to film and produce the show," Jann said, "and we put the all-star jam session to rest, as we were now primarily inducting groups instead of solo artists."

The eighth annual ceremony was held at the Century Plaza Hotel in the City of Angels—the first time the event was not staged at the Waldorf. It was a gargantuan year. In addition to Cream, three West Coast juggernauts—the Doors, Sly and the Family Stone, and Creedence Clearwater Revival—would be inducted, which made Los Angeles even more logical. With many artists residing nearby, it also lowered travel expenses, making the show theoretically more profitable.

The induction of Cream would arguably be the greatest reunion in rock history, so the change in format was fortuitous: All band members were alive, healthy, and willing to play. The blues rock trio had formed in 1966 and was only together for three years. There had been no reunions since then.

Gallen was already in touch with Roger Forrester to discuss logistics for the performance, and everything was on track—that is, until Jann Wenner and Robbie Robertson asked Tom Petty to be the presenter.

For some unexplained reason, Eric Clapton didn't like the idea of Petty doing the honors, and so Roger relayed the news that Tom was a non-starter. Momentarily, everything was in limbo. In the end, Petty was disinvited to the ceremony. (Prior to this point, Jann and Ahmet had carte blanche in terms of choosing presenters and speakers.)

Who did Clapton want to bestow the honors upon Cream? ZZ Top, the Texas-blues power trio. They were musical brothers, and it made perfect sense. The fact that ZZ Top was a trio was important to Clapton. The band's musical structure and interaction were similar, especially the stripped-down nature of a trio playing live. The Hall of Fame was becoming more established and more meaningful to the artists, so starting with Clapton, some of the artists being inducted began insisting on approval over who would honor them, often choosing a close friend who could deliver a personal, heartfelt speech. This was a big shift.

I flew out to LA on January 8 and went to Cream's rehearsal with Suzan. It was held at a sound stage in the Valley that had been booked by producer Gallen. Suzan's husband, Mitchell, drove us, and we got lost along the way, with Mitchell blowing his top about missing the rehearsal and speeding like a madman to make sure we arrived on time. We were three New Yorkers lost in Van Nuys in the pre-GPS navigation era.

When we arrived, Ginger Baker was already at his drum kit, and his tech was doing some last-minute adjustments. A few minutes later, Jack Bruce showed up and plugged in his bass guitar as Ginger started to play. Jack was laying down the bass line to the song "Born Under a Bad Sign" from Cream's 1968 album *Wheels of Fire*—a song that was cowritten by Booker T. Jones. Jack and Ginger laid into the groove again and again, for ten minutes or so.

Eric Clapton arrived, smiling and nodding to his former bandmates, and soon plugged in his sunburst Fender Stratocaster and began to play. When Jack started singing, the room seemed to levitate. There were only seven or eight of us in the small space, but I think we all would remember this as one of those impossible-to-describe moments. I mean: *They hadn't played together in twenty-five years!*

The next afternoon, other historic reunions were underway: The Doors were to be inducted, and on another soundstage, I saw Ray Manzarek, Robby Krieger, and John Densmore rehearsing "Light My Fire." Eddie Vedder from Pearl Jam would step in for the lead vocal duties. Eddie was full of charisma and angst, and his deep, howling voice could do Jim Morrison justice.

Manzarek told me, "In true rock 'n' roll style, Eddie and his girlfriend have decided to drive down from Seattle instead of flying. No one for sure knows when he will arrive."

Suzan Evans recalled, "We were worried and asked Eddie to call and check in every hour."

Ultimately, Vedder arrived on time and was in great form; he nailed the rehearsals. After witnessing the Cream rehearsal the previous day and seeing the Doors performance, I knew that the ceremony itself was going to be extraordinary.

While all this was happening, there was yet another rehearsal going on. Creedence Clearwater Revival was being inducted, and while John Fogerty wanted to perform, he was unwilling to speak with, let alone perform with, his former bandmates due to bad blood and long-term disputes. Instead, Fogerty hatched the idea to form an ad hoc supergroup for the evening to play a set of CCR songs and enlisted Bruce Springsteen, Robbie Robertson, and producer Don Was to fill in. The board was torn on what to do, but since Jann acquiesced, it went forward. Suzan called me right after Fogerty's rehearsal—she was very upset and told me it was a terrible idea and would reflect poorly on the Hall of Fame.

On the day of the ceremony, I was a fly on the wall at Cream's soundcheck at the Century Plaza. They played at full volume, and there was no security there—just me, Gallen, and a few roadies, along with Eddie Van Halen and his brother, Alex, both of them Cream superfans. I couldn't believe it. After a few minutes Eddie Vedder stormed in, livid, grabbed a folding chair, and hurled it across the room—he seemed to be upset that he had missed the beginning of the soundcheck.

Afterward, I managed to snag Ginger Baker for a short meeting in a hotel suite I had rented. Ginger was again dressed in head-to-toe denim and sat in the chair directly across from me, but while I gave him my standard pitch about preserving his history, he was clearly off thinking about something else. I wrapped up my meeting and let him go on his way—this just wasn't the right time.

At the actual induction, the members of ZZ Top gave eloquent speeches—they were touched that Clapton had asked them to be there.

"Tonight, I get to hear Ginger Baker play drums," drummer Frank Beard said. "Starting out in the '60s, there were one hundred drummers in Dallas, and when Ginger and Cream came out, we all set our drums up like Ginger. We all had two bass drums now, and we all had tom-toms set sideways, and we all put two cymbals on each stand. He was the one drummer that we all wanted to be like. And we all studied his work and listened to the records and said, 'How did he do that? How did he make that sound?' So when we get through introducing Cream, and the gentleman tries to lead me back to my table over here, I'm not going. I'm going to be hiding over here behind an amplifier and I'm gonna be watching Ginger Baker play drums."

From Cream, Jack Bruce spoke first, and he thanked his former bandmates along with Ahmet, who had signed the band to Atlantic Records in 1966. Clapton spoke next: "I have to be honest and say that, until very recently, I just didn't believe in this institution at all," he said, talking about the Hall of Fame. "I don't believe in institutions, I suppose, but it seems to me that rock 'n' roll should never be respectable. And then a friend of mine not long ago, Robbie Robertson, pointed out to me that minor and major miracles take place in here. It moved me, and I looked at this from a different point of view, and I saw that a lot could be gained by coming here tonight. I've been united with two people that I love very dearly. It's very moving, and yesterday, we played together for the first time in twenty-five years. It was pretty amazing, it was wonderful, and we're gonna play again in a little while. I don't know how it will be. . . . The last time we were together, we were on acid down at my house, and we were in the garden, and this drug dealer that owed me money or drugs or something came around the corner, and he stopped about thirty feet away, and he couldn't get any closer—it was like there was a force field." By this point, Clapton was beyond emotional; he was crying onstage as he finished. "And that kind of symbolizes to me what happens when the three of us get together—it can be good or bad, you never know. I'm very, very grateful to be here tonight."

Right then, the institution's stock skyrocketed, with Cream's short set moments later another major victory: It was the first time in the Rock Hall's history that a true reunion had taken place. There would be other reunions years later, but nothing ever compared to this one.

The evening wasn't all sunshine and rainbows, though. After the CCR awards were presented, John Fogerty and his pals played an incredible set, but CCR bassist Stu Cook and drummer Doug Clifford had left the ballroom before Fogerty and his pals started to play, both of them very hurt and angry.

"Right now, I feel pretty hollow," said Clifford. "John refused to play with Stu Cook and myself because he doesn't like us. What can I tell you? *Creedence* was inducted, not John Fogerty. The love and the grooves will never be taken out by the hate in his heart." (Fogerty sang "Born on the Bayou," "Who'll Stop the Rain," and "Green River.")

After the fallout, Springsteen felt uncomfortable that he had been involved, as he was unaware that Stu and Doug had been intentionally sidelined.

The board had made a poor decision. The performance wasn't in the spirit of the Hall of Fame's mission, and it turned out to be a low point in the organization's history. The controversy didn't overshadow the show, however, which had made news around the world.

And next we'd make some real groundbreaking news.

Ozzy Osbourne, the one and only Prince of Darkness, who jumped out a window at his home in the English countryside while meeting with Rock & Roll Hall of Fame curator Craig Inciardi in 1996. PHOTO CREDIT: Jeffrey Mayer / Rock Negatives / MediaPunch

Craig Inciardi in his office at Sotheby's in New York, shortly after joining the auction firm, 1988. PHOTO CREDIT: Author's Collection

Jerry Lee Lewis, Fats Domino, and James Brown beaming with pride in the ballroom of the Waldorf Astoria Hotel at the first annual induction ceremony, 1986. The ceremony was like a high school reunion for the pioneering artists. PHOTO CREDIT: Associated Press

John Fogerty, Keith Richards, Neil Young, and Chuck Berry kick off the first ever jam session at the Waldorf Astoria Hotel in 1986. Berry was the first artist inducted, and Richards did the honors. PHOTO CREDIT: AP

Chuck Berry scoops up Suzan Evans at the second annual Rock & Roll Hall of Fame induction ceremony at the Waldorf in 1987. (Left to right: Jerry Leiber, Jann Wenner, Suzan Evans, Bruce Springsteen, Chuck Berry, John Fogerty [partially obscured], Henry Stone, and Roy Orbison [partially obscured].) PHOTO CREDIT: Ron Galella / Ron Galella Collection via Getty Images

ob Dylan, George Harrison, and Mick Jagger at the third annual induction ceremony at the Waldorf storia Hotel in 1988. This ceremony is widely regarded as the most historic of the induction ceremonies, ears before it became ubiquitous for rock stars from different groups to perform together. CREDIT: Sonia Ioskowitz / Getty Images

Ruth Brown at the podium after her induction into the Rock & Roll Hall of Fame in Los Angeles, 1993. PHOTO CREDIT: Jeff Kravitz / Getty Images

Debbie Harry striking a pose while wearing a stage outfit that Inciardi collected from her for exhibition, 1980s. PHOTO CREDIT: Maureen Donaldson / Getty Images

Yoko Ono exclaimed, "Cleveland . . . look what you've done!" Left to right: Seymour Stein, Jann Wenner, Lewie Steinberg (original bassist for Booker T. & the MGs), Ono, Little Richard, Dennis Barrie, and Suzan Evans at the ribbon cutting ceremony for the opening of the Rock Hall in Cleveland on September 1, 1995. PHOTO CREDIT: AP

Bruce Springsteen and Chuck Berry performing at Municipal Stadium in Cleveland on September 2, 1995, for the concert celebrating the opening of the Rock & Roll Hall of Fame. PHOTO CREDIT: AP

Paul McCartney and his daughter Stella McCartney, on hand at the 1999 induction ceremony at the Waldorf Astoria Hotel. Stella's shirt made vividly clear how annoyed her father was that h induction as a solo artist took way too long. PHOTO CREDIT: Kevin Mazur / WireImage / Getty Images

The Beatles' iconic *Sgt. Pepper's Lonely Hearts Club Band* costumes as exhibited in the *Rock Style* exhibition at the Costume Institute, the Metropolitan Museum of Art, 1999. PHOTO CREDIT: The Metropolitan Museum of Art

rince taunted a very pissed off Tom Petty during the memorial tribute to George Harrison in March 004. Prince's guitar solo became the most significant musical event in the institution's long history. After oncluding his solo, the Purple One threw his guitar straight up into the air, disappearing into the night. eft to right: Tom Petty, Dhani Harrison, and Prince.) PHOTO CREDIT: Timothy A. Clary / AFP via Getty nages

Inextricably linked: Jann Wenner, Mick Jagger, and Ahmet Ertegun on stage during Wenner's induction into the Rock & Roll Hall of Fame in 2004. PHOTO CREDIT: AP

Better late than never. KISS is finally inducted into the Rock Hall at the Barclays Center in Brooklyn, 2014. (Left to right: Paul Stanley, Peter Criss, Ace Frehley, and Gene Simmons, alongside their champion Tom Morello.) PHOTO CREDIT: Charles Sykes / Invision / AP

Craig Inciardi and Keith Richards at Richards's home in Connecticut in 2014. They were horsing around with Richards's uncooperative Jaguar when he donated it to the museum. PHOTO CREDIT: Jane Rose

CHAPTER EIGHT

GROUNDBREAKING IN CLEVELAND

The year 1993 was the year the delays and the bullshit excuses came to an end. On June 7, we *finally* broke ground on construction of the museum. Ahmet coaxed a bunch of artists to show up, including Chuck Berry, Pete Townshend, and the "Queen of R&B" Ruth Brown. Jann brought Billy Joel and Yoko Ono. It was a joyous day. Townshend theatrically asked, "Is there any liquor? Is there any liquor here?" I think someone handed him a beer. Pete and Chuck Berry played air guitar with their commemorative shovels; Jann had handed out dozens.

An enormous guitar-shaped stage was built for the groundbreaking. There were close to five thousand fans and the Goodyear Blimp on hand at the construction site to witness the event. Ahmet was genuinely appreciative. From the podium, he said, "Many people have asked us over the years why we chose Cleveland to be the site of the Rock & Roll Hall of Fame and Museum, and my answer to them is that we chose Cleveland because Cleveland shows us the quality of the people who represented the city. When they came to see us—[it] was so far superior to everyone else we met that there was no doubt in our mind that this was where we wanted to be. This is a great moment for the music industry, for the city of Cleveland, and the state of Ohio."

From the podium, Pete Townshend said, "It was music that came from people that were in trouble, and spoke deeply and hugely and heroically. From deep down in their soul—that's what we inherit here. It's a real living, breathing religion. Let's hope it doesn't become a monolith to a bunch of dinosaurs; then the cynics would have their way with us."

Ahmet and I had wanted to leverage the event to secure some donations, so we had called up Townshend when we were together in the Atlantic Records office in New York. Hanging up the phone, Ahmet said, "Pete is going to bring something special over from London." I imagined a broad spectrum of possibilities. *What will it be?*

At the construction site in Cleveland, I greeted Pete, whom I had met a few months earlier in New York when he was casting the Broadway production of *Tommy*. Pete handed me his Gibson J-200 acoustic guitar and said, "This is the guitar I used to write 'Pinball Wizard.'"

Townshend strummed a few chords and said, "I haven't touched this guitar for over ten years, and when I looked at it back in London, it was still perfectly in tune." It was the first important musical instrument that I collected for the museum.

Remember my visit to Art Garfunkel's home? Well, that wasn't the end of it. Back at his penthouse, I was continuing to make progress. I had settled into a routine over the past few months, working upstairs.

One day, Art told me that he'd be working downstairs for the next few hours, and not to disturb him. About an hour later, I started to hear Simon & Garfunkel songs being played. And I thought to myself, *What artist plays their own records at home*? It seemed very odd. I was puzzled. So I quietly walked halfway down the spiral staircase to listen. The music continued. I heard "Mrs. Robinson," and then I heard the song abruptly stop. I heard Garfunkel talking, and then I heard him say the words *harmony* and *leap octave*. At that moment, I realized that Art and Paul were sitting on a sofa about twenty feet below me rehearsing for a concert! Paul's acoustic guitar sounded magical; his fingerpicking was magnificent. He was able to do so much with an acoustic without being a showoff. I sat motionless for the next thirty minutes and listened to them run through some of their greatest songs—"Mrs. Robinson," "The Sound of Silence," "El Cóndor Pasa," and a section of "Bridge Over Troubled Water." I was tearing up. It felt as if the world were standing still. I walked quietly back up the spiral staircase while they were still playing and stared out the window to Seventy-Ninth Street, watching the traffic and the people below while they continued to sing. Not a single one of those people on the street had any idea of what was occurring high above. It was that great magic of New York.

Art made a substantial donation to the museum—one of the first collections that included important manuscripts, which showed two artists developing their craft. In many ways, they were lucky they had started off as that duo, Tom & Jerry. They learned the music business as teenagers, and when Clive Davis signed them to Columbia Records in 1963, they were already seasoned recording artists and negotiated a record deal that would make the Beatles envious.

Around this time, I was also realizing that I apparently had a talent for befriending rock stars' mothers. I was striking up a friendship with Jim Morrison's mother, Clara Morrison. (Yes, the Lizard King had a mother.) She and her husband, George Morrison, a retired US Navy rear admiral, were so proud of their son, even though he had written them off and told the press they were dead. A month or so into my correspondence and conversations with

Clara, a beaten-up cardboard box arrived at my office via Federal Express. Inside were dozens of loving handwritten notes and cards from Jim to his mother, his first poem ever written entitled "The Pony Express," his Cub Scout uniform, dozens of child photos, early poems inspired directly by Rimbaud, drawings, and letters from his father discussing Jim's legal troubles—all in all, an amazing representation of his formative years.

The collection humanized Morrison, who by this point had been typecast as a sexy, wild-shaman poet. While much of that might have been true, that wasn't the whole story. Viewing all of the materials revealed a man who had had a rich and interesting childhood—an army brat who moved from town to town many times. What happened in his teen years to stoke the dramatic transformation that he eventually underwent has still never been completely uncovered, though, and after reading many of the notes that he had written to his mother, I still couldn't imagine what caused him to leave home, cut himself off from his family, and tell the press they were dead. The collection was head and shoulders one of the most significant gifts made to the museum.

Meanwhile, my conversations with Keith Moon's mother were starting to pay off. In October 1993, she called me up and said, "I've got some things for you if you can have somebody pick them up." Seymour was in London at that moment and he had his assistant pick it up. Soon, a trunk filled with a large quantity of Keith's stage clothing, handwritten letters, and report cards (filled mostly with C's and D's) arrived at our offices. Finally, I was beginning to build a collection worthy of the artists in the Rock Hall.

In August 1993, the board had hired Dennis Barrie as director of the museum. While there had been many acting directors who had shepherded the project along, none of them had museum experience. With Barrie at the helm, we had a real museum professional with a résumé that included the Smithsonian Institution and, later, the Contemporary Arts Center in Cincinnati, where he had been charged with obscenity for presenting the Robert Mapplethorpe exhibit *The Perfect Moment* (He and the museum were acquitted of all charges). Despite Barrie's credentials, though, Jann made it clear that he shouldn't be *too* confident in his new role.

"Jann told me I had the job," Barrie recalled, "and told me that I had fifty-one percent of the vote." He laughed. "That's classic Jann." The reality was that Wenner wanted to run the museum from his corner office at *Rolling Stone* in midtown Manhattan—and, to an extent, that is what he did for decades to come.

CHAPTER NINE

BEAT THE CLOCK

By 1994, Cleveland was on track, with the museum barreling toward completion. The whole thing had been one big Hail Mary. We were improvising the way the Grateful Dead or Phish might approach a jam. Sure, we had subjects, locations, and periods to cover. But unlike fine art museums, where paintings were hanging on the gallery walls, when visitors entered our new music museum, they likely *already* possessed the art: The music we were honoring was on the records, tapes, and CDs in their collections at home, and on their car stereos.

As self-proclaimed rock music curators, we sought to create a museum experience that relied on supporting evidence—the debris, the tools that made music, the iconography, and the fashion associated with the artists and their fans. All of that could be assembled and presented to tell stories. Using a combination of artifacts, musical instruments, photography, film footage, and posters, we sought to document, honor, and preserve more than a half century of music.

I flew back to London for another sweep. The primary focus of this trip was to secure a collection from the Stones. I met Alan Dunn, who had worked for the band since 1967; he was a big, imposing figure, but inside he was a teddy bear. Alan, who had also worked for Dusty Springfield, did all the logistics for the band's tours and often accompanied Mick Jagger as a bodyguard.

"My first assignment was in 1967," he told me. "I had to go out into Central London to locate Brian's Rolls-Royce, which he had abandoned one night after overdoing it."

I met Alan at the band's headquarters in Wandsworth Plain in South London. He had a small but nice office, with a morning fire burning in the fireplace when I arrived. Alan was immediately receptive to helping me, and over the years remained a tremendous advocate for me and the museum. The Stones' offices comprised several townhouses, with a courtyard in the middle and more buildings in the back. I saw one of Mick Jagger's Ferraris parked in a garage. Alan let me loose in an old stone garage that housed, among other items, band wardrobes that I recognized from past tours. I spent hours looking at things.

Curators, of course, always wear many hats, and on this day, I felt very much like a twentieth-century archaeologist. When I was finishing up, I noticed a couple road cases that I had seen in photos from the 1970s and behind them, a large object with a blanket thrown over it. I uncovered it and saw that it was a hulking keyboard. As I examined it more closely, I got very excited: It was a Mellotron, which was a precursor to the synthesizer. It was completely analog—each key was connected to a separate spool of recording tape that played a specific note. The instrument played the actual sounds of trumpets, violins, saxophones, and other instruments. (Perhaps most famously, the Mellotron is what the Beatles used to record "Strawberry Fields Forever.") I took a couple of Polaroids and went back to my hotel. (I had brought some books about the Stones to London, and I was able to identify the keyboard as one that the band used on their psychedelic album *Their Satanic Majesties Request*.) I located a photo of Brian Jones playing the keyboard on several of the tracks, including "2000 Light Years from Home." It was an extraordinary discovery.

In the end, I came away with a fantastic collection that included the Mellotron (which would be shipped to Cleveland), one of Mick Jagger's iconic Ossie Clark–designed jumpsuits from the 1972 tour, one of his football-style outfits from the 1981 tour—replete with white Capezio ballet-style shoes—and his plastic punk outfit from the late 1970s, along with various garments from Ron Wood. A snare from Charlie Watts was all they could spare in the drum department. Maybe best of all, though, was the dulcimer I secured that Brian Jones played on the recording of "Lady Jane." (Jones, the band's multi-instrumentalist, could extract a great sound out of virtually everything he touched.)

Back in the States, I headed to TAIT Towers—one of the premier stage-building and stage-designing firms in the world—in Lititz, Pennsylvania, where I was able to secure some of the scenery and staging from the 1989 Steel Wheels Tour.

Meanwhile, back in Cleveland, Dennis Barrie realized that the museum needed more edginess and pizzazz. I. M. Pei's design was elegant, but very austere—it didn't exactly scream rock 'n' roll. Compounding that fact, the Burdick Group had an interior aesthetic quite similar to what Pei was doing. We needed to be unique. So Barrie did his best to make changes, though he had come late to the party and most decisions had already been made years earlier.

In a masterstroke, however, Barrie hired the cult fashion designer Stephen Sprouse as an overall stylist. Sprouse, who found his calling in the late '70s after working for American designer Halston, was a fashion innovator who incorporated graffiti into his designs. In Cleveland, Sprouse provided the appropriate amount of punk-rock fairy dust to sprinkle throughout the museum; he even designed the uniforms for the museum's security guards. Sprouse also knew that a standard fashion mannequin was not going to work to display garments, since most rock stars are not six feet tall. He hired a skeletal, five-foot-seven male model whose body would be cast in plaster to make a custom mannequin for the museum.

"We need a mannequin that will fit the clothing of a typical singer who's a heroin addict," Sprouse said.

The model arrived at a mannequin-making studio in Brooklyn's Dumbo neighborhood. He tried on one of Sid Vicious's outfits, and it fit perfectly—he had passed the test, and a life cast was made of him. Then we commissioned designer and fabricator Ralph Pucci, who had worked with the Costume Institute at the Metropolitan Museum of Art, to produce the mannequins for the Hall of Fame. There were, of course, exceptions to the rule—Robert Plant, Joey Ramone, and Brian May were all well over six feet tall, and we also employed a female mannequin based on a petite model.

The following week, I was back working with Sprouse. I woke up super excited about the day's assignment and took a taxi to collect Sprouse at his apartment, where the walls, floors, and ceilings were all painted flat black. It was jarring, made you feel uncomfortable—which I suppose was the point. It seemed like punk rock's answer to Andy Warhol's aluminum foil–decorated spaces at the Factory. But no matter: On this day, Sprouse would be introducing me to my high school crush and idol, Debbie Harry.

Sprouse was friends with Debbie and had designed some of her most famous stage outfits when they were neighbors on the Bowery during Blondie's early days. We headed over to Debbie's apartment in the London Terrace complex on West Twenty-Third Street. Inside, her space was decorated with animal skin rugs, and on the wall, I spotted a Warhol portrait of her. Soon she began pulling out a ton of her most famous outfits as Stephen and I sat on a sofa; a moment later, Debbie laid on the floor in front of us on a carpet, vamping and putting on a show for us. Stephen and I selected several outfits for exhibition—some of them designed by Stephen himself, including a black off-the-shoulder micro mini dress with thigh-high boots. On the spot, Stephen grabbed a Sharpie and sketched out a recreation of his original design, entitled "Detroit 442," and handed it to me as a souvenir.

Debbie was happy to help us out. And I knew, unquestionably, that Blondie would be inducted in a few years, when they became eligible—at least twenty-five years after an artist's first released recording.

At the moment, our punk exhibit was coming along nicely. We had collected from Jamie Reid, who designed many of the Sex Pistols' most famous album covers and graphics, as well as from Debbie, and more was coming. Next on my list was visiting Chris Stein, Debbie's ex-bandmate, ex-boyfriend, and songwriting partner, who lived down in Tribeca off Desbrosses Street in a cavernous loft right around the corner from the film production company we had hired to produce films that would eventually be incorporated into the museum's exhibits. Amid what looked liked human skulls and other creepy artifacts in Chris's apartment, I procured Debbie and Chris's lyric manuscript for "Rapture"—one of the first commercial pop hits to include a rap. Hanging on the wall was the original painting for Blondie's album *Autoamerican.* (Six months later, I saw that very same artwork hanging in the Upper East Side apartment of its new owner—a former Sotheby's client.)

Next stop: The Ramones. I went to see the band at a studio in Chelsea, where they were finishing up a rehearsal. I introduced myself to Joey Ramone, Johnny Ramone, Marky Ramone, and the band's new bass player C. J. Ramone., who had replaced Dee Dee Ramone. Everyone was very friendly—except Johnny.

"What's the point of this," he said, as I introduced myself, "and why do we have to shake hands?"

I explained that we were building a new punk exhibit at the Hall of Fame, and that we wanted the Ramones to be well represented. I felt like a door-to-door salesman, but I knew it came with the territory. I was always asking for a favor. We all walked out of the building together; Johnny's bicycle was leaning up against the wall, and he just got on it and rode away. I told the other guys I'd be in touch. It was becoming a game of inches.

Onward, I went over to Keith Richards's office at 1776 Broadway to work on our Rolling Stones exhibit. I was able to collect some amazing papers and artwork, including a setlist handwritten by Richards from 1978's *Some Girls* tour. Between what I had collected from the band members and from some serious Stones collectors, we had enough to curate a solid exhibit for the museum's opening.

Meanwhile, Jann was making more moves. That year he made Jon Landau cochair of the nominating committee with Seymour Stein, who had been in charge since 1988. Landau was close friends with Jann and had written for *Rolling Stone* since the magazine's first issue. He'd also produced MC5, and after leaving *Rolling Stone* in the mid 1970s, he became Bruce Springsteen's manager and producer. Landau provided additional gravitas to the committee and helped bring a certain amount of order to the sometimes long-winded and meandering meetings that Seymour Stein had presided over. Of equal importance, Landau shared the same musical tastes as Jann. Together—and with the help of a lot of other like-minded journalists—they had essentially invented rock 'n' roll music criticism. The Beatles, Bob Dylan, and the Stones—along with blues greats like Muddy Waters—were categorically supreme. Conversely, entire genres like heavy metal and progressive rock received poor record reviews in *Rolling Stone* or weren't covered at all.

Since its inception in 1985 (and continuing today), the annual nominating committee meeting has been greatly anticipated. Members mark their calendars almost a year in advance, and it's a rarity that anyone missed the meeting. Being on the committee affords the approximately thirty-five members great prestige and bragging rights—for many members, it's part of their identity.

Most of these meetings were held in the boardroom of Wenner Media—*Rolling Stone*'s parent company—with the committee typically nominating fifteen artists each year. That ballot was sent to the voting committee, comprised of approximately a thousand people in the music business, including artists, producers, journalists, record executives, and agents.

The top-five-to-seven vote-getters were inducted.

If the sixth or seventh vote-getters were deemed essential to the financial success of the ceremony, they were also inducted. In addition, there were various awards for non-performers, side performers, and early influence categories.

Suzan Evans always made sure there was a gargantuan spread from the Carnegie Delicatessen at these meetings: piles of pastrami, corned beef, chopped liver, and—non-negotiable—a pound of sliced tongue, all washed down with Dr. Brown's Cream Soda and Cel-Ray. Five hours later, by the time the initial ballot was tallied, some of the attendees looked like they needed to be carted away.

Seymour Stein's animated and undisciplined personality had made him a curious choice to head up the nominating committee, but he was dedicated, passionate, well-liked, and knew his music backward and forward. The meetings he ran were often unwieldy and rollicking, very much like Stein himself. There was singing and reminiscing, and people were allowed to go off on twenty-minute tangents to speak about an obscure doo-wop group. His leadership was a reflection of the Hall of Fame's freewheeling early years, when an "anything goes" ethos permeated the entire organization.

Phil Spector would typically arrive at the meetings with his long hair still wet, straight from the shower. (Of course, everyone knew he wore a wig.) Some members of the committee were in awe of Phil, many were afraid of him and his influence, and others were in awe of him *and* afraid of him. Spector held a lot of grudges, in particular against artists whom he had worked with and invariably fell out with, and he had a famous penchant for faxing cruel, misogynistic notes with oddly scrawled caricatures, singling out whomever he felt deserved punishment. His ex-wife Ronnie Spector, the lead singer of the Ronettes, was a prime target of Phil's influence on the committee, ensuring that the Ronettes would never be nominated on his watch.

Phil also held a grudge against George Harrison. He and George had, of course, worked together in the early '70s, with Phil bringing his Wall of Sound production to George's album *All Things Must Pass*. There were creative differences, especially with the amount of reverb Spector put on the album. George was inducted to the Hall of Fame as a solo artist only posthumously, and it is suspected that Spector had maneuvered behind the scenes to keep him off the ballot when he was alive.

I attended the meetings as a notetaker and vote counter, and I was there to check dates if someone had a question about the eligibility of an artist, or when they had recorded their first songs. Popularity was not a criterion for nomination, nor were record sales.

In the winter of 1995, I flew to London to view the Victoria and Albert Museum's rock 'n' roll collection in the hope that we could negotiate a significant loan for the museum. The V&A's collection was then part of London's Theatre Museum in Covent Garden, but their warehouse was located near the Olympia tube stop in Kensington, West London. The majority of their collection had been acquired in the 1970s, and they were particularly strong in costumes and stage outfits. There were several sets of the Beatles' iconic collarless suits from the early '60s, designed by the Soho tailor Dougie Millings. I examined the labels and the linings of the jackets, each one with the name of each band member sewn into the inner pockets (one jacket had John Lennon's name stitched into the collar).

There were numerous fake Beatles stage suits so it was important to check the labels and stitching. On a strange instinct, I reached into one of the jacket pockets and, to my surprise, found a square, tortoise shell–colored guitar pick—a tiny object, but so unique and important. I dropped it back into the pocket and went on to look at a giant garment rack of stage costumes donated to the museum by Adam and the Ants; or the most part, they were the same pirate-style outfits I had seen the band wear onstage at Pier 84 on the West Side of Manhattan when I caught their concert in high school. (The band made a memorable entrance on an old pirate ship flying the Jolly Roger.)

There were also several fantastic outfits from Led Zeppelin, including Jimmy Page's iconic poppy suit and the outfit that John Paul Jones wore during *The Song Remains the Same* film; guitars from Pete Townshend; and Mick Jagger's handwritten notes for the London choir that sang on "You Can't Always Get What You Want." I negotiated a significant loan from the V&A for the museum's 1995 opening, and their staff couriered the artifacts to Cleveland and helped install them in the exhibits.

Building on my maternal success with Kit Moon, I decided to spend even more time focusing on the mothers of artists. Jim Henke and I had sketched out an idea for a two-part punk rock exhibit for the museum's opening—half focusing on London, and the other half on New York. I called Patti Smith, who put me in touch with her mother, Beverly Smith, and she immediately invited me down to her house in Mantua, New Jersey. Beverly lived in a modest ranch house and had lots of scrapbooks and other material related to her daughter; I could immediately tell she was Patti's biggest fan. Beverly ended up donating the pair of black leather boots that Patti wore onstage every night during the 1970s, wrapped with duct tape, along with some other stage clothing, photographs, and postcards. Even though Patti hadn't yet been inducted into the Hall of Fame, I knew she was a shoo-in once she became eligible. (Early on, I made the decision to cast my net for acquisitions quite wide: Limiting myself to the artists who were already inducted made no sense on many levels.)

Once every six weeks or so, I traveled out to Cleveland to meet with Henke and my colleagues and to check out progress on the new building. Turner Construction was in charge of building the museum, and there were a number of challenges. For one, those bitter, lake-effect Cleveland winters made it nearly impossible to properly cure the museum's foundation; the builders ended up having to build tents and blowtorches to keep temperatures warm enough for the concrete to properly cure. Also, I. M. Pei's ambitious design included a complicated cantilevered theater that would hang directly into the harbor of Lake Erie.

But with construction of the building well underway, whenever a major artist was in town for a show, we would invite them to take a hard-hat tour of the building site. And on August 28, 1994, the Stones were playing at Cleveland Municipal Stadium, which was just a couple hundred yards from the museum. When Jim Henke went over to say hello to the band before their sound check, Mick Jagger told him that the Mellotron keyboard that he had loaned to the museum—that same Mellotron I'd uncovered at the band's offices in South London—was used to record "Jumpin' Jack Flash." I was pumped that it would be displayed at the museum's opening.

By 1995, less than a year away from our opening date, we were collecting at a feverish pace. There were so many different eras to cover, so many different musical genres and styles. We were having particular trouble collecting from the pioneering artists of the 1950s.

Elvis wasn't a problem. It was almost one-stop shopping: We had secured a fantastic collection from Sam Phillips and Graceland.

Chuck Berry had given us a guitar, the lyrics to "School Days," and a jacket—not much, but they were substantial enough for us to tell a story.

For some reason, though, we were having difficulty with the piano players. We were nowhere with Little Richard or Jerry Lee Lewis.

I had been telephoning Richard in Los Angeles for five years now. He lived in a hotel room, and when I called, he usually pretended to be one of his brothers on the line—an easy way for him to screen calls. We also had no success with the Killer.

So one day I called Seymour Stein and told him our plight.

Seymour suggested that we make a trip down to New Orleans to see Fats Domino. He knew Fats and felt confident that we might make some inroads. Our meeting was arranged with the help of Philadelphia DJ Jerry Blavat, "the Geator with the Heater" I didn't know anyone like Blavat. He rubbed shoulders with Chuck Berry, Fats Domino, and Frank Sinatra—half rock 'n' roll, half Rat Pack—and he had that wise-guy vibe that could help you on occasion. Lord knows we needed it now; we were pretty much dead in the water with some of the most important artists from the '50s.

The three of us checked into a grand old New Orleans hotel. In the elevator on our way up to our rooms, Jerry's cell phone rang.

"Hi, Vic, how are you?" he said.

The conversation was brief.

"That was Vic Damone, calling from the coast."

Blavat had a warm bond with the old-timers and seemed pleased with himself. I felt confident he was going to make a difference.

Fats Domino's driver and valet Rip soon arrived with Fats in tow, and the conversation immediately turned to food. I was in heaven—I had never been to New Orleans, and as a foodie, I could not have been in a better place. Seymour was another glutton like me, so I knew there was going to be a lot of eating on the trip—and let's just say that walking into a restaurant in New Orleans with Fats

Domino was like arriving with royalty. Over the course of two days, we dined at Antoine's, Brennan's, and Galatoire's. I had a great conversation with Fats about his gumbo, and Rip explained how he made turtle soup—a tale which included some fairly graphic details about the poor turtle in question. Fats eventually convinced me to have a bowl of it—loaded with heavy cream and sherry—at Brennan's. I'm glad I didn't develop gout on that trip.

Antoine "Fats" Domino was such a gentle and humble man. It's extraordinary how someone so influential—you could argue that the music he was playing in the late 1940s was already rock 'n' roll—had seemingly no ego and was so self-effacing. As with Chuck Berry, we got a small but significant collection from Fats. One of my favorite items was the short-sleeve shirt he wore in the '60s that had actual dominoes on it. When you saw that shirt, you immediately knew who had owned it. A few years later, Fats was up in New York shopping a record deal and met with Seymour at the Sire Records office in Rockefeller Center. Seymour had a Steinway upright brought in so Fats could play some of his new songs, and I was there when they wheeled in the piano. Fats started playing immediately. In the end, he and Seymour couldn't make a deal; he wanted a record of duets pairing Fats with artists like Elton John, Billy Joel, and Stevie Wonder. Though Fats was nice about it all, he simply wasn't interested. (He did ask me how my gumbo was coming along.)

Back in New York a few weeks later, I went to see Joey Ramone again. When I met him in the lobby of his East Ninth Street building, Joey was carrying a coconut that a fan had mailed to him, with a note written right on the shell and encrusted with postage stamps. I couldn't believe it actually made it through the postal system, but there it was. Joey's apartment was a kind of man-child cave, decorated with Godzilla memorabilia; his mother was there doing his laundry, and he was still distraught over losing his girlfriend to none other than his guitar player, Johnny.

"She's like Anita Pallenberg," he said. "I lost my girlfriend to another guy, and of all people in the world, it's someone I share the stage with." (In his comparison, he was referring to the infamous love triangle between Keith Richards, Pallenberg, and Brian Jones.) Eventually, Joey gave us one of his iconic black leather jackets.

Later, as Jann looked back on the experience of building the Hall of Fame in Cleveland from several decades' distance, he was very candid: "It took ten years to build the actual Hall of Fame," he wrote. "In the first place, I didn't really know what I was doing, and I was the one who knew the most."

Ertegun had unilaterally decided on I. M. Pei from the get-go, knowing that it would be easier to raise money for the construction of a building with a world-famous architect. But that meant there was no bid process or competition. The board—many of whom only had experience working with architects on their residential projects in the Hamptons or Europe—placed their complete trust in Pei and his colleagues.

With less than a year before the museum's opening, it was becoming apparent that the building had a long list of shortcomings. As a curator, I was responsible for collecting and conceiving exhibits—and, on a practical level, deciding where those objects would be located. I had not given any thought whatsoever—nor had my colleagues—to how these objects would enter the building. There were several rude awakenings, with Dennis Barrie being the first canary in the coal mine.

"I. M. Pei was a fascinating choice," Barrie said, "because you wouldn't associate him with rock 'n' roll. He was a true gentleman. When I went to meet him as the building was going up, he said, 'You have a great building with many problems.' That's a quote."

When Barry asked him to elaborate, Pei admitted, "Well, the limits of the building, the way it goes up, precludes you from doing certain things."

We soon realized what that meant: There were no freight elevators, for instance—heresy for a museum—so we were forced to use small passenger elevators and high riggers to hoist large objects to the upper floors. Also, the glass-centric design caused far too much daylight flooding, which could damage objects on exhibition; the office space was all below grade; and storage was limited. The building was elegant, but cold and austere—it certainly didn't scream rock 'n' roll. The Burdick Group, who were in charge of interior and exhibit design, didn't have a rock 'n' roll aesthetic either.

We were also butting heads with Pei about where some of the artifacts would be displayed in his new building. U2 loaned the museum several automobiles that they had used as stage props during their Zoo TV Tour—Russian Trabants that were covered in fur, lights, and colorful paint. I had the idea of suspending them from the soaring ceiling of the building so that they could be seen when you entered through the doors. Pei, though, felt this would spoil the sight lines inside the building. In the end, we did install the U2 cars, and they still hang there to this day, along with other large props including a gigantic hot dog that I acquired from Phish, who used it during their famed New Year's Eve performances at Madison Square Garden. (They even borrowed it back once for the Garden shows, returning it a few weeks later.)

The challenge was unique: The Rock & Roll Hall of Fame is a museum about music, but since music is invisible, the museum needed to become a series of storytelling experiences on a visual level, supported by both the tools of the trade and the visual detritus that exists from the making of music.

Not surprisingly, there are artists and fans who question if there even should be a museum dedicated to rock history. Since rock 'n' roll was built on a foundation of anti-establishment ethos, it was only natural that the Rock Hall's existence would be controversial. Among the artists who refused to attend their inductions and accept the honors were David Bowie, Joni Mitchell, Van Morrison, and Thom Yorke. They all had their reasons for not attending. However, some of the most anti-establishment artists like Bob Dylan and Neil Young were there at the podium and came back for more. At the Kinks induction in 1991, Ray Davies had it both ways. He arrived at the ceremony wearing his tuxedo, and standing at the podium, he announced, "Seeing everyone here tonight, it makes me realize that rock 'n' roll has become respectable. What a bummer."

Naysayers worried that we were going to drain rock of its passionate rebellion, presenting it like a lab experiment—mummified specimens in glass cases. But Ahmet and Jann had made it clear early on that our mission was righteous and nothing was going to hold us back from doing our job.

"This fringe culture being somewhat enshrined in a temple, with formalized architecture—there were antithetical elements in that idea," said Jann. "I heard it a lot at the beginning: You guys are going to violate the spirit of rock 'n' roll."

Many artists questioned the whole idea of the museum, or made jokes about it, but I like to think they came around—even if from the grave. Yoko Ono, speaking for her late husband, put it like this: "I think John might have been suspicious of the idea of the museum at first. And then be very glad that it was there."

In May 1994, Joan and I decided to buy a beach house in East Hampton, an old fishermen's shack from the 1920s on a peninsula called Louse Point. The house had water on two sides, and we could walk out the door and go clamming. Jackson Pollock and Lee Krasner's old house—now a museum—was across the harbor; and three doors away was the writer George Plimpton, who owned an old barge that had been converted into a beach cottage. Plimpton had an out-of-tune piano that we could hear when he was hosting parties, and since a lot of his friends were retired singers from the Metropolitan Opera, we could hear them howling late into the night. Lou Reed and Laurie Anderson had a nice house around the corner, and Paul and Linda McCartney were nearby. They could have bought any house they wanted—the biggest mansion with the most beachfront that anyone could have dreamed of—but what they craved most was privacy. They had an extraordinarily large piece of property, so big that even during the winter, when the trees were stripped of their leaves, you still couldn't see their house from the road.

Toward the end of the summer, Jann got more involved in the collecting process. He knew that we needed a solid representation of the Beatles, and Yoko was his ace in the hole. They had been close for a long time, despite Jann and John Lennon falling out with each other in the early 1970s.

Oh, Yoko! She delivered the motherlode of collections: At a press conference held at the Sony Club on Madison Avenue on October 13, 1994, she announced that she would loan the museum a number of pieces from her personal collection, including John's *Sgt. Pepper* outfit; several of his handwritten lyrics, including "In My Life"; and his Rickenbacker guitar from the Beatles' Shea Stadium concert—with the setlist still attached.

"John would have been pleased to have his work presented in this context," she said, "and I hope his collection will inspire all who see it."

In less than three years, we had somehow managed to build a very solid collection that, in some areas, was downright extraordinary. But again, we were running out of time: We had only another seven or eight months to finish collecting before the museum's opening.

Next, I was on to visit one of Sid Vicious's closest friends, Patti Palladin, an American expat from the band Snatch, who handed over Sid's leather pants, boots, and T-shirts, designed by Vivienne Westwood and Malcolm McLaren and splattered with Sid's own blood. Some of these T-shirts had images so disturbing they could not be displayed. I had everything air-shipped to Cleveland.

As if getting the museum ready to open wasn't enough work, the team also had the 1994 induction ceremony—the ninth annual—to plan and execute. And though I was the editor of the induction program again, Seymour Stein was always in charge of the cover art. What did he want this year? He wanted to use his friend James Holdsworth, a pop art artist from London who had worked on the previous cover. I loved James's work; Joan and I had just bought a very large canvas by him, which was inspired by Anthony Burgess's novel *A Clockwork Orange*.

Suzan Evans and I grabbed a cab and headed down to James's enormous rented studio in a landmark building on Bond Street in Lower Manhattan. It was pouring out, and once we arrived, we had a horrible time trying to figure out which buzzer to push to get into James's studio. As there were no names on any of the buttons, I ended up pressing every single one. Finally, James called down from the intercom, told us to come up to the third floor, come right in, no need to knock, and he buzzed us in.

Suzan and I trudged up the stairs and walked into the third-floor studio, which was dimly lit, and I called out for John. Soon I heard a rustling sound, and from across the room I saw a figure running toward me at full speed—a tall, stunning woman with blonde hair holding a frying pan. She took a swing, aiming for my head, but missed. I could have been killed!

"Get the fuck out of here!" she screamed at us. I held my hands forward while she continued to swing the frying pan, and I explained that we were here to see James Holdsworth.

She soon calmed down and said, simply: "That asshole lives upstairs."

It was at that moment that I recognized the woman: It was the actress and model Lauren Hutton. We were about an inch away from each other, and I could see the famous wide gap in her two front teeth. I apologized, and we left her apartment and climbed the stairs to James's studio on the fourth floor, laughing hysterically. Nobody was hurt.

At the ceremonies that year, John Lennon was inducted as a solo artist, with Paul McCartney there to do the honors (Paul was also eligible but hadn't gotten the nod—more on that later.) Paul's speech was presented in the form of a letter to John: "Dear John, I remember when we first met in Woolton, at the village fête. It was a beautiful summer day."

McCartney reminisced about the first songs they wrote, smoking tea, and dreaming about being famous. He never would have written a letter like this to Lennon if he were alive, but it opened an extraordinary window to fans and the public about their earliest days. I especially liked hearing what it was like when the band was on the road:

> We'd be in the van touring later, and we'd have the kind of night where the windscreen would break. We'd be on the motorway going back up to Liverpool, and it was freezing, so we'd have to lie on top of each other in the back of the van, creating a Beatles sandwich. These were the ways we got to know each other.

After the ceremony, McCartney went over to see Yoko Ono and Sean Lennon at the Dakota, where Yoko handed him cassette tapes containing John's demos for the songs "Free as a Bird," "Real Love," and others, which eventually became post-Lennon Beatles' recordings where Paul, George, and Ringo overdubbed new music onto Lennon's work.

That night, Bono delivered another one of the most powerfully moving speeches as a presenter—one which would be emulated in future ceremonies—inducting the legendary Bob Marley:

"We are both islands. We were both colonies. We share a common yoke: the struggle for identity, the struggle for independence, the vulnerable and uncertain future that's left behind when the jackboot of empire has finally retreated. . . ."

The content, the cadence, and the delivery of Bono's speech was up there with his best song lyrics. It was visceral to hear his thoughts about Ireland's and Jamaica's similarities and connections as artists. And the humor, too, especially joking about both people's penchant for procrastination. For the Hall of Fame, the speech was groundbreaking. It elevated the entire night, adding a poignant and erudite nugget.

Bono had created his own spoken word piece of art—an immediate standout among countless brilliant induction speeches.

Phil Spector, meanwhile, was quickly establishing another tradition after the induction ceremonies. He came every year, bought many tickets and many tables—but it was the lavish afterparties in his suite that were most memorable. Phil was a character, and his presence was always felt.

This time around, Phil had rented out the presidential suite at the Waldorf. There was a grand piano the artists were taking turns playing, and well over two hundred people in attendance. I was talking to Seymour Stein, who said to me, "Look over there! Phil Spector is kissing your wife!" I turned around, and there was Spector on one knee, dressed in his tuxedo, kissing Joan's hand.

Seymour knew Joan fairly well—we had just attended the same New Year's Eve party in St. Barts, and they saw each other at the Park

Avenue Armory antiques shows. And while I'd been corresponding with Spector and trying to convince him to work with us at the Hall of Fame, we'd never actually met. What better time, I thought, to say hello? Joan and Phil were yucking it up, having a grand old time. Joan looked gorgeous in a silver dress, her hair piled high on her head. I introduced myself. "Hi, Phil, I'm Craig Inciardi from the Rock & Roll Hall of Fame. Joan is my wife." Spector mumbled something unintelligible.

I continued. "I'm the curator who—" Phil cut me off mid-sentence and said, "I know who you are. You're that fucking greaseball who keeps sending me letters and calling my office!"

I noticed a revolver bulging out of his jacket. I knew about his reputation with guns—knew that he had threatened both John Lennon and the Ramones, among others, with them. I whisked Joan away to a connecting room. Suzan Evan's assistant at the time picked up the phone, calling room service to send up a case of champagne—billed to Spector's room.

At that point, I had basically given up on pursuing Phil. I stopped calling him, stopped writing letters to him, but I didn't care about his rejection. I knew he was a wack job, and I had much bigger, better fish to fry. I was salivating because on the horizon was the Big Kahuna, the Hammer of the Gods, the Monolith . . . Led Zeppelin.

CHAPTER TEN

LED ZEPPELIN REUNITES

At the induction ceremony in 1995, Jann Wenner stepped up to the podium and gleefully stated: "George Voinovich, who was mayor of Cleveland when we decided to locate the Hall of Fame there, is now the governor of Ohio. I don't have to stand up here and promise you again that we're gonna build this thing. It's the end of making bullshit promises. This is the year we're going to deliver."

There was thunderous applause.

"The museum will open on Labor Day weekend."

The naysayers were finally vanquished, and that "phantom temple of rock in Cleveland" would be a reality.

"They had many legitimate reasons to think that we were really crazy," Jann continued. "We did some crazy things."

The Hall of Fame was like *Rolling Stone*: Both entities had missions and goals that were so brilliant that they survived—indeed, thrived—despite Jann's sometimes nutty decisions. Ahmet had been a great ambassador, but without Jann, there would have been no Rock & Roll Hall of Fame, period. Nobody put in more time, sweat equity, and sheer force of personality to get the place built.

As if that wasn't enough excitement for the evening, Neil Young, the Allman Brothers Band, and Led Zeppelin, among others, would all be enshrined that evening. Led Zeppelin's induction in particular—both the anticipation and the significance of it—was a singular moment in the institution's history, much like Cream coming together at the inductions in 1993.

I bumped into Rex King, who had been working for Zeppelin for years, near the concierge desk at the Waldorf and sheepishly asked him where the band would be rehearsing. Rex snarled at me in Cockney, "*We* don't rehearse!" I always got a kick out of managers and roadies who used the first-person plural, as if they were a band member. What instrument did Rex play—the cowbell? I guess it made sense, though, that there would be no rehearsal: For the Atlantic Records' fortieth anniversary concert at Madison Square Garden in 1988, Jimmy Page flew into New York on the Concorde, and they rehearsed for just six minutes.

When the Allman Brothers Band were inducted that evening, Gregg Allman gave a heartfelt speech and talked about his brother, Duane, and how much he missed him. Neil Young played a high-octane set with Crazy Horse, and then a Pearl Jam–backed version of "Fuckin' Up."

While Ahmet was at the podium joking about Led Zeppelin's debauched lifestyle and the eclecticism of their music, huddling in the kitchen of the Waldorf were Jimmy Page, Robert Plant, and John Paul Jones hastily deciding what they could play. Page and Plant were annoyed with each other as they discussed song options. Steven Tyler and Joe Perry were there, too, trying to inject enthusiasm. When it came time to accept their awards, Jones had the chance to voice his feelings about being cut out of Page and Plant's reunion album and tour: "Thank you, my friends, for finally remembering my phone number."

It had been three years since the last of the unrehearsed induction-ceremony jam sessions. When Page, Plant, and Jones—along with their late drummer John Bonham's son, Jason, on drums—were joined onstage by Steven Tyler and Joe Perry, a.k.a. the Toxic Twins, they ran through the Yardbirds' hits "For Your Love" and "Train Kept A-Rollin'," Zeppelin's "Bring It On Home," the blues standard "Baby Please Don't Go," and Muddy Waters's classic "Long Distance Call." When the legendary bluesman's song concluded, Page took off his guitar and was about to exit the stage when Neil Young ran up and said to him, "We've gotta jam!" Before Page could react, his friend Perry Margouleff, who had graciously stepped in to be Page's guitar tech for the evening, placed Joe Perry's Les Paul sunburst around his neck.

Margouleff recalled, "I basically said to Page, 'You're not getting out of this.'" Meanwhile, Melissa Etheridge asked Plant if she could join in. (His answer: No.)

Joe Perry was soon looking up at the stage, wondering why Page was playing his guitar. Soon, Neil joined Page on the stage while Michael Lee, who'd been drumming with Page and Plant, stepped behind the kit and kicked off a ferocious version of "When the Levee Breaks."

Page played the main riff with a menacing tone, and Neil unleashed a careening solo that sounded like bombs dropping out of the sky. It seemed like an impossible feat, but Neil had—unintentionally—upstaged Led Zeppelin. He was simply so excited that he couldn't help himself. (Page, for his part, seemed happy to lay back. There was also a brief head-scratching moment as Robert Plant, of all people, strapped on a Gibson Les Paul, holding the guitar awkwardly while furiously strumming a few chords for a moment. I suppose since it was just a shambolic jam, he was allowed to have a little fun, though Page didn't exactly look pleased to see his singer playing guitar.)

It was the highlight of an incredible evening. They closed with Buffalo Springfield's classic "For What It's Worth." I was standing near the side of the stage and was struck by the stark difference in tone and guitar attack: Page played a stabbing rhythm behind Neil's shaggy but piercing soloing, and Zeppelin melded into some sort of British version of Crazy Horse. It was a unicorn moment featuring guitar gods from each side of the Atlantic; another reminder, to quote Eric Clapton, that "major and minor miracles can occur" at the Rock & Roll Hall of Fame.

Young's performance with Zeppelin inspired him to write the song "Downtown," which would appear on his album *Mirror Ball*, name-checking Zeppelin and Page in the song. Even with all of the tension, nevertheless, it was a joyous musical reunion, and the musicians all had a ball.

When I was heading home in the early morning, I saw Gregg Allman seated at the grand piano in the lobby mezzanine. He was playing quietly and looked despondent. For the Allmans, it had been an evening of highs and some lows, especially for Gregg, who was still deeply mourning the loss of his brother, Duane.

My outreach on behalf of the museum collection continued apace. Seymour Stein had given me Tina Weymouth and Chris Frantz's telephone number. I idolized Talking Heads, especially mesmerized by Weymouth's entrancing bass lines. I called to introduce myself and ended up spending more than an hour on the phone with her. A few weeks later, I drove up to their house in Westport, Connecticut, joining them for breakfast with their two sons and some friends. Knowing that I was coming, they pulled out all the stops, bringing out a great deal of material for me to look at—stage clothing from the Jonathan Demme *Stop Making Sense* film, several of Tina's basses, handwritten lyrics, and the twelve-string guitar that David Byrne played on the original recording of "Psycho Killer"—and I ended up returning to their house every few months for a long spell, securing a wealth of donations and loans. It was the beginning of a long-working friendship.

Later that year, I went to see David Byrne at his townhouse in Lower Manhattan. Like Tina and Chris, he seemed to have kept everything important related to his career, and I came away with two jaw-dropping artifacts: The famous suit that he wore in the *Stop Making Sense* film, its jacket custom-fitted with oversized shoulder pads to make his head look small; and a shoebox of the old, stained Polaroids the band had used to create the artwork for their iconic album *More Songs About Buildings and Food.* I had the Polaroids restored by a conservator and framed just as they had appeared on the album cover.

Our last big get came from Sam Phillips, the inductee and the owner of Sun Records. He delivered a motherlode: a big chunk of the studio equipment that he used to record Elvis Presley, Carl Perkins, Johnny Cash, Jerry Lee Lewis, and so many other Sun artists. We cobbled together enough gear to recreate Sun's control room and installed it behind glass.

Phillips's Sun Records was one of the most significant incubators for rock 'n' roll's birth. It was a fitting acquisition, knowing the museum would open in a few months. Artists were so attached to this studio that they would visit when they were in Memphis. A few musicians helped themselves to a memento, such as an acoustic ceiling tile from the original space.

Art imitates life, and vice versa. Band members of Spinal Tap: Michael McKean aka "David St. Hubbins," Harry Shearer aka "Derek Smalls," and Christopher Guest aka "Nigel Tufnel." PHOTO CREDIT: Associated Press

Craig Inciardi and Jimmy Page gaming things out for the interview and film shoot at Abbey Road Studios, 2019. Page brought along his entire recording rig and his principal instruments for the day. Inciardi's ludicrous idea that he hatched years earlier at Keens Steakhouse in New York became a reality with the enthusiastic participation of Page, Keith Richards, Eddie Van Halen, and Tom Morello. PHOTO CREDIT: Scarlet Page

Jimmy Page's guitar rig as it appeared on exhibition at the Metropolitan Museum of Art. See appendix for more. PHOTO CREDIT: The Metropolitan Museum of Art

mmy Page's custom Gibson double-neck and his famous dragon stage outfit on exhibition at the
letropolitan Museum of Art. See the appendix for more. PHOTO CREDIT: The Metropolitan Museum of Art

Keith Richards's rig on exhibition at the Metropolitan Museum of Art. Richards's distinctive guitar tone comes from his unique open tunings and just two 1950s high-powered Fender amplifiers. See the appendix for more details. PHOTO CREDIT: The Metropolitan Museum of Art

Keith Moon's iconic "Pictures of Lily" drum kit assembled for the exhibition from various owners, including the Victoria and Albert Museum. Moon famously blew up the kit during an appearance in the late 1960s on *The Smothers Brothers Comedy Hour*. See the appendix for more. PHOTO CREDIT: The Metropolitan Museum of Art

ob Dylan's Fender Stratocaster electric guitar famously layed at the Newport Folk Festival in 1965 when he ent electric, changing the course of popular music orever. The guitar had been left on an airplane in the 960s and resurfaced some forty years later. See the ppendix for more. PHOTO CREDIT: The Metropolitan Iuseum of Art

Jimi Hendrix's iconic white Fender Stratocaster electric guitar, most famously played at Woodstock in 1969. It was later sold by his bandmate Mitch Mitchell at Sotheby's in the late 1980s and purchased by Microsoft cofounder Paul Allen. See the appendix for more. PHOTO CREDIT: The Metropolitan Museum of Art

Tom Morello's rig as it appeared at the Metropolitan Museum of Art. He was highly influenced by Eddie Van Halen, who was also a participant in the "Creating a Sound" sub section of the *Play It Loud* exhibit. PHOTO CREDIT: The Metropolitan Museum of Art mmy Page's hand-painted Dragon Fender 'elecaster guitar, famously played when mmy was in the Yardbirds and during ıe recording of Led Zeppelin's debut lbum. Page brought the dragon Tele to bbey Road to demonstrate his use of armonics on "Dazed and Confused," ɔgether with his Supro amp and tage-worn shawl. PHOTO CREDIT: The Ietropolitan Museum of Art

Eddie Van Halen with his iconic "Frankenstein" guitar. Van Halen reinvented what it meant to be a guitar player. He was a brilliant songwriter and innovator. Not since Jimi Hendrix had a guitarist caused other rock players to be so envious and insecure. PHOTO CREDIT: Kevin Estrada / MediaPunch / IPx

Tina Turner was inducted into the Rock & Roll Hall of Fame as part of Ike & Tina Turner and as a solo artist. PHOTO CREDIT: AP

CHAPTER ELEVEN

THE HALL OF FAME OPENS

"Cleveland, Look what you have done!" screamed Yoko Ono from the stage.

Wielding scissors two feet long, Ono, Little Richard, Sam Phillips, Ahmet Ertegun, Jann Wenner, Suzan Evans, Ohio Governor George Voinovich, and others cut the ceremonial ribbon, opening the Rock & Roll Hall of Fame in front of more than ten thousand people as a squadron of jets ran a high-octane commemorative flyover. It was September 2—Labor Day Weekend—and all of us who had been involved felt an overwhelming sense of accomplishment and joy. We had all delivered: I. M. Pei, the New York and Cleveland boards, the artists, and the museum's fledgling staff.

Yoko Ono was ecstatic.

"John," she said, "would have loved the fact that he's here and not anymore in my closet."

She meant, of course, that John's *Sgt. Pepper's* outfit, along with so many of his other iconic pieces of clothing, had spent many years hanging in a wardrobe closet at their New York City home in the Dakota. I knew that because I had been the person tasked with getting them for the museum.

There had been a parade that day in Cleveland with fireworks and confetti, and it seemed like there was a costume party all over town.

Girls were dressed like Madonna, and I heard that there were parking attendants dressed like Elvis.

Jim Henke and I gave a tour of the museum to a bunch of artists including Jackson Browne, Chrissie Hynde, John Fogerty, and Bruce Springsteen. Bob Dylan was in town for the concert but, unsurprisingly, we couldn't get him into the building.

On the night of the opening, a gala concert had taken place at Cleveland Municipal Stadium, which already had an important musical history: the Beatles played there in 1966, and in the 1970s, Pink Floyd and Fleetwood Mac were among the performers who appeared there. In later years, U2 and Bruce Springsteen played the stadium.

After spending many furious years—and nail-biting final weeks—getting the museum ready, I was more than happy to take a moment to check out the backstage scene. I saw Bob Dylan exiting the trailer where he had been hiding out. He would be the big unannounced guest of the evening for the broadcast on HBO. (We'd all been keeping track of his logistics very closely; when he finally arrived on-site, I remember someone handing me a relieved message: "The eagle has landed," it said.) There was a massive catered spread assembled, and it was a surreal experience waiting in line: Ahead of me were Aretha Franklin, chatting with Ahmet; James Brown; Lou Reed and Laurie Anderson; Iggy Pop; Johnny Cash; and Garry "Diaper Man" Shider from Parliament-Funkadelic, who was wearing his customary diaper and smoking a cigar.

It had taken so much work to convince all these artists to perform. "When I asked Chuck Berry, the whole not-getting-paid part of the equation was, of course, a sticking point. Ultimately, I just threw my hands up and said, 'Nobody's getting paid! Can't we just do this? It's such an important event, and you were so instrumental,'" said Suzan Evans. The two of us went back and forth, until finally he gave in.

"I don't know how you always convince me to do this," he said, seemingly amused.

Let's also remember: It was Labor Day weekend, so the sun set late. This fact turned out to be oddly crucial, because we had scheduled Little Richard in at the beginning of the show.

"Well, when Little Richard showed up in Cleveland," Suzan Evans recalled, "he announced to us that he was now an Orthodox Jew, and since it's Shabbos, he would have to walk to the concert venue—and, also, he said he couldn't perform until after sundown!"

Joel Gallen, the producer, had to change the whole running order of the show for the self-proclaimed "Architect of Rock and Roll."

Earlier, at rehearsals, we had a nearly impossible number of bodies to move around and countless minor tremors to tamp down—or, simply, to wait out and watch them pass. Jerry Lee Lewis, who was doing a number with Bruce Springsteen, got upset about something during rehearsal, but Bruce just went over to Jerry Lee, talked to him in a low, soft, musician-to-musician manner, and the two of them worked it out. And that's why we call him the Boss.

HBO was very hands-on with the production, and Gallen and Nancy Geller from the network were banging heads the whole time.

As with most everything else we'd been doing, though, we gritted our teeth and ultimately made it happen. *Et voilà*: Chuck Berry opened the show in a white tuxedo, backed by Bruce Springsteen and the E Street Band, in front of fifty-seven thousand people. The stadium was outfitted with two stages, one of which had a large rotating platform so that one band setup could be assembled while another band was performing; after that, it was as simple as rotating the new setup into place.

Dylan, of course, was fantastic—as was Chrissie Hynde and the Pretenders playing "My City Was Gone," a melancholy ode to her nearby hometown of Akron, Ohio. It was the ultimate punk rock maneuver, singing a song about the hollowed-out Rust Belt and the overdevelopment that had destroyed the greener pastures of her childhood, which had been "paved down the middle / by a government that had no pride."

Berry returned to close the show with Bruce, the E Street Band, and a host of other musicians. The plan was to close with "Rock & Roll Music," but Chuck disregarded anything about the song that we'd planned in rehearsal—he even changed key onstage with no notice. (Keith Richards had run into the same trouble when he was working with Berry during the filming of *Hail! Hail! Rock 'n' Roll* in 1986. Berry always felt that since he had written the songs, he could play them any way he wanted—even if that meant they were sloppy, or in the wrong key, which had annoyed Richards to no end.) As Nils Lofgren from the E Street Band recalled:

> We're all looking around at each other—the cast of characters and the backup band; these are pros, decades in, and we are making these horrible sounds, collectively, in front of a sold-out stadium. We're looking at each other, like, *This can't be happening—right?* But no one has any idea how to fix this. Chuck looks at us all and starts duck-walking off the stage—leaving us all out there playing in six different keys with no band leader—gets in his car, and drives away: Now *that's* rock 'n' roll.

There were many fantastic performances—the Kinks were another standout—but unquestionably, the musical high points were Lou Reed and Iggy Pop, both backed up by Soul Asylum. Reed played "Sweet Jane," and Iggy played the Doors' version of Willie Dixon's "Back Door Man," and they were head and shoulders above everyone else. In spite of the ragged ending, the night had been glorious. Joel Gallen had pulled off a fantastic five-hour-marathon balancing act with dozens of artists and no interruptions. Although a few artists that had been advertised didn't make it to the show, including Dr. Dre, Snoop Dogg, Prince, and Brian Wilson, thirty-six groups performed two- or three-song sets, including Al Green, John Fogerty, Aretha Franklin, Johnny Cash, James Brown, The Allman Brothers, and Nancy and Ann Wilson from Heart.

At the official opening the day after the performances, Jann had hatched a surprise for Ahmet: Unbeknownst to his dear friend, the main exhibit hall had been named after the legendary label boss, and even though Jann had done most of the heavy lifting, he gave Ahmet his due.

"He was the guiding moral and aesthetic sensibility and consciousness all along the way," Jann said. "Decisions had to be made on every level: How do you reconcile the formality and elegance of a museum with the rudeness of an art form like this? What would be appropriate, and what would be in good taste, and what would not? In the end, it was always: 'What does Ahmet think?' Because Ahmet had the vision."

The museum? It was a joy to witness the fans' reaction, especially after all the hard work of building the collection. Visitors both past and present have been overwhelmed by the contents. Much of this is simply because music has given them so much joy, but many visitors have found that the exhibits are also a unique and sometimes profound way to mark time. Songs and albums are linked to a person's life, and walking through the museum often feels like a trip back through their personal history. The amount of work and brainpower expended was off the charts, but we were only on the starting line; now, we had to figure out how to keep the place open.

CHAPTER TWELVE

AT HOME WITH LEMMY AND HUNTER S. THOMPSON

Having the museum open was a huge relief, but that didn't mean my work building the collection was over. We were already planning two major new exhibits: one on heavy metal and another about the psychedelic era. There was no time for rest as I continued to pursue the artists on my endless punch list.

On another trip to Los Angeles, I was again feeling like a traveling salesman. I rented a car and booked more appointments than I could conceivably pull off, assuming that at least one or two would be canceled at the last minute. I went to see Black Sabbath's drummer Bill Ward, who lived near Venice Beach, and left his house with a carload of cymbals and drums—check. From there, I was off to see Dave Davies of the Kinks in Hollywood Hills. My goal had been to secure the little green Elpico amp that Dave used to record the Kinks classic "You Really Got Me" after famously slicing holes in the speaker cone with a razor blade to get the nasty sound that, ultimately, launched heavy metal—a Holy Grail. But Dave didn't show up for our meeting, and later I was devastated to discover that the famed amp was long gone.

Next up: Lemmy Kilmister. Lemmy's band Motörhead occupied a unique position in heavy metal. There were very few successful heavy metal *trios*—most metal groups had five members: think Deep Purple, Judas Priest, Scorpions. Nevertheless, Motörhead made an awful lot of noise with only three instruments and a voice. They checked all the required metal boxes and had some additional attributes: Lemmy, "Fast" Eddie Clarke, and Phil "Philthy Animal" Taylor were grizzled, lewd, and downright ugly. Today they could have been cast as soldiers fighting for Jon Snow in the "Battle of the Bastards." Lemmy's amphetamine-fueled, live-fast-die-young songs weren't completely grim, though, and they had a charm of their own. "Ace of Spades" said it all: "You know I'm born to lose / And gambling's for fools."

I loved Motörhead, and their live album *No Sleep 'til Hammersmith* was one of my favorites. When I was about ten minutes away from Lemmy's apartment in West Hollywood, my brand-new Motorola StarTAC flip phone rang. I dreaded when my cell phone rang when I was traveling for work: Not that many people had my number back then, and this usually meant that a meeting was being canceled. I answered the phone—it was an assistant who worked for Lemmy's manager.

He asked me: "Are you Jewish?"

I thought to myself: *This is very odd.*

"No, I am not," I said.

"Okay good, I just needed to check," the assistant said.

I hung up the phone and laughed to myself.

Five minutes later, my cell rang again: "Are you *sure* you're not Jewish?" the assistant asked me.

At this point, I was getting annoyed, and I responded, maybe a little too firmly: "I am Catholic. I went to an all-boys Catholic high school in Brooklyn, New York."

The assistant seemed to breathe a sigh of relief.

"Okay, I just needed to double-check. It's just that Lemmy collects Nazi memorabilia. But I want to assure you: He's not anti-Semitic."

I sputtered out an "Okay."

Before hanging up, the assistant warned me: "You might be shocked when you see his place."

When I finally arrived, Lemmy—his face was adorned with moles and assorted growths—invited me into his home. When Lemmy spoke, he sounded just like his singing voice: blunt and gnawed down by a lifetime of cigarettes and booze.

"Craig, I need to make it clear to you that I am not anti-Semitic."

I nodded.

"What can I say?" he continued. "The Nazis had great style. I just collect this stuff because I think it looks cool."

His two-bedroom apartment looked like a prop room from a World War II movie, jammed with swastika banners, SS daggers and guns, and Prussian-era pith helmets going back to the nineteenth century. There were loads of weapons and uniforms, and the whole scene made me so uncomfortable that I considered leaving. It may be the understatement of my lifetime to say that I'd never ever seen anything like this before. Lemmy was so proud of the collection, though, and he showed me several hand-forged daggers. And if that wasn't enough, there were a half dozen or so filthy ashtrays overflowing with cigarette butts.

Eventually, though, we got around to talking about my heavy metal exhibit, and Lemmy told me that he had been a roadie for Jimi Hendrix. We talked about his progressive rock days in the pioneering band Hawkwind, and about music in general. Then Lemmy pulled out a fantastic pair of white leather boots, a great leather jacket, and one of his most important Rickenbacker basses. I recognized all three pieces and knew that he wasn't holding back. More than once, artists have presented a guitar that was brand new and literally still had the tags on it—useless for a museum collection. Lemmy was genuine, so it wasn't surprising that he was handing over something real. I was grateful for the pieces—and very happy to get out of there.

The next morning, I went to see the family of the late rockabilly hero Eddie Cochran, who died tragically in a car accident while on tour in England in 1960. (Cochran's rocker friend Gene Vincent, another passenger in the car, was severely injured.) Cochran's career was so brief, but nevertheless immensely impactful, channeling teenage outrage and rebellion with songs like "Twenty Flight Rock," "Summertime Blues," "Somethin' Else," and "C'mon Everybody," influencing everyone from the Rolling Stones and the Who to the Sex Pistols.

The Cochran family lived in a modest ranch house, and soon after I arrived, Eddie's nephew Ed Julson asked me to follow him to the garage to look around. I was a bit concerned that such an important collection would have been stored in a garage, but when he rolled up the door, there was no memorabilia to be seen. Instead, resting on tables, were five or six large tortoises in hibernation—another extremely bizarre (if far less unsettling) show-and-tell.

I didn't know it yet, but this would be one of the most consequential days in the museum's history. With the tortoise show now concluded, Julson showed me Eddie's great stage clothing, his personal photographs, his amp—all incredibly impressive.

And then he showed me one of rock 'n' roll's Holy Grails: Eddie Cochran's Gretsch 6120 hollow body modified Chet Atkins guitar, which had been beside him during the car crash.

The guitar—considered one of the most important and rare in the world with an unusual patina—was in perfect shape. More than a dozen of the world's wealthiest guitar collectors had been salivating over the chance to acquire this guitar for their private collections—it seemed a miracle that it hadn't been scooped up.

Julson informed me, though, that separate factions had inherited the Cochran estate. Soon, I was meeting with an attorney who represented the estate, and a few months later, I met the other side of the family in the parking lot of a restaurant in LA to continue the conversation. Eventually, I convinced both sides of the family to loan the entire collection to the museum, and in 2021, the family decided to donate the guitar to the museum permanently. I was overjoyed. The Hall of Fame wasn't used to receiving single gifts of such historic importance. I had reeled in a whale, and twenty-five years later, I still feel good knowing this historical piece would be at the museum forever.

The New York board decided that we should mount our first major temporary exhibit to commemorate the thirtieth anniversary of the Summer of Love. The plan was to call it "I Want to Take You Higher." It would have been a great idea if we could have added a few years to plan it out, but of course that anniversary date—1997—was looming. And there was another enormous obstacle: Our fabulous I. M. Pei–designed museum did not possess a temporary exhibit space large enough to accommodate a big show of ten thousand square feet—another major design flaw that we had to navigate and finesse as best as possible.

The exhibit plan was ambitious, with an object list that was impressive by anybody's standards. But where would we mount the exhibit? At the previous year's induction ceremony, when Jann said the board members had done a lot of crazy things, he wasn't exaggerating. Meanwhile, those insane decisions continued: Jann decided, after much deliberation, that we would rip up more than half of the permanent exhibit space, which literally had just been installed six months earlier. Our staff was still recovering from the ramp-up and the opening of the museum. It had been a huge success, and people were still talking about the concert; and now dumpsters arrived for us to throw out hundreds of thousands of dollars of display cases and lighting. I was hardly shocked, as I was still new to the whole museum thing, but I didn't really realize what the repercussions would be.

Jann's general concept was a comprehensive exhibit that covered the entire psychedelic era, from 1965 to 1969, examining how rock 'n' roll came of age in the late '60s and influenced everything, from fashion and art to politics and literature and youth culture and sexuality, and showcasing the icons of the era, including the Beatles and the Rolling Stones. I suggested that we include actual tabs of acid in the display—though this idea was ultimately shot down for legal reasons.

Many of the artists, promoters, and writers from the era had signed on to participate in the exhibit, and they were all gung ho about making the show as real and visceral as possible: Peter Jenner, Joe Boyd, and Barry Miles from London were there, and from San Francisco we had the help of Chet Helms, Victor Moscoso, Paul Grushkin, Paul Kantner, Jorma Kaukonen, Jack Casady, Country Joe McDonald, and Charles Perry. In short, we had an all-star crew.

It seemed a minor miracle that so many of the movers and shakers from the Summer of Love were still around. I mean, they had consumed so many drugs and lived such wild lives that we were beyond lucky to have them clear-headed and enthusiastic to help us create an incredible exhibition.

At the top of our list of writers was the legendary gonzo journalist Hunter S. Thompson, who was inextricably linked to *Rolling Stone*. When Jann asked me to go see Hunter at his home in Woody Creek, outside of Aspen, Colorado, and convince him to be part of the exhibit, I was simultaneously thrilled and petrified. The stories of Hunter were, of course, legend: I already knew about his penchant for guns, explosives, and drugs.

Having never been to Aspen before, I started feeling the effects of altitude sickness—headaches, a kind of lethargy—almost immediately upon arrival. But I gamely drove out to Woody Creek and Owl Farm, Hunter's longtime home, where iron buzzards mounted on top of metal gates seemed to watch over the property. But meeting with Hunter turned out to be easy—he was a real Southern gentleman from Kentucky, and was in a jovial mood when I arrived. He seemed excited at the prospect of being a part of this exhibit, which, of course, also included his contemporaries like Tom Wolfe, the Stones, the Beatles, and so many others. I loved all the taxidermy in the house, and we talked about Deyrolle, the famous shop in Paris that sold a vast array of taxidermy including baby elephants, tigers, and giant exotic insects preserved in amber. The kitchen was Hunter's workspace, so that's where we spent most of the time, though I tried hard to ignore the rifles on the counter next to me, along with the cattle prod. Now and again, I went down to the basement to grab piles of papers and letters and manuscripts, which were just a jumbled mess and in desperate need of a proper archivist. Then again, I would have been shocked if Hunter's papers had in fact been properly organized and archived—the mere thought of it seemed anathema to his whole persona. He seemed to feed off chaos—in fact, he had made a career of it.

I was there primarily to look at material related to Hunter's 1967 book *Hell's Angels*—a classic work of participatory journalism that chronicled Hunter's experience embedding himself with the notorious motorcycle club in California. I found some amazing material, including a working manuscript that included a vivid description of members of the Hell's Angels stomping Hunter and nearly killing him. Amphetamines were their drug of choice, and Hunter—who, while reporting the book, was well on his way to becoming a living, breathing laboratory of drug consumption—was more than happy to partake.

After five or six hours of looking at papers stained by coffee mugs and riddled with holes from cigarette ash, I was ready to return to my hotel room and get some sleep. I went back upstairs to say goodnight to Hunter and let him know that I would be back in the morning, and found him still in his kitchen, now in an animated discussion with Ed Bradley from *60 Minutes*. They were neighbors and close friends, and they seemed to be in a highly spirited mood.

Suddenly, Hunter had other plans for my evening.

"Let's go see Lyle Lovett; he's playing down in Aspen, and he's a good friend of mine."

I loved Lyle's music and was very excited to go. I worked another hour or so, or until Hunter came down and said, "You worked enough today—let's go have some fun."

We jumped into Hunter's car—I'm not sure what happened to Ed Bradley—and he started driving down the winding mountain road as snow pounded down on us. Hunter seemed really drunk, and for a second, I imagined us ending up frozen in a snowbank, discovered the next morning, Joan now a widow. (Yes, I was learning that being a museum curator could be dangerous. I had already been injured at Sotheby's when I lifted a carved wooden carousel horse that was so heavy that I ended up needing surgery. And after the museum opened, I was trying to move Alice Cooper's full-scale stage-prop guillotine from a storage unit in the bowels of Encino when it almost crushed me.)

Hats off to Hunter: He was driving really fast, considering how bad the weather conditions were, but we arrived in one piece.

The show was fantastic. Somehow, Hunter managed to drop me at my hotel and he found his way back to Wooden Creek.

While in Aspen, I received a phone call from a woman I'd been trying to track down for more than two years. Her name was Cynthia Albritton, better known as Cynthia Plaster Caster, half of the infamous groupie duo who made plaster sculptures of men's erect penises. I was trying to convince her to entertain the idea of loaning her collection to the museum for an exhibit.

I can admit now that the idea was a bit naive: For starters, the crowd in Cleveland was fairly risk-averse and far more conservative than the New York board members. And while many of the Rock Hall's inductees had been willing participants in the Plaster Caster's performance art—including Jimi Hendrix, the Lovin' Spoonful's Zal Yanovsky, Eric Burdon, Wayne Kramer, and others—the exhibit idea was quickly shut down when I was informed that the girls had also done casts of several record executives.

In the morning after the Lyle Lovett concert, I resumed culling material from Hunter's papers. We were hanging out in his living room now, in front of a great old fireplace that he kept feeding wood. There was now a blizzard raging outside, but inside it was almost shockingly peaceful. We were just shooting the shit, talking about music and our favorite concerts we'd seen. We talked about the Stones, both of us in awe that their shows continued to be stunning.

Hunter asked me: "How is it that Keith Richards can make so much money from the music he made in the '60s and '70s? *I* can't do that."

I understood what he meant.

"Keith is a performing artist, and people still want to see the Stones perform," I told him. "It can bring them back and make them feel young."

Hunter agreed.

"Keith's art is in a different medium than yours," I added.

Hunter nodded and sighed, seemingly resigned to this unfortunate fact. I was thinking that a lot of Hunter's hijinks these days weren't just part of his identity—they were also masking something that seemed like depression.

Back in New York, Tom Wolfe was next on deck. I was in search of material related to the original manuscript of his iconic work of New Journalism, *The Electric Kool-Aid Acid Test*. Jann gave me his phone number, and I was feeling bullish after my successful visit to see Hunter, so I set up a meeting immediately and I met Tom—dressed, as per usual, in one of his many beautiful white three-piece suits—at his elegantly furnished apartment on Park Avenue. Tom and his wife had exquisite taste. As with Hunter, no arm-twisting was necessary: Tom and I simply jumped in the elevator and went down to the basement of his building, where his archive was stored. Considering how important his papers and manuscripts were, I was shocked to find them sitting in a cage alongside the dusty luggage and boxes of old family photographs belonging to the other people that lived in his building. And while there were some leaky pipes in the vicinity above his boxes—which were at least, thankfully, stacked on shelves—miraculously, everything was in excellent shape, and about as well-organized as one might expect from someone like Tom Wolfe.

When, a few weeks later, I found myself in London again working on the show, I decided to pop over to County Cork for the afternoon to meet with Donovan. Don and his wife, Linda Lawrence (who had had a son with Brian Jones in the early '60s), lived in an old church about twenty minutes from the Blarney Stone. He ended up lending us a wonderful collection, including his Zemaitis acoustic guitar and some of his most important early manuscripts. The maker, Tony Zemaitis, built custom-made guitars for many British rock stars, including Ron Wood, George Harrison, and Eric Clapton. All the collecting I had done thus far was for America from Americans, and it was important that the exhibit also represented the English artists who were so important to the psychedelic movement.

On my way back to the airport, I had a beer with Pete Townshend's old friend Happy Jack—yes, the namesake of one of the Who's most popular songs is an actual person. Jack was a lovely guy. We'd had several phone conversations over the years, and we agreed that we'd have to share a pint of Murphy's at some point. Sadly, the only artifact that Jack still had from his days with Pete was a pair of his socks—not exactly Hall of Fame material.

CHAPTER THIRTEEN

MACHINATIONS, THE LIZARD KING, AND THE E STREET MOBSTER

One morning in the early 2000s, I received a call from Clara Morrison. The Rock Hall was now the repository of her son Jim's early papers, and whenever Clara called me, I think she was able to reconnect with her son in some way. Today, Clara informed me that Père Lachaise Cemetery in Paris had requested that the Morrison family relocate her son's remains to another cemetery due to all the crowds and vandalism on both Morrison's gravestone and the neighboring graves close by. Clara was deeply upset, told me that she wanted to have the graffiti removed, and asked me if I had any suggestions of what kind of equipment might be needed. I recommended a special machine, which she purchased, and a team she hired successfully cleaned up the gravesite. To her great relief, Père Lachaise stopped pressuring the family to relocate the grave. (The bust of Morrison, which was stolen from the gravesite in the 1980s, was recovered in a police search in 2025.)

Music fans, of course, have long claimed a kind of ownership over or kinship with their idols, whether they are alive or dead, often referring to them by their first names. I'm willing to venture, though, that most of those fans don't think about the parents of the deceased artists. For Clara Morrison, living with her son's legacy—and his fan base—was painful. *Rolling Stone* put Morrison on the cover in 1981 with the now famous headline "Jim Morrison: He's Hot, He's Sexy, He's Dead." The magazine codified something that had already happened: Both the music business and the fans claimed ownership of Morrison.

At the 1996 ceremony, the Velvet Underground were finally inducted after being passed over many times—the snubs over the years an extreme example of the disconnect between the erudite tastes of the nominating committee and the more populist taste of the general voting body. VU's drummer Maureen Tucker had to quit her job at Walmart to attend the ceremony. David Bowie, another inductee, was a no-show; Madonna did the honors, thinking he was going to be there. It was also Jefferson Airplane's big night, though Grace Slick declined our invitation to attend—she had retired from performing and now felt rock 'n' roll was only for the young.

Another major change: After many years of keeping the induction ceremonies private and videotaped for archival purposes only, we had earned the respect of the artists—so much so that for several years, the artists themselves had been suggesting that we televise these inductions to share them with the public! And so, starting in 1995, we agreed to broadcast an edited version of the ceremony on a limited basis—first with MTV and then VH1. After that, the whole thing just took on a life of its own, eventually ending up on HBO, ABC, and Disney+.

After the city had clamored to host the ceremony for years, Cleveland finally held the inductions in 1997. It helped their case, of course, that this was part of the deal that got the museum built there. The enormous class that year included the Bee Gees; Buffalo Springfield; Crosby, Stills & Nash; the Jackson 5; Joni Mitchell;

Parliament-Funkadelic; the Rascals; Mahalia Jackson; Bill Monroe; and Syd Nathan, founder of King Records. But while the Jackson 5 were inducted, they didn't perform. Michael Jackson requested that he be able to rehearse his speech and deliver it from a teleprompter—a Rock Hall first. It felt symbolic of the more highly produced, scripted event the induction ceremonies were quickly becoming. During his rehearsal, Jackson was complaining about the placement of the television cameras, and he kept holding out his right hand to block the side view of his face.

As Jackson familiarized himself with the speech, he asked the production crew to add the word *applause* to the transcript in various spaces, so he would know when to pause and let people clap. The director politely said to Jackson: "This isn't that kind of show. There isn't going to be applause until you finish your speech."

There had been huge anticipation that Buffalo Springfield would reunite for the evening, like when Cream was inducted, but Neil Young was a no-show. He was uncomfortable because the show was going to be broadcast on television, and he had concerns that the band wouldn't be able to play well enough. Not everyone, it turned out, was on board with the new, more commercial event that management was crafting.

In the summers between induction seasons, I was still traveling frequently and meeting with artists to expand the collection. In 1996, I went to see the Who's bassist John Entwistle at his immense country estate in Gloucestershire near Stow-on-the-Wold. Entwistle's girlfriend, Lisa Pritchett-Johnson, picked me up from the train station in a custom-made Rolls-Royce station wagon that had been designed to ferry around his Russian wolfhounds. Lisa was incredibly friendly and excited that I was visiting; John was a little grumpy when I arrived, but made time for me regardless.

The house, called Quarwood, was by far the largest estate I had ever seen. Updated from the mid-nineteenth century, the main house had more than fifty rooms, and there were outbuildings, barns, and fountains.

"John's son, Chris, lives in that house," Lisa said, gesturing toward one property, "and Bobby Pridden [the Who's soundman] lives over there."

Inside, the house had all the trappings of a gentleman of landed gentry: knights in full armor and loads of taxidermy (including whole sharks). John frequented Harrods and had truckloads of niceties delivered after the end of each Who tour.

When I entered, it was apparent that there had been a party the night before—there were loads of broken glass, furniture turned over, a dozen or so overloaded ashtrays, and a player piano playing a furiously fast boogie-woogie.

"Keith Emerson was here last night," Entwistle said, referring to the renowned keyboardist of Emerson, Lake & Palmer, "and that's a recording of him playing."

John was famous for parties—sometimes it seemed like half of the Cotswolds were at his house on any given evening.

I was looking for some early posters from when the Who were called the High Numbers and the Detours. Entwistle had an amazing framed poster collection in one of his many drawing rooms, amid a collection of armored knights, and soon enough he offered them to the museum. In my excitement, I started to remove a few of them from the walls to get some measurements, and had taken four of them from the walls above a large sofa—truly, some of the rarest posters I had ever seen—and as I was in the process of taking pictures of them with my Polaroid, John suddenly said, "Sorry—you can't have them: Look at the walls."

I glanced over and quickly deduced that the posters likely hadn't been removed from these walls in thirty years or so: The paint in the room was evenly faded across the entire well, *except* where the posters had been hanging. John explained that since the room was so huge, it would need to be completely repainted, so instead, we simply put the posters back and moved on to other parts of the house and ended up at an old stone barn filled with instruments and amplifiers.

A kind of faded grandeur pervaded the entire estate. There were vast gardens, beautiful statuary, and just enormous acreage. It must have cost vast sums of money simply to maintain such a place. Of course, there were once many estates just like Entwistle dotted throughout the UK, but as they're generally money pits, many of them had been converted to hospitals, schools, and old-age homes. I applauded him for continuing to maintain this extraordinary property as a private home.

In the end, I walked away with one of Entwistle's custom B.C. Rich basses, along with an amplifier.

I was also pounding the LA pavement that summer, working on our upcoming heavy metal exhibit, which would open on September 20. And while I knew that most of the collection would come from England and California, a week before I left for LA I spoke with Leslie West, the incredible guitarist from the trio Mountain. West produced one of the most identifiable and iconic guitar tones in rock 'n' roll—thick as a tree trunk—from his Les Paul Juniors, and I was thrilled when he invited me to meet him at a restaurant in Manhattan on lower Broadway.

When I arrived, I was taken aback to see Leslie standing right up front, dressed in a tuxedo and greeting customers, until I suddenly realized: This is his day job now. The restaurant was packed, loud, simply too chaotic for me to properly explain what we were doing. West, of course, was far from the only legendary musician who'd had to resort to other types of work in order to keep the lights on—

Buddy Guy had to do extra work too. He drove a truck in Chicago in 1967, years after he had recorded "Hoodoo Man Blues" with Junior Wells in 1965. It reminded me of the great Elmore James's days moonlighting as a house painter.

The following summer, I went to see Jimmy Page in London. We met at his house in Kensington, a landmark Grade I -listed estate called the Tower House—one of the most extraordinary private homes in London. We went to dinner at Nobu, the famed sushi restaurant, in Hyde Park. At the time, Jimmy and I both had newborns, my first, and our conversation ranged wildly from music to changing diapers. I mentioned to Jimmy that I had seen the opening night of the Page and Plant tour in Boston when the band tried out the song "Achilles Last Stand" from *Presence*.

"I was happy I got to be there," I said, "when you guys were bringing out unusual songs."

More so than most Led Zeppelin songs, "Achilles Last Stand" is inherently challenging to pull off and perform, and ultimately, they decided not to add it to the setlist. Page seemed impressed that I had noticed all of this.

After dinner, he asked me if I wanted to visit the recording studio where he and Plant were recording *Walking into Clarksdale*. And while I tried my damnedest to contain my growing excitement, when the cab pulled up in front of Abbey Road, I thought I was going to have a stroke. And it got better: They were working in Studio Two, where the Beatles had recorded most of their albums. All of Page's instruments were there in front of us, including the Harmony acoustic guitar he used to write "Stairway to Heaven." Sitting on music stands were all of his favorites including his

Number One Les Paul Sunburst, the Gibson double-neck, and the Danelectro.

Steve Albini, who recorded and mixed the album, was there, setting up for the next day's recording session. "Years ago, we'd record into the early mornings," Page said.

No more early-morning recording sessions.

Soon after, I met with Page's bandmate John Paul Jones at his exquisite hideaway in West London. I could hear the fog horns blowing from the nearby River Thames when I approached the house. Jones was soft-spoken and charming. By now he was building his own instruments and showed me his workshop where various basses and guitars were being built. Four- and eight-string basses, some really exotic shaped, modern instruments. He ended up giving me his eight-string Olympic bass, which he used to record Zep's album's *Presence* and used on tour in the late '70s. The side of the neck was fitted with LED guide lights so that the instrument could be played in the darkness.

A few months later, Page loaned his Harmony acoustic guitar, which was his primary writing instrument and one of the most sacred artifacts in rock history. In addition, he lent his iconic Dragonstage outfit and the small Supro amp that was used to record Led Zeppelin's debut album. It was remarkable that so much extraordinary sound could come out of such a small amp.

Back stateside, I was invited to join the Hall's induction dinner committee and began taking more of an active role in the induction ceremonies, occasionally making suggestions for presenters. It was exciting to be more hands-on in the show, and I began to learn more of the nuts and bolts of how the event was built from the ground up.

The foundation was getting ready for the first Cleveland-based induction ceremony, the 1997 event to be held at the Renaissance Hotel and featuring the large class mentioned earlier in this chapter, which included the Rascals. As we were casting around for a presenter for the Rascals, I suggested Stevie Van Zandt. He wasn't the committee's first choice, but Suzan Evans agreed that it was a great idea and called Steven—who, at the time, was no longer with Bruce Springsteen and the E Street Band.

"I was completely out of the business by then, walking my dog," he recalled. "And they chose me to induct the Rascals into the Rock & Roll Hall of Fame!"

I thought Steve was the perfect choice: Like the members of the Rascals, he was a Jersey guy; more importantly, he was—in the mold of Pete Townshend—a true believer in rock 'n' roll, unhesitant to proselytize about rock's power and virtue. Steve was a disciple, and I was confident he would deliver a great speech.

On the night of the ceremony, Steve went to see the Rascals before the show kicked off. The old bandmates were arguing, their reunion seemingly on the verge of falling apart, but they—momentarily, at least—put their differences aside, and the original group performed together for the first time with singer Eddie Brigati since he left the band in 1970. (Flying back to New York the next day, I was seated next to the Rascals' guitarist Gene Cornish. I congratulated him and asked him how things went. He was grumpy. "It's like dancing with your ex-wife," he said. "You know every move exactly, but do you really want to do it?")

Steve's speech was glorious. He had just enough Jersey schtick and sarcasm, and when he revealed his Rascals-style stage outfit (the Rascals were infamous for recording in knee socks, rounded-collar shirts, and schoolboy ties), he brought the house down.

"Some people may not realize it," Steve said, "but the Rascals were the first rock band in the world. In the '50s, we had vocal groups and solo people, and then the '60s on the West Coast there were the Beach Boys . . . and okay, over there in England, some guys will make some noise, but in the *real* world, in the center of the universe—New Jersey—the Rascals was the first band!"

Van Zandt questioned why it took so long for the hall to induct the band and joked that perhaps it had to do with their stage clothing. "You know, their stage garb was a little bizarre. People think that you're dressed funny? Now *this* is a subject I know something about.

"The first time I saw the Rascals was at the Keyport Roller Drome in Matawan, New Jersey—that's right: It was no Fillmore; there were no arenas in those days—rock 'n' roll played skating rinks, where it belonged (and the way rock is selling, we may back be back in skating rinks next year)."

Van Zandt waxed poetically about seeing the Beatles, the Stones, and the Who during the early 1960s. All as a setup for the Rascals.

"The first time I ever heard the song—I'll never forget it; I was with my girlfriend at the time, Loretta Gorgonzola (she had brains, she had everything), and we're there, you know, her mother was out, and 'I Ain't Gonna Eat Out My Heart Anymore' comes on the radio, and I just stopped. She says, 'What's wrong, what's wrong?' It was like she wasn't even there anymore. I couldn't . . . it was just . . . I don't know how else to describe it: It was the sexiest record I have ever heard in my life. The melody, the chords, and his voice—the texture of Eddie with Felix and David. The guitar solo was even sexy. This record was sexier than the sex I was having with my girlfriend—let's face it. New Jersey soul was born right there."

I never imagined in a million years that my casual suggestion that Stevie be the Rascals presenter would lead to the creation of his iconic role as Silvio Dante on *The Sopranos*. David Chase, the creator of the show, saw Stevie inducting the Rascals on television and instantly knew he wanted him to be part of *The Sopranos*. It didn't bother Chase that Van Zandt had no acting experience—he was electrified by his look and his performance and was convinced he had to be part of the show. The Hall of Fame sometimes created this kind of synergy.

On *The Sopranos*, Stevie became Silvio, the consigliere to Tony Soprano, the character played by the late James Gandolfini. It was a role that Stevie had played in real life with Bruce Springsteen.

"That became very comfortable for me as an actor," Van Zandt told an interviewer. "I knew exactly what those dynamics were all about." All these years later, I still think it's crazy that I inadvertently had a hand in Stevie being cast to play this iconic mob character—one whom I loved so much.

CHAPTER FOURTEEN

BRUCE, BILLY, AND PAUL

In 1999, Bruce Springsteen, Paul McCartney, and Billy Joel were inducted—in fact, presented like a kind of Holy Trinity, with their own mini program printed and distributed at the ceremony. From a fan's standpoint, it was a dream scenario—but the drama leading up to the ceremony needed its own program.

In his first year of eligibility, Bruce was inducted on his own, without the E Street Band. And although Springsteen eloquently acknowledged every member of the band when he accepted his award, they were all hurt, especially Van Zandt. There had been internal discussions within the committee that perhaps the hall should wait a few years, until twenty-five years after the E Street Band's name appeared on an official recording, and nominate them all—but the board, along with Jann and Jon Landau, didn't want to wait; more importantly, they felt Springsteen deserved to be inducted on his own. The E Street Band, after all, were an unusual entity—super sidemen, if you will, who were employed by Springsteen.

Bono, who had previously inducted the Who and Bob Marley, was the presenter. As an orator, Bono was quickly becoming a master, his speeches on the same level of genius as his lyrics:

"Bruce is a very unusual rock star," Bono said. "He hasn't done the things most rock stars do. He got rich and famous. He never embarrassed himself with all that success. No drug busts. No blood changes in Switzerland. Even more remarkable: no golfing! No bad hair period. Even in the '80s, no wearing of dresses in videos—though there were those fingerless gloves. No embarrassing movie roles, no pet snakes, no monkeys. No exhibitions of his own paintings. No public brawling or setting himself on fire on the weekends. Rock stars are supposed to make soap operas of their lives, if they don't kill themselves first. You can't be a big legend and not be dysfunctional—it's not allowed. You should at least have lost your looks. Everyone else has. You see them? It's like Madame Tussaud's back there. Then there's Bruce Springsteen . . ."

When it was Paul McCartney's turn to step up to the podium, he was accompanied by his daughter Stella, who was wearing a white tank top that read IT'S ABOUT FUCKING TIME. McCartney was angry it had taken so long for him to be nominated as a solo artist—and that he hadn't been inducted the same year as John Lennon. A few years earlier, when Jann had called McCartney asking him to induct John Lennon, the Beatle nicknamed Macca recalled: "I said, 'Yeah, sure.' And then I put down the phone and thought, *What about me?* The thing about Lennon-McCartney is we were equal."

McCartney alleged there had been a quid pro quo with Jann and that Paul would be inducted the following year.

"I rang Jann Wenner and said, 'I'm getting all the papers, and I don't appear to be in, you fucking bastard.' We had a deal—a verbal contract that was not worth the paper it was written on—so that didn't endear me to him."

Wenner strongly disputed McCartney's memories.

Billy Joel, never a critic's darling, knew that his induction would receive a mixed reaction: "I know I've been referred to as derivative," Joel said, accepting his nomination. "Well, I'm damn guilty—I'm derivative as hell. And let me just suggest this to anyone who is derivative like I'm derivative and should be automatically excluded from this institution: It would mean that there wouldn't be any white people here! I know we're on TV, but we gotta get some outrageous shit started here."

As for the performances: Besides the rehearsed sets, there was a little of the old spontaneous magic that crept in. Sony president Tommy Mottola, who was seated up front, shouted out, "Let It Be!" Hearing the cue, Billy Joel suddenly rushed onstage and began playing "Let It Be," with Paul Shaffer and his house band quickly jumping in. Paul McCartney was still seated at his table, but he eventually sauntered through the crowd taking up to the stage and took control of the band, to thunderous applause—but there was a noticeable shift away from the joyous, anything-goes speeches and performances of the early ceremonies.

Curtis Mayfield was also inducted into the hall that year as a solo artist (he had already been inducted as a member of the Impressions back in 1991). Mayfield had been gravely injured years earlier, when a lighting rig fell on him during a concert in Brooklyn, paralyzing him from the neck down. Earlier that year, I had reached out to him in Atlanta, where he was living with his wife, and we spent the day together at his house. At one point he sent me up to the attic and into various closets to pull out specific items—one of them being his famous Thinline Telecaster with the f-hole. Curtis was such a kind, gentle, and thoughtful man, and it was terrible to see him in such a state, but he still seemed to have a spark in his eye. As I was leaving his house at the end of the day, he gave me a T-shirt with the movie poster for *Super Fly*—his landmark album of the same name serves as the film's soundtrack—on the front.

Around this same time, we negotiated a deal to collaborate with the Met's Costume Institute to cocurate a show about rock 'n' roll fashion. Designer Tommy Hilfiger signed on, with a generous multi-million-dollar sponsorship, and as the Hall's curator stationed in New York, I was ecstatic: New York was a center of the art and fashion worlds, and *Vogue*'s all-powerful Anna Wintour—a trustee of the Met and the orchestrator of the Costume Institute's gala, a.k.a. the Met Gala—had also greenlit the project. As a curator whose work was, until now, exclusively on display in Cleveland; this show would be a major departure for me. In Cleveland, we had always struggled to get prominent national and international press coverage. When we opened a new show in the Rock Hall's home city, we received local and regional press, but we were lucky to get a stringer from a major outlet to report on our newest showings. This exhibit—harnessing both the Met's prestige and Tommy Hilfiger's money—would be a game changer.

I made it clear to the Rock Hall's curatorial team that the opportunity of working with the Metropolitan Museum and the Costume Institute was once-in-a-lifetime, and I insisted that we leverage the Met's prestige and expertise to both mount a great show and simultaneously forge new relationships with major artists who had been unwilling to work with us before.

I came to the first planning meeting with Harold Koda, the curator-in-chief of the Costume Institute, armed with an exhaustive wish list.

"We need a Holy Grail to anchor the show," I began, before laying out my dream of reuniting all four of the Beatles' *Sgt. Pepper's* uniforms from the iconic album cover.

Since the Hall of Fame museum's opening, the Beatles have been well-represented. We already had John Lennon's outfit on loan from Yoko Ono, and we had managed to cobble together several solid Beatles exhibits with pieces from major collectors, but thus far, we'd had zero success convincing Paul McCartney, Ringo Starr, or George Harrison to be involved with the museum. Of course, for decades, both individuals and institutions had been asking the Beatles for favors, and they were understandably concerned about their treasured property.

I enlisted Jann to write Paul, Ringo, and George letters asking them to loan their uniforms, and we quickly received positive responses from Paul's people and from Ringo—but George decided to pass. We really needed that fourth uniform, so I did something that I had promised myself I would never do: I found a replica costume, in London, and it looked perfect—the only difference was that the fabric was slightly brighter than the others, since the garment was much newer.

It was thrilling to work on something taking place in my hometown: Every day for a few months, I hopped on the subway uptown from my office to the Met to work on the show. One evening after my work at the Met, though, I headed far downtown, to see Grace Jones—whom I had approved to be part of the *Rock Style* exhibit—on Bank Street, just a few blocks away from where Joan and I were living. When I arrived at her apartment, her assistant greeted me and told me that Grace would be out in a few minutes. Two hours later, Grace came in and sat down, and we discussed the exhibit. She was happy to be part of the show and agreed to lend a metal bikini designed by Issey Miyake, the designer to whom she served as a muse in the '70s and '80s.

In the meantime, David Bowie, Mick Jagger, and Keith Richards had also agreed to participate, and we already had some fantastic punk rock costumes—including an incredible Vivienne Westwood outfit worn by Sid Vicious—in our collection. We were definitely on a roll. In the end, more than forty major artists, from the '50s to the '90s, were represented in the exhibit, including all of the above plus Bono, Madonna, and Elvis.

The opening party for the exhibit, on December 8, 1999, was a great success, as was the exhibit itself, which ran through March 19, 2000, in New York and then traveled to Cleveland. It was a major achievement for us. Anna Wintour was by then the chair of the Costume Institute's Met Gala, and the party didn't disappoint. It was strange to see people smoking at the Met, including Harvey Weinstein who was puffing away in the museum's Great Hall. (We were also able to parlay the loan of Ringo's *Sgt. Pepper's* outfit into a more substantial loan from him the following year.)

Six months after the Rock Hall museum's opening, Dennis Barrie resigned as the Hall's CEO, and for the next few years, the museum cycled through three replacements. Finally, in 1999, the museum hired Terry Stewart as president and CEO. Stewart was a dapper Southern gentleman from Alabama who had degrees in engineering and education, along with an MBA and law degree from Cornell, and had worked in mergers and acquisitions before becoming the president of Marvel Entertainment in New York.

I met Stewart in New York when he was still interviewing for the job. His credentials were impeccable, and I knew he had the right kind of personality, but what sealed the deal for me was that he was a big collector—not just someone with a lot of stuff, but one of us; somebody who had a good eye and an insatiable appetite for records, posters, documents, and memorabilia. After Stewart was hired, he bought a mansion on Lake Erie with two swimming pools and filled it with great furniture, great art, and a collection of music history that could rival the Smithsonian. Over the years, he donated an extraordinary collection to the museum.

That same year, I began working on the museum's first exhibition about hip-hop, to be entitled *Roots, Rhymes, and Rage.* The earliest hip-hop artists were still not eligible for induction, based on the twenty-five-year rule, but we dove in head-first, creating a blockbuster exhibit. I flew out to LA again to do one of my sweeps and met with Snoop Dogg at his Mediterranean-style house in Claremont, which had become infamous after being shown on *MTV Cribs* and was now surrounded by metal fencing. When I arrived, a pack of giant Dobermans were barking and jumping on the other side of that fence, and when one of Snoop's assistants emerged from the house and opened the gate, I was utterly petrified, figuring that I had about five seconds before I'd be torn to shreds. It turned out to be unwarranted fear; the dogs were well-trained. Snoop was charming and sat for an interview that was candid and insightful.

From there I hopped in my rental car and drove over to see Ice-T in the Hollywood Hills, where he had a stunning contemporary home. We met in his private recording studio, which had an enormous fish tank built into a wall, with a shark swimming around inside. We discussed the exhibit for a while, and Ice seemed impressed with our plans, sending me off to see his manager Jorge Hinojosa the next day. I left LA with a fantastic collection, including the original lyric manuscript to Ice's notorious song "Cop Killer."

Returning to New York, I met with Biggie Smalls's mother, Voletta Wallace, who donated an extraordinary collection that included some of Biggie's fantastic stage outfits. She was soft-spoken and so proud of her son's achievements. Then I swung by Chuck D's house in Queens to pick up a collection. The exhibit's opening party featured an utterly fantastic performance by Slick Rick, and after closing in Cleveland, the show went to the Brooklyn Museum where it drew huge crowds.

Back in Cleveland, we had decided to extend the run of an exhibition centered on Bruce Springsteen, which had been occupying the fifth and sixth floors of the museum. The curatorial staff, as per usual, had a lot of other work going on with future projects, but the National Constitution Center in Philadelphia had also shown an interest in taking the Bruce show, which would be an exciting opportunity for the museum to show their work and gain a wider audience from another part of the country. The Boss himself slipped in to see the show right before it was dismantled—a low-key visit with no press—and while I wasn't there, I heard from colleagues that he was very pleased, even humbled.

When Ahmet and Jann first conceived the idea of a museum, it was always with the plan of building an accompanying repository where music historians, journalists, and students could conduct serious study, a place—like the music library at Lincoln Center, or the Downtown Collection at NYU's Fales Library—that would become a kind of academic mecca. In early press coverage from the 1980s, in fact, the library and archives were mentioned in the same sentence as the museum. Since the museum could generate income, though, it was decided that it should be built first, with the library and archive coming later.

In early 1999, the New York board decided that the time was now, and we started to collect for the future research center. Jann and Ahmet charged me with heading up a team to begin the process. The museum had now been open for four years, and they knew how time-consuming the collecting process could be, so I hired a team of six consultants, much like when Jim Henke was brought in to ramp up collecting in Cleveland. The new center would be installed at a university in Cleveland, most likely Case Western Reserve.

In some ways, this new assignment was an even heavier lift than any previous one. We weren't seeking the artists' sacred musical instruments and flashy stage clothing—what I called the "sexy stuff" that filled our exhibits—to have on loan from the artists, their families, and collectors. Libraries and research archives don't accept loans; everything must be donated or purchased. The collections have to be permanent, so researchers will know they can return years or even decades later to do follow-up research.

For decades, the established precedent or academic tradition for collecting the personal papers of individuals—artists, politicians, writers, and scholars—didn't start until that figure was deceased. It took a scholar named Howard Gotlieb—later to be known as the "father of modern archiving"—to break that norm and start collecting the personal papers of people still very much alive and well. Gotlieb was then the founding director of Special Collections at Boston University, and one day, Suzan Evans, a BU alum who knew Gotlieb, suggested we head up to Boston to pay him a visit.

"When I was in college, I got him a manuscript from Doris Lilly, whose book for *How to Meet a Millionaire* was adapted into the well-known movie *How to Marry a Millionaire*, starring Marilyn Monroe," Evans said. "Doris had been a close friend of my grandfather, and I was having dinner with her one night and she said, 'Oh—Boston University is trying to get my manuscript; I should just give it to you, and you can give it to them for me.' That's how I met Howard."

Gotlieb, who earned his doctorate from Oxford and then taught at Yale before settling in at BU in the early 1960s, was generous with his time. He explained that he came into archiving while serving in the Army Signal Corps after World War II, when his many assignments included organizing the correspondence and documents of Germany's Nazi party.

In the 1960s and '70s, when collecting papers directly from individuals was still thought ill-advised, Gotlieb simply felt the opposite and began corresponding with the Hollywood actors whom he had a particular interest in, reaching out to Betty Davis, Joan Fontaine, and Angela Lansbury.

I instantly realized that Gotlieb and I were on a similar mission—he'd just started thirty years before me, collecting from (in addition to the above) Fred Astaire, Douglas Fairbanks Jr., writers Elie Wiesel and Isaac Asimov, and journalists Oriana Fallaci and Dan Rather. Most extraordinary of all, he'd cultivated a relationship with Martin Luther King Jr., whose papers would end up at BU. In his 2005 *New York Times* obituary, Gotlieb was quoted as saying that he "groveled" to snare some of his prized papers. I knew how he felt: When he told me how, when he acquired Peter Benchley's papers relating to a book initially entitled *Great White*—later, of course, changed to *Jaws*—he felt the exuberance of a hunter bagging a twelve-point buck, I smiled in recognition.

Gottlieb organized four lavish and (his words) "highly successful" parties every year, each one in a different city, to thank his donors and cultivate new ones. When I asked him for advice, though, he simply said that one has to be "relentless" and "imaginative." I did feel like he let me in on one secret, however, when he casually mentioned that he also had a staff of twenty working for him. With this knowledge, I went to the board and asked for a budget to hire a bigger staff.

CHAPTER FIFTEEN

DILDOS, MAGGOTS, RITALIN, PHIL SPECTOR'S LAST STAND—AND MY SOBERING EXPERIENCE AT THE DAKOTA

In the late '90s, Yoko Ono and Jann Wenner began hatching the idea of an exhibit at the Hall of Fame dedicated to John Lennon's sixtieth birthday in October 2000. It was a great idea with one major problem: budget. Although attendance at the museum was strong, many of the corporate sponsorships that had been sold for the museum's opening were simply not being renewed, and that lack of cash had serious implications for the still-fledgling institution. And then—miracle of miracles—a Cleveland board member, a mysterious and wonderful woman who went by the name "H," somehow found a tech executive with $1,000,000 to fund the exhibit, and once again we were off to the races with the kind of "seat of the pants" acumen that was becoming our trademark.

In September 2000, I was busy finishing up my work on the Lennon exhibition when I went over to the Dakota to pick up what would be the most solemn and precious artifact I'd laid my hands on in my thirty years at the museum. I signed some forms and gave Yoko's registrar our insurance certificate and was then handed the eyeglasses that Lennon was wearing when he was murdered—stored in a heavy steel briefcase with a very large paper evidence bag that was covered in dried blood stains and stamped ROOSEVELT HOSPITAL. Yoko had never opened it, and it remained sealed. Inside the bag was John Lennon's clothing and what appeared to be a pair of boots. I could hear the jangling sound of his keys and some coins. From there I took a car to JFK Airport, where a security guard accompanied me to my gate. I discreetly placed everything on the conveyor belt, and the guards ran everything through the metal detector. It was a year before 9/11, so nobody questioned what I had, but my heart was racing the entire time: After all, I was transporting some of the most important objects in rock history. Sometimes there was a surrealness to my job, and this was one of those days.

A few weeks later, I found myself on the phone with Ahmet Ertegun, talking about a twenty-foot penis. "Good morning," Ahmet began. "Do we have any need for the Stones' lotus stage from the '75 tour?"

I was simultaneously thrilled to hear from him and caught off guard: The lotus stage he was referring to weighed ten tons and was hydraulically operated, so the flower petals that were its centerpiece could move up and down.

"It has over three hundred lights," Ahmet said. I already knew that; it was designed by Robin Wagner, who had created much of Broadway's most iconic and imaginative staging for shows including *Jesus Christ Superstar*, *Hair*, and *A Chorus Line*.

Wagner's lotus was widely considered to be one of the most sophisticated performing stages ever built, and bearing in mind that it dated from the mid-1970s, that's saying something. Without missing a beat, I asked Ahmet, "Does that include the giant inflatable twenty-foot penis that Mick rode in on?" Ahmet howled, and then said, "Sadly, no—I asked already, and it's long gone."

Back in those days I was game for almost anything. But I knew there was really no good place we could display the lotus stage, and Ahmet explained that there was only one person in the world who knew how to operate it—and he was located in Perth, Australia. After I passed on it, the entire structure was shipped to a scrapyard somewhere in the Midwest.

Earlier that year, I had a memorable meeting with James Taylor and his mother, Gertrude. (By this point, I was known as the horse whisperer of rock stars' mothers and widows.) James was among the class of 2000's inductees, and I'd had an early and very personal relationship with his music: "Fire and Rain" was among the first songs I heard as a young child that meant something to me. It was my hope that JT could contribute a significant collection to the museum, so I flew out to Martha's Vineyard just a few weeks before the ceremony—a quick up-and-back trip with a lot to cram in just a few hours.

James collected me from the rural airport in a pickup truck, and we drove out to Gertrude's stunning oceanfront house. There was snow on the ground, and the waves were crashing on the beach behind us. Gertrude was a wonderful woman with an innate calmness and gentility; we had some coffee, and then she began pulling out several things for the exhibit.

The two of them were soon showing me James's first guitar, a very cheap plywood acoustic that James's brother Alex had painted with blue house paint—the whole thing: neck, body, even the strings. James said, "It's ruined, unplayable—you can have this." I loved it and insisted that it told a great story. I also realized that instruments that were no longer playable were easy for artists to hand over and low-hanging fruit for the museum. Gertrude, meanwhile, gave us a collection related to James's childhood, including family photos and letters he had written that had never been seen by the public.

At one point, I looked at my watch and realized that I needed to be heading back to the airport soon, just as James was telling me about the new house he was building on a tract of oceanfront property he had purchased in the early 1970s with some of his first big royalty checks. As the two of us were walking out of the house on our way to the airport, James pointed out a separate smaller house on the property that he, Carly Simon, and their children had lived in years earlier; I told him about my fishing shack on Long Island. Amid more small talk, James turned to me and asked: "Hey—would you be able to help me move something before I drop you off? I just bought a stove for the new house, and I need to deliver it to the site. Could you help me get it in the back of my truck and bring it over?"

It was a funny request, but I loved that he asked me. We drove over to an industrial park where, sitting on the loading dock, was an enormous eight-burner restaurant-grade stainless steel stove. James backed his pickup truck right up against the loading dock, the two of us lifted this enormous thing onto the truck and brought it over to the new house—and JT got me back to the airport with five minutes to spare.

The next day, I drove out to see an attorney in New Jersey who represented the estate of Billie Holiday. Holiday, one of the all-time greatest jazz artists, had been inducted in the early influence category of the hall in 1999. While her connection to rock 'n' roll was tenuous, her vocal phrasing and her raw voice—not to mention her hard-boiled biography—made her a kindred spirit of many rock 'n' roll singers.

Mifflin Hayes had been working with the estate for decades and had met many people who knew Holiday. "I've got something you need to see," he told me, before leading me to a back room and unstrapping an old leather suitcase that looked like it was at least sixty or seventy years old, revealing a treasure trove of artifacts dating back to the 1940s and '50s that belonged to Holiday—a time capsule that hadn't been opened in decades. Inside was one of Billie's ball gowns, a fox stole (the fox's head included, along with a black and white photograph of her wearing it), autographed photos and utility bills, and signed contracts covered in glue which showed how money was being diverted away from her.

At one point, I reached into an elastic pocket inside the suitcase and found ten or so empty pill bottles, dated 1959, for the amphetamine Ritalin, prescribed in her name with her Upper West Side address. While the entire discovery filled me with a deep sense of dread, I marveled that these artifacts still existed, since Holiday had led such a tragic and tumultuous life. The materials were from the estate of her last husband and manager, Louis McKay, one of many men who had victimized Holiday.

In the wind-up for the induction ceremony in 2001, I was over at SIR Studios on the west side of Manhattan checking out the rehearsals of Aerosmith and Queen—both of whom were being inducted. Paul Shaffer and I spoke with Steven Tyler after Aerosmith finished up, and I remember Steve saying to us: "Can you believe a schmuck like me from Yonkers is going to be inducted into the Rock & Roll Hall of Fame?!? That's fucking crazy!"

As the roadies were loading out Aerosmith's gear and swapping in Queen's for the next rehearsal, I went on a reconnaissance mission upstairs, where many artists, especially New York–based ones, stored their equipment in cages. Peering through the fencing at equipment from Keith Richards, Bruce Springsteen, Stevie Van Zandt, and Joan Jett gave me the idea for an exhibit: Because only a small percentage of their vast collections could be seen by the public, some museums, including the Metropolitan Museum of Art and the Brooklyn Museum, had ingeniously created exhibits from open storage. And from a rock 'n' roll perspective, SIR's storage upstairs was the real thing.

My head in the clouds, I headed back downstairs to Queen's rehearsal, but my reverie was soon interrupted by an urgent phone call from Suzan Evans.

"We still don't have a presenter for Steely Dan," she said. "Do you have any ideas?"

"Ask Moby," I replied.

When she asked me why, I just said, "I know it doesn't seem to make sense, but trust me."

To be honest, I wasn't giving Suzan my full attention because watching the Queen rehearsal was another revelation. Brian May was there with his Red Special, the guitar that he used to record virtually every Queen song. (Brian and his father made the guitar from a chunk of wood from their fireplace mantle.) Dave Grohl and Taylor Hawkins from Foo Fighters would be sitting in with Queen, and the initial rehearsal was just the two of them standing in a huddle with Brian May and Roger Taylor with no instruments—just talking. The two drumming Taylors ran through the entire sequence to Queen's classic "Tie Your Mother Down"—with no drums: They just played air drums while humming the song, tapping their feet, and hitting imaginary toms and cymbals with their fingers, running through the whole thing a few times until they were satisfied. Taylor Hawkins was a Queen fanatic and knew every single one of Roger Taylor's moves. The entire thing was just a fascinating analog exercise to witness. Steven Tyler popped back in for a minute, and when Grohl saw him, he said hello by playing the opening riff to Spinal Tap's "Tonight I'm Gonna Rock You Tonight."

Moby agreed to induct Steely Dan, and on the big night, I don't think I was the only one curious as to what he was going to say from the stage. He began: "A few weeks ago, when I got a call asking me to induct Steely Dan into the Rock & Roll Hall of Fame, I immediately asked myself a few questions. The first of these questions was, *Why are they asking me?* Because as far as I know, Steely Dan seems to hate everybody. So I was flattered but very suspicious."

In truth, Moby had reason to be suspicious. A good friend of mine lived in a downtown loft on Mott Street, and her apartment was on the same floor as Moby's. Years earlier, Moby had invited her to a party at his loft, and "as guests arrived, Moby handed everyone a dildo as a conversation starter," she had told me. My friend was unimpressed—but it was knowing that Moby was into dildos that convinced me that he was the man for the job.

Moby continued: "The truth is, we are talking about two men who named their band after a dildo in a William S. Burroughs book. So after I got over my suspicions that this was a practical joke—although, to be honest with you, I haven't quite gotten over my suspicions, and I do have a fear that there's a carload of giant rubber chickens waiting offstage . . ."

The idea that I had hatched went off according to plan. I knew that Moby would not be able to help himself—he'd *have* to reference the connection to *Naked Lunch*. It's only rock 'n' roll, right?

Phil Spector was on hand for the show with his new girlfriend Nancy Sinatra, with two enormous bodyguards in tow, dressed in suits with matching grizzled faces. I made sure to stay clear of Phil.

In the summer of 2001, it was time for yet another Los Angeles sweep, and among the people I planned to visit this time was music business legend Lou Adler, whom I had now known for five or six years. Lou was one of those guys that turned whatever he touched to gold. Just a few of his achievements: managing the Mamas & the Papas, producing the Monterey Pop Festival, and producing Carol King's landmark album, *Tapestry*. As if that wasn't enough, in the 1970s, he made a B-list movie, *The Rocky Horror Picture Show*, and we all know where that went!; was a partner in the famed Whisky a Go Go on the Sunset Strip; and owned the Roxy, among other clubs.

When in LA, I would often pop out to Malibu to see him at his house built on the cliffs with its magnificent view of the Pacific. Lou had been asking me for a few years if we would be interested in mounting an exhibition about the painter Guy Peellaert, who had published a book of his fantastical and surreal paintings of rock stars in 1976 called *Rock Dreams*. Lou had quite a few of Guy's best pieces, which he proceeded to show me, and I was intrigued—but though I knew that they'd make for a great show, there just didn't seem to be enough of them. When I asked him if he knew anyone else who had a lot of Guy's artwork—we'd probably want thirty or forty paintings for an exhibit—Lou pointed me in the direction of one of his best friends.

"Jack Nicholson's got a huge collection of Guy's work," he said. "You should go see Jack and then make a decision."

From my days at Sotheby's, I knew that Nicholson was an art collector, but I had thought that he had very expensive taste—mostly Picassos and that kind of thing.

In any case, the next afternoon, I drove over to Jack's sprawling ranch house at the top of Mulholland Drive, where I found Jack outside, putting on his putting green. When I asked him about the house, he told me he had bought it in 1969—around the time that he had written and produced the cult classic film *Head*, with its soundtrack from the Monkees—and had put on some additions over the years. I was so impressed he was still in the same house for all of those years; he was someone who was comfortable in his own skin. (He had also had the foresight to buy an amazing piece of property.) The house was jam-packed with art—lots of Picassos, yes, including pieces from the artist's Blue Period, along with some extraordinary cubist works. There was easily over a hundred million dollars' worth of art on the walls in his living room, bedrooms, and hallways. He had seemingly run out of wall space; there were even paintings hanging in the bathrooms.

I spent a few hours there, and in addition to all the artwork, he showed me some of his autographed photographs of professional golfers including Sam Snead, Ben Hogan, and Bobby Jones—autographs that he had purchased.

"As you can imagine, I've met everyone," he said to me, "musicians, actors, artists—and looking back on it, I should have asked for their autographs. I love autographs."

I told him I understood, but that in my capacity as a curator, I didn't ask for autographs.

"I just didn't think it was right to ask," Jack said. He seemed to be saying that he was too cool to ask. It was such an honest admission.

When we finally got around to talking about the Guy Peellaert paintings, he led me into a large bathroom, where a few of them were hanging on the walls, with the rest of them tucked into a guest bedroom—all of them terrific examples, just like Lou's.

In the end, we abandoned the idea of mounting that exhibit, but I was happy to have spent that afternoon with Jack.

Later that day, I drove back to Lou's house and asked to see a certain something that had become one of my favorite objects of all-time. Lou simply laughed, said, "Of course," and led me back to his living room, where a lamp with a lampshade sat on a table next to a sofa. During John Lennon's famous "lost weekend"—an eighteen-month period around 1974 when, separated from Yoko Ono and on a wild bender culminating with him being thrown out of the Troubador for being drunk and violent—he had gone back to Lou's house, where he was staying at the time, and trashed the place. When Lou got home, "there was broken glass everywhere, broken furniture—the place looked like a pile of shit," Lou said. John left a sort of apology note written on the lamp shade. It's one of those singular artifacts: There's simply no single better object to sum up that period of John Lennon's life than that lamp.

At the time, I was also working on our upcoming teen idols exhibit, which would open in Spring 2002, and so I paid a visit to Pat Boone, who had an office in a Beverly Hills high-rise, and to Shaun Cassidy, who was then working on a pilot for a new television show. I saw some rushes Cassidy's team had shot, and they had just added the Rolling Stones' song "Paint It Black" to the intro credits. The sequence worked really well, but the team wanted to know how much I thought using that Stones song would cost them. I simply informed them that it would likely be very, very expensive, and told them to get in touch with Allen Klein, the band's notorious former manager, who still controlled the publishing.

That evening, I met up with Seymour Stein and Andy Paley, a former Sire Records artist and now a producer who was doing some consulting work for me collecting for the library and archives. Paley had recently composed songs for *SpongeBob SquarePants*, and my daughters were wholly impressed. We had dinner at the legendary Musso and Frank in Hollywood. There were lots of revelry and many martinis and steaks. Seymour always made me pay the bill with my meager expense account. The next morning, I looked at the credit card receipt and saw that I had written in a tip for $1000—instead of the intended $100. I drove over to the restaurant and the maître d' saw me when I came in and he had mercy on me. He said, "We realized exactly what had happened."

Next stop: Las Vegas, to meet with Shaun's half-brother David Cassidy, one of the biggest teen idols of the 1970s. I had loved *The Partridge Family*, truly one of the iconic TV shows of its era, and I thought it essential to lock down David's involvement. Cassidy had famously decided to end his teen idol career by appearing in a soft-core photo shoot by Annie Leibovitz in *Rolling Stone* in 1972, with Jann more than willing to provide the vehicle for Cassidy's transition into a more mainstream career. I went to see Cassidy at a mansion he was renting at the time with his wife Sue Shifrin. It was surreal to meet the guy that had been on my lunch box when I was in first grade. At the time, Cassidy was starring in a one-man show at one of the casinos.

"I'm trying to save my voice for tonight," he told me, "so I'm gonna have to whisper today when we talk."

He had a fantastic collection of stage clothing, photographs, and instruments, and generously loaned a large part of it for the upcoming exhibit. I was especially thrilled that he was willing to loan his main guitar—a custom hand-carved Gibson SG that he had played throughout the 1970s.

The 2003 nominating committee meeting was more dramatic than usual. The attendees included many from the old guard, including Ahmet Ertegun, Jerry Wexler, Seymour Stein, and Columbia Records' Don DeVito. But then Phil Spector entered the room just as the meeting was about to begin, and the entire room erupted in applause. In retrospect, I think everyone in attendance realized that celebrating his arrival was inappropriate, but it was really just a nervous reaction, given that Spector was out on bail for the murder of actress Lana Clarkson, whom he had shot in the head just a few weeks earlier at his house in California on February 3. After the room settled down, writer and MTV executive Bill Flanagan, realizing how surreal the entire situation seemed to be, said out loud, "Hey, Phil, what's new?" This was the last time Spector attended a nominating committee meeting. He was eventually convicted of second-degree murder in 2009 and sent to state prison, where he died in 2021.

Around this time, the makeup of those attending the ceremony had begun to change. With all of the consolidation among the record labels, there was less and less money to fly people in and buy tables for the dinner. Wall Street to the rescue: The masters of the universe, after all, could buy anything—except access, and cool, or access to cool. Still, it was jarring to see hedge fund moguls sitting up front, sharing tables with the likes of Eric Clapton and Bono. This sort of shoulder-rubbing might cost $250,000 for the night, but for those who could afford it, the big payoff was bumping into, say, Keith Richards a few months later at a tropical bar in Turks and Caicos and saying, "Hey, we met last year at the Waldorf—can I get you a drink?"

When it was announced in November 2002 that the Clash would be inducted into the Hall of Fame, it sparked an excitement and anticipation that, frankly, hadn't occurred since Led Zeppelin's induction. It promised to be a reunion for the ages. I had seen the Clash perform at Shea Stadium when they were opening for the Who in 1982, with Terry Chimes on drums. To see them again would be a gift from the punk rock gods.

Talk of a full-on reunion was immediate. When Joe Strummer was interviewed by *Rolling Stone* shortly after the announcement, Strummer said: "When I heard the news, I just put my fist up and said, like Babe Ruth: I just didn't know what to say." Strummer was excited about the prospect of the band playing at the ceremony. "I'm sure I'll do it, and I'm sure Topper would do it, but it's only fair and polite to inquire of the others."

A week later, Strummer played a benefit concert for striking firefighters at Acton Town Hall, just a few minutes from Mick Jones's studio. Jones was in the audience, and Strummer invited him onstage for a last-minute three-song encore of Clash songs—the first time they had been onstage together since 1983. Mick, as it turns out, was also willing to play at the ceremony.

Then, in mid-December, Strummer went to see Topper Headon at his house in Dover, hoping to rehearse a few songs for the ceremony. Joe hadn't seen Topper in many years, and when he arrived, he found his old drummer sound asleep. Joe tried to wake him up, to no avail. Topper had been off heroin for many years, but he had also disappointed Joe countless times. The Clash, of course, had always been a combustible band, but despite all this, Strummer was still hopeful. A few days later, he sent bassist Paul Simonon a text: "Come on Paul—give it a try, you might even like it."

Joe Strummer died from a congenital heart condition the next day at his house in Somerset.

A year or so later, in the winter of 2004, I found myself on a train heading from Paddington station to Somerset to visit with Strummer's widow, Lucinda Garland, in the beautifully rustic farmhouse they'd shared on a rambling property with eighteenth-century outbuildings. We connected immediately. Luce made us some tea, and I was sitting on a bench in the kitchen.

"That's exactly where Joe died," she said, matter-of-factly, gesturing toward the living room. He had been out walking his dogs and came back in and expired.

Luce was very charming and welcoming. As she showed me around the house, I noticed a Damien Hirst artwork from his famous butterfly series hanging in her living room, and just as I was about to comment on it, Hirst himself—a close friend of the couple—walked into the room.

The three of us strolled over to a large brick barn, which was mostly empty. Luce explained that it was where Joe's recording studio had been located, and then Hirst told me that after Joe died, he and his staff had meticulously photo-documented the entire studio and all of the equipment in it, photographing everything just as Joe had left it from dozens of different angles, before Hirst's staff numbered and packed up every single object and carefully placed them in Hirst's archival storage vaults, so that the studio could be reassembled at a later date. Hirst showed me some of the photographs, and it was astonishing—everything was there: guitars, amplifiers, cord jacks, setlists, cigarette butts, beer bottles, tools, magazines, books, every imaginable piece of debris.

When I went back to Luce's house the following day, she pulled out a bunch of Joe's military-style stage clothing from the *Combat Rock* tour. Damien Hirst was still hanging around, and as I was finishing up, he told me that he was heading over to his studio, and he invited us to join him, so we all piled in the car and headed out. I was a big fan of his work and was excited to see his operation.

Hirst's studio was located in an enormous compound of eighteenth- and nineteenth-century buildings on a beautiful property a short drive away. We entered the main space, where his assistants were working on a new collection of butterfly paintings, with boxes and boxes of butterflies of all different species and colors organized on tables, which his assistants were meticulously attaching to boards and canvases. There was also a giant sculpture entitled *Charity*, based on the charity boxes featuring disabled children which were common on British streets. A Sarah Lucas sculpture incorporating an actual car was hanging from the ceiling.

Hirst was excited to give me a tour of the place, and his energy and enthusiasm was contagious. On one wall was a large painting which, from far away, looked like it could have been a Rothko. As I approached it, though, I could see that it had a thick impasto texture, and when I was mere inches away, I realized that the entire painting was covered with flies that had been painted black. It was mesmerizing.

"Where the hell did you get all those flies?" I asked Hirst.

Grinning, he replied: "Do you really want to know?"

Hirst led me outside to yet another outbuilding about a hundred yards away. Inside, cow carcasses hung from the ceiling, rotting specifically in order to create maggots. It seemed to me that there were literally millions of maggots crawling and flies swarming throughout the barn. After the flies had died—or had been killed; this part was still unclear, and I was afraid to ask—Hirst mixed them up with paint and whatever other ingredients they used and applied them to his paintings. It was genius.

The following year, I went back to Somerset to continue working on Joe's collection. Luce had found Joe's original notebook containing the first draft of "London Calling," which at the time was called "The Ice Age."

Conveniently, I also timed my trip so that I was able to catch one of the Cream reunion shows at the Royal Albert Hall. I met with Pete Brown, who had cowritten many of Cream's songs with Jack Bruce. To my amazement, Brown still had his original working lyrics to "White Room," "I Feel Free," and "Sunshine of Your Love." I was blown away to see these manuscripts in person: Not only did they actually exist, they looked really cool, too, with all sorts of sketches and doodles of airplanes on them. When I got back to New York, I hoped to raise the funds from a few board members so the museum could acquire them—but before I could even shake the trees, an exotic car dealer from the West Coast swooped in and bought them for himself.

Meanwhile, Suzan Evans was scouting around a bit to see if there might be another, larger venue in New York that might accommodate more fans at some point, but most everything she saw that was big enough proved to be tricky: "We wanted to keep the essence of what we already had, with a seated dinner as a kind of centerpiece to build around, but we were already getting pushback from people that lived around the Park Avenue Armory about potential noise issues," said Evans.

She was also concerned about the acoustics in the armory, because they weren't very good for music. The Javits Center was also a possibility, but I. M. Pei, who designed it, actually told Evans not to have the induction ceremony there because the acoustics were not good for musical performances.

While all of this was going on, we were making enormous progress collecting for the future library and archives—but Jann was getting impatient with the Cleveland board's lack of progress in securing the funds and selecting a suitable site in Cleveland for the future research center. Because the collecting operation was based out of New York, this had become Jann's pet project, with everything that we collected shipped to a climate-controlled warehouse in Chelsea. One day, he asked me to start pursuing NYU—because of its prestige and its New York location, but also to put further pressure on the Cleveland board to cut a deal with Case Western Reserve. This was the same tactic he had used in the late 1980s and early '90s when the Cleveland board was still struggling to raise the necessary capital to build I. M. Pei's building.

Jann also started calling in favors: He asked the philanthropist Jonathan Tisch, whose family were major benefactors at New York University—they founded the Tisch School of the Arts—to arrange for me to meet with Mary Schmidt Campbell, the Tisch School's dean, and the head of the university's sprawling library system, and I was given a tour of the iconic Elmer Holmes Bobst Library on Washington Square Park, which was designed by Philip Johnson and Richard Foster.

Jann was thinking of his own collection, too, and it's a good point: Jann, as I knew, had an amazing archive of his own. He had kept seemingly everything—every bit of paper from boarding school on into high school, and Berkeley, and from his time working at *Ramparts* magazine—and then, of course, *Rolling Stone*. When we were working on exhibits, Jann had generously given me access to the collection—we would often borrow items and then return them the following year.

NYU's library team was sufficiently impressed with my presentation, and soon I was giving them a tour of the vault in Chelsea to inspect what we had already collected. They were blown away with our collections, and I was personally elated that NYU was showing serious interest. The staff resources and infrastructure at the university were, of course, world-class. I thought about what Howard Gotlieb had built at Boston University and knew that partnering with an academic powerhouse could further ensure our success.

I had also met with the ARChive of Contemporary Music in New York and made significant progress with the leadership at NYU, who were enthralled with the idea of installing our archive in their famed Philip Johnson building. I'd also met with EMI executive Phil Quartararo, who floated the idea that he could give us two floors in the famed Capitol Records Building in Hollywood. I went out to see the tower a few months later. The floor, of course, was circular, and it wasn't clear how we could install a 30,000- or 40,000-square-foot library in the building, but I was certainly game to keep the conversation going.

Soon, though, Jann informed Terry Stewart—and, by extension, the Cleveland board—that NYU was a genuine contender for the library archives, and that if Cleveland couldn't quickly find a suitable partner, he would simply install the archive in New York. For Jann, it made great sense: The music industry was in New York, as was *Rolling Stone*. There was also the small fact that New York City was a cultural capital of the world. Jann wasn't bluffing.

Jann's threat pushed the Cleveland board into high gear to find their own location. One idea was installing it in Tower City in downtown Cleveland in an enormous complex owned by the Ratner family, who were on the Cleveland board. The idea was that the library would take over the ground-level space that had been occupied for many decades by the defunct Higbee's department store, and while this was a very generous offer, the library and archives really needed to be located at a university to ensure that it was that it was well-utilized by scholars and faculty.

After months of discussions, NYU suggested that they could allocate two floors of the Philip Johnson building for our archive—but only after they completed a major renovation, which would take years. At the same time, the prestigious Case Western Reserve University in Cleveland generously offered a location on their campus, but the amount of square footage was inadequate.

In the end, Terry Stewart negotiated a generous deal with Cuyahoga Community College, which was located about ten minutes from the museum. The college was constructing a new building and offered the Hall of Fame a substantial thirty thousand square feet of space. The facility itself would be spectacular.

There was some high-level drama on the horizon that absolutely nobody predicted. But the end result was extraordinary.

CHAPTER SIXTEEN

WHEN PRINCE'S GUITAR WEPT

In March 2019, I was standing in a gallery at the Metropolitan Museum of Art, wearing a pair of white cotton gloves and holding a Telecaster electric guitar. I was there to help place the instrument behind glass, where it would remain for the next six months. To be clear: This wasn't a *Fender* Telecaster—it was a Hohner knockoff made in Japan in the 1970s, and the last time I had seen it was fifteen years earlier, hanging around Prince's neck: The Tele was his principal instrument, and the one he played during his historic 2004 performance at the Rock & Roll Hall of Fame.

After Prince's guitar was secured in place, I stood back and admired it—marveled, really, that I had touched it and seen it up close. On that night of Prince's epic performance honoring the late George Harrison, I was standing at stage right in the Waldorf's ballroom, taking in the entire spectacle as the Purple One delivered the most significant musical performance in the institution's nearly forty-year history. His solo on "While My Guitar Gently Weeps" deserves some kind of Hall of fame recognition of its own. The YouTube video has been viewed millions of times, and the performance has been written about extensively in the press. But the real story about how it all came about is virtually unknown.

Prince, who was being inducted that year, had to be coaxed into playing in the posthumous tribute to Harrison. Initially George's widow, Olivia Harrison, had only wanted musicians who had personally known her husband to be onstage, but it was producer Joel Gallen who had the genius idea. When he finally sold Olivia on the idea of adding Prince to the lineup, Gallen went to Prince—communicating through one of his bodyguards—and he finally agreed.

There was just one problem, which only emerged during rehearsals: Tom Petty and Jeff Lynne did not want Prince involved in the tribute. Suzan Evans was at the rehearsal and remembers it vividly.

"Prince was being completely ignored by Tom and Jeff," she says. "Joel Gallen and I were shocked—we were shaking our heads at each other. We couldn't believe this was happening—it wasn't right."

Ultimately, Prince was there because he admired George Harrison—but George's son, Dhani, was the only person in the room willing to speak with him. "They stuck me in between them [Tom and Jeff] and Prince to kind of be a buffer zone," Dhani remembered. Marc Mann, a session guitarist who had worked with Lynne, was brought for the solo on "While My Guitar Gently Weeps," giving Prince absolutely no room to play.

"I went to go see Olivia and explain what was happening," Evans says, "but Olivia [Harrison] had no reaction."

Dhani was in a tough position: Tom and Jeff were his father's closest friends.

After the rehearsal at SIR, Prince walked out onto the street carrying his guitar in hand—no case—and looking annoyed.

What happened next, of course, is the stuff of legend. Petty and Lynn sang the verse and chorus, and the session man played the note-perfect version of Eric Clapton's solo, uncredited when it originally appeared on the so-called "White Album" in 1968. Then, at three minutes and twenty-seven seconds—just about the time the song was going to start wrapping up—Prince stepped to center stage slightly in front of Petty.

I was quoted about the solo in the *New York Times*: "Prince seemed like he was levitating—you hear all these sorts of harmonics and finger tapping, sort of like what you'd hear Eddie Van Halen do. He ran through all these different guitar techniques that are all sort of astonishing. You hear what sounds like someone cocking a shotgun. There are all these strumming power cords that really, really connected. Then he plays his version of the Eric Clapton solo—he evokes Eric's solo in a sort of truncated fashion. And as he ends the song, he plays this flourishing thing that sort of ends up sounding a little bit like *Spinal Tap*, but in a good way."

Petty just stood there grim-faced, strumming his guitar. Dhani Harrison was laughing hysterically. Prince was taunting Petty and having a ball, mouth wide open in a broad and wicked smile.

The day after the ceremony, Tom Petty's management had the gall to call Suzan Evans to ask if they could post the footage from the performance on Petty's website. It was no secret, of course, that the music business could be ugly.

When the *New York Times* interviewed Joel Gallen, Tom Petty, and me after Prince's passing, Petty completely changed his account, employing a large dollop of revisionist history to simultaneously honor Prince and make himself look good. The unique opportunity to pay tribute to their friend George had brought out a territorial competitiveness in him and Lynn; they wanted to own that moment alone.

It again demonstrated how the Hall of Fame could elicit emotion and brilliance—but there were so many other incredible moments; some hysterical ones, too. This was the year Jann himself would be inducted, with no less than Mick Jagger and Ahmet Ertegun doing the honors. This was back in the days when the speeches were still long—sometimes way too long—as the ceremony typically ended well after midnight.

Keith Richards was also at the ceremony—there to induct ZZ Top. The Hall's go-to photographer Kevin Mazur and his crew were there, as usual, and had always managed to be unobtrusive, but when they saw Mick and Keith seated together at a table up front, they went into full-on paparazzi mode, with four of Mazur's hired shooters crowded together, almost knocking Robbie Robertson off his chair while trying to get the best shot of the Glimmer Twins seated together in their tuxedos.

Ahmet spoke eloquently about Jann and then said: "I present to you a great pioneer of rock 'n' roll, Sir Mick Jagger."

It was a fascinating moment: Jann idolized Mick, possibly more than he idolized John Lennon or Bob Dylan. And here was Mick to present Jann with his Hall of Fame induction. The two had been good friends since the late 1960s, and Mick of course knew how important it was to Jann that he had agreed to do the honors. This wasn't something that Mick did very often; the last time he was a presenter was back in 1988 when he inducted the Beatles. Mick delivered a brilliant speech (with a little assistance from Lorne Michaels) that included some heartfelt comments about Jann's love for rock 'n' roll and his talent as an editor. But he also didn't pass up the opportunity to land some fabulous zingers.

From the lectern, Mick said, "When I was first asked to come up and induct Jann into the Rock & Roll Hall of Fame, my response was immediate: *Why?* But, you know, they wouldn't take no for an answer, so here I am."

Jagger explained that Jann was among the first journalists who truly understood how musicians felt and was a kindred spirit. Jagger rarely doled out compliments in this way. You could tell he meant it even with all of the sarcasm. Jann Wenner almost single-handedly pioneered the idea of popular music, and rock 'n' roll in particular, as a vibrant art form, not just a collection of flash in the pan mediocrities.

"He's kept an incredibly high standard for thirty-six years without even batting an eyelash—no mean feat. Jann Wenner has made an invaluable contribution to the appreciation of our music. This is a wonderful, heartfelt occasion, and I will treasure the memory of it all the way to the airport."

Mick's speech was all very interesting, especially when you consider that the Rolling Stones' New York attorney had sent Jann a cease-and-desist letter on November 1, 1967, which I found in Jann's extensive archives, accusing the magazine of "misappropriation of clients' property rights in the name of the Rolling Stones for your own commercial benefit. . . . Let me assure you that unless you immediately cease and desist from the continuation of the sale of your publication, and you destroy all works of art or other material containing my client's copyright, and furnish us with written proof that you are taking immediate action with regard to same, this matter will be forwarded to our California council with instructions to take immediate legal action, including an injunction and a suit for treble damages."

Rolling Stone, of course, kept its name—in fact, a year later, Jann and Mick were in negotiations to start a UK version of *Rolling Stone*. They remain close friends to this day.

After Prince was inducted, the inventory of artists most preferred by the nominating committee was dwindling. In 2005, U2, the Pretenders, and Buddy Guy were inducted, along with Percy Sledge, who had been eligible for nomination for twenty years. There had long been discussions about whether Sledge's recording career was distinguished enough for consideration, or whether an artist should be inducted for essentially one extraordinary song ("When a Man Loves a Woman," a song Sledge didn't even write). But he made it to the ballot anyway.

U2 accepted their awards and took to the stage, with Bono grabbing a bottle of champagne off one of the tables, shaking it up, and spraying the audience—less a celebration than an acknowledgment that the record exes up front were sitting on their hands.

In 2005, Jon Landau took over as sole chairman of the Hall of Fame's thirty-five-or-so-strong nominating committee. Soon after, he created subcommittees, where small groups could focus on specific genres of music, such as hip-hop, heavy metal, alternative, etc. These subcommittees would prep for the big meeting and have sidebar conversations months in advance before presenting potential nominees to Landau. He added more structure to the proceedings, which enabled him to keep tabs on where the committee was going.

While Seymour Stein had worn his passion on his sleeve, Landau was more buttoned up—but he was equally committed to maintaining ultra-high standards. He often described the voting process as "purposefully opaque," and asked that participants not discuss the proceedings even with each other outside of our meetings—and of course certainly not with the press.

On occasion, though, members were removed from the committee for being disruptive or unwieldy. Going forward, Landau periodically cleaned house, purging five or six members from the committee to make room for new blood. And yes, there were some hard feelings—no question. Landau also felt that the meetings were dragging, with too many people who loved the sounds of their own voices, and so one year, he showed up with a large three-minute hourglass timer. That lasted for two years.

The committee always had a lively and varied group of members, which would stay relatively constant. For many years, Ahmet and Jerry Wexler existed as founding father figures on the committee—after all, they were there when rock 'n' roll was born and, as producers and record company executives, had unique insight. Journalists, of course, were the mainstay of the committee—and for the most part, they either worked at *Rolling Stone* or had grown up reading the magazine, and so the entire school of rock criticism which Jann had helped create permeated these meetings.

Each year, the museum's president Terry Stewart would bring up the names of artists who had been overlooked, and every year he would get some pretty cranky, nasty emails, letters, voicemails, and in-person diatribes as he walked around the museum. There were always lots of letter-writing campaigns with fans hoping that the nominating committee would take a more populist approach to the ballot. KISS was kept off the ballot for well over a decade, as conventional wisdom carried the day; since the band was considered derivative and weren't top songwriters, they did not deserve the honor despite how influential their costumes and makeup had been. The KISS Army was furious; their beloved group had sold millions of records and concert tickets.

Since the Hall of Fame's opening, exhibits focused on a specific genre or artist. Now that the museum was open for nearly ten years, I felt that we were ready to take on an exhibit that focused on a single work. The museum had been most comfortable doing retrospectives, but when I suggested an exhibit about the Who's rock opera, *Tommy*, Jann was immediately on board. He was friends with Pete Townshend, and my colleagues in Cleveland didn't hesitate. *Tommy* was a singular work in rock. It debuted in 1969 and, over the years, there were many incarnations, including the motion picture directed by Ken Russell and starring the Who, Ann-Margret, Elton John, Eric Clapton, Tina Turner, and others. There was the ballet and now multiple Broadway productions as well. If there was a rock album that had legs, it was *Tommy*.

Townshend was very cooperative, providing manuscripts to songs like "See Me, Feel Me" and "Pinball Wizard." He had, of course, already donated the Gibson J-200 he used to write "Pinball Wizard," and I secured other materials from collectors and people who worked with the band. When I went to Pete's office in Richmond to pick up the manuscripts, I arrived with a small, custom-made wooden crate to hand-carry his precious cargo back to the states.

Tommy: The Amazing Journey was groundbreaking; occupying the two top floors of the Hall of Fame, it was the first time a major museum had curated a show on a single rock 'n' roll album. Having so much real estate at our disposal to focus on the work was a luxury, but also added pressure to go deep.

I was back in Cleveland in September for the Rock Hall's star-studded tribute to folk and blues icon Lead Belly. The concert was held at Severance Hall, the Cleveland Orchestra's home venue. After checking into my hotel, I stepped into the elevator to head to my room and ran into Robert Plant, of all people, who was on the bill for the show the following evening.

We had met a few times, and Plant was aware of the many entreaties I had made over the past few years in the hopes of mounting a major Led Zeppelin exhibit at the hall. But the answer had always been no, and I had long ago given up hope that he would cooperate. Today, I just told him: "I know there's no chance you will be part of a Zeppelin exhibit—but don't you realize how many people on this earth would want to see the original working handwritten lyrics to 'Stairway to Heaven'? It's like the Magna Carta!"

Plant laughed and said, "I certainly understand your point . . . it's just something I don't wanna do."

Then he looked at me intently.

"If the public sees the lyrics to 'Stairway,'" he said, "it will demystify the song."

My jaw dropped. As we parted ways, I thought to myself, *Another* Spinal Tap *moment!* David St. Hubbins could have said the same thing. Life imitating art, imitating life.

The next night's Lead Belly tribute was astonishing.

"This is a great way of saying some kind of protracted *thank you* for all of those great songs," said Plant from the stage.

One of the highlights of the show was Plant's amazing duet of "In the Pines" with Alison Krauss. It was at this concert in Cleveland where they met for the first time, and they, of course, went on to work brilliantly together. Plant in particular found a new way to sing and collaborate. Meanwhile, Odetta and John Hiatt were also on the bill.

CHAPTER SEVENTEEN

BRUCE SPRINGSTEEN SENDS IN THE GOONS

In 2005, one of my former clients from Sotheby's, Ed Kosinski—a prominent lender to the museum—landed one of the most significant collections in the history of twentieth-century pop culture: Bruce Springsteen's "Born to Run" spiral notebook, which contained more than thirty drafts of that single song. (Kosinski had purchased it from the writer Charlie Cross, who had acquired it from Bruce's old manager Mike Appel.)

I immediately thought the notebook would be great for the Hall of Fame, and presented the idea to Jann Wenner, who discussed it with his friend and fellow board member (and Bruce's longtime manager) Jon Landau. Ed's price: one million dollars. Jann proposed that the foundation would put up $500,000, and the museum, in turn, would put up the balance.

I showed the notebook to the museum's director Terry Stewart. It contained nearly one hundred pages and included evolving drafts of not only "Born to Run" but also "Thunder Road" and "Jungleland"—and in each case, the early versions of the songs had almost no resemblance to the final product. It showed an extraordinary creative evolution and was a hands-on guide to the way that Bruce's exquisite songwriting craft unfolded. Years later, Springsteen jokingly described himself as a "sociopath" when he was writing the *Born to Run* album: His revisions took months. It was a process so different from, say, Neil Young, whose songs seemed to shoot out of him like a firehose. Neil could write two or three songs in an afternoon fever dream.

Unfortunately, that deal fell apart, and a few months later, things got weird when Springsteen's attorneys became involved.

"Two retired FBI agents showed up unannounced at my apartment," Kosinski told me; they pushed past the doorman at his Manhattan apartment building and knocked on his door, armed, asking about the notebook and how he'd come to acquire it—all on Yom Kippur. Bruce's "man of the people" persona, it would seem, had its limits. In the end, everything worked out. Kosinski and Bruce Springsteen made a deal.

Similar manuscripts were now coming into their own as investments. In today's dollars, the "Born to Run" notebook is probably worth \$4–\$5 million—and that single page of Jimi Hendrix's crumpled-up lyrics for "Purple Haze" that Seymour Stein bought from my auction at Sotheby's way back when? It's now worth a cool \$1 million.

When Springsteen's manager Jon Landau became the sole chair of the nominating committee that year, he began to bring in new blood, diversifying interest and attention away from an earlier focus on the blues and R&B and toward somewhat more modern music. Miles Davis's name came up, with the big-time music attorney Peter Shukat, who had represented the estates of Miles Davis, John Lennon, and others, making noise and calling members of the committee in the time leading up to the next meeting on September 19. For him, it was a simple business decision: He wanted to promote the Davis catalog.

Landau made his thoughts clear at the nominating meeting that Miles Davis should not be inducted, but he was overruled: His personal vision of what the Hall of Fame should be was being challenged.

That spring, I was back in England, resuming work on Joe Strummer's collection. I had already made two visits to his old farmhouse in Somerset, and each time I showed up, his widow, Luce, seemed to have found more material for me to sift through. She knew me well by this point and allowed me to wander around the outbuildings to look for additional artifacts.

Soon after my arrival, Luce pulled out Joe's two most important guitars: his iconic blackish-gray Telecaster, which was covered in stickers (while many guitars now are decorated in a similar way, this was among the first of its kind, with dozens of setlists pasted or taped to the top the guitar), and its companion, a natural-colored Tele that served as a backup.

We rummaged through some more trunks in the house, and from there, Joe's former assistant—his nickname was Pockets—and I walked over to a large eighteenth-century brick barn. The structure had a leaking roof and no electricity, and it was dark and dank inside—certainly not the kind of place where you'd expect to find any treasure.

I was scavenging around on my hands and knees, but it all began to seem like a waste of time. Eventually, though, I came upon an old beaten-up trunk filled with papers that were mostly damp or soaking wet. There was also evidence that rats had been in the trunk—not just droppings, but chunks of paper had bite marks on the corners, and chew-sized pieces of other pages were missing.

As I sifted through the debris, I located a section of papers in the middle of a stack that was dry—and soon realized that many of these papers were Joe's handwritten lyrics from the Clash's *London Calling* album and were in pretty good shape. It was an astonishing discovery: I first found a lyric fragment to "Lost in the Supermarket"—one of Strummer's most brilliant songs, a lament about a world that is becoming increasingly commercialized, which was sung by Mick Jones—scribbled on an Ernie Ball guitar string envelope. Next, I found the lyrics to "Clampdown" and "Death or Glory." I felt like Indiana Jones excavating the past. These were some of the most important relics from the twentieth century, and I had rescued them from destruction and oblivion. After that, I found a version of the "London Calling" lyrics that had sustained some water damage but was still readable. The lyrics of other songs, of course, were mere meals for some starving rodent.

Riding on the train back to London, I knew I had the makings of a blockbuster exhibit.

A couple months later, I was back in London continuing the hunt. Next stop was a trip to see Mick Jones at his recording studio inside a warehouse in Acton. Jones had an amazing archive of posters, papers, and his stage clothing, along with newspaper clippings and magazines. The studio was jam-packed with many of his guitars, including his Les Paul Jr., and I recognized a bunch of them from his days with the Clash.

That night, we went to a club that was owned by John Mayall's son Gaz. Jones was a huge Stones fan, and he told me that he had been lucky enough to go to their legendary concert in Hyde Park in 1969. He and his school friends had also learned where Mick Jagger lived, at Forty-Eight Cheyne Walk in Chelsea, and they'd walk there and simply hang out in front of the house, just staring into the windows.

"One day, Mick came over and pulled the curtain shut right in front of us," Jones told me. He and his crew were thrilled.

Jones had a fantastic sense of humor, and he was extremely enthusiastic about our exhibit. I think the fact that he himself was a collector of pop culture made it that much more interesting for him. He told me he planned to attend the opening.

I was also thrilled to find myself back at Abbey Road again—this time for an EMI party in honor of Sir George Martin, the Beatles' famous producer. I got to see Studio One, the big orchestra room where many of the most important and historic movie soundtracks from the modern era were recorded, including *Raiders of the Lost Ark*, *The Last Emperor*, and *Braveheart*, to name just a few. Then I popped upstairs to see Studio Three, where Pink Floyd recorded their first album while the Beatles were downstairs in Studio Two. The most unexpected surprise, though, was seeing the microphone room. Lester Smith, who had been working at Abbey Road since 1970, was the keeper of Abbey Road's microphone collection, which then totaled eight hundred-plus—all of them kept in good repair and still used to this day. He showed me one of his handwritten logs that detailed which microphones were used on recording sessions, and I saw many of the microphones used to record the Beatles, including what Lester said was the most requested microphone at Abbey Road: the Neumann U 47 that Paul McCartney used to record the vocals for "Penny Lane."

That summer, Suzan Evans stepped down from her position as executive director of the Hall of Fame for personal reasons, though she remained on the board. Evans was succeeded by Joel Peresman, who had cut his teeth in the mailroom at William Morris and later booked acts like David Bowie, Genesis, and Pink Floyd. In the mid-'90s, Peresman worked at Madison Square Garden and helped produce the concert for New York City after 9/11. He knew the concert side of the business well, and he's the best salesman ever for the Hall of Fame's brand.

I've already explained that the work of a curator can be painstaking, requiring scholarship dedication and perseverance. It can take years or even decades to reel in an important collection; but sometimes things just fall into your lap. That has happened to me many times under different circumstances. Sometimes, it comes down to misfortune or somebody losing their job.

Right after Joel started, I received a call one morning from a friend of the acclaimed music journalist Robert Christgau who said that I should immediately get over to his office at the *Village Voice* to grab the remnants of his reference library. I had heard the day before that Christgau had been fired from the *Voice*, so I jumped in a taxi and rushed downtown to the paper's famed headquarters. When I arrived, it looked like the last days of Pompeii—the offices were a mess; staffers were crying as they packed up their desks, and many of them angry. Christgau seemed disgusted. He pointed to a huge pile of books and told me I could take what I wanted. (I had a sense the books were all duplicates of copies he had at home.) I was there to scoop up some crumbs. I grabbed them and left; five or so boxes of reference books. But it just didn't feel satisfying.

Other times, I would swoop in at the last moment to haul away truckloads of material that would otherwise go to another institution or into a dumpster. One such instance happened when the *Philadelphia Inquirer* decided to get rid of a massive chunk of their reference library and record collection. I showed up with moving vans and whisked away an immensely important collection that was easily worth well over $100,000. If I had hesitated even for a day, a librarian or archivist from one of Philly's many universities would have surely taken the haul. That was an immensely satisfying get.

There was more change afoot. In October 2006, Ahmet Ertegun was attending a Rolling Stones concert at the Beacon Theatre, a fundraiser hosted by Bill and Hillary Clinton, and was backstage saying his hellos—Keith Richard's manager Jane Rose, who was friends with Ahmet, had just taken some photos of Ahmet with the band—when he fell and hit his head on a concrete floor. Ertegun was taken to the hospital, having fallen into a coma, and passed away on December 14.

His passing was a tragedy, but we took solace in knowing he was active until the end, never letting up on his hectic schedule.

"I think it's better to burn out than fade away," Ahmet had said. "It's better to live out your days being very, very active—even if it destroys you—than to quietly disappear."

It was somehow fitting that he was with the Stones when he checked out.

I attended Ahmet's memorial celebration at Rose Theater in Lincoln Center. Many Atlantic artists, of course, were on hand, and the diversity of the crowd of twelve hundred reflected well on his epic life: There were old bluesmen, British rockers, politicians, and women in high society. Soon, a corps of drummers and horn players piped up, and Wynton Marsalis, the artistic director of Jazz at Lincoln Center, emerged from a side door playing "Oh, Didn't He Ramble," a tune typically performed at funerals in New Orleans.

Eric Clapton was also among those who performed and spoke that evening. "I loved Ahmet," he said. "He was like a father figure to me. In the old days, we'd have a drink and do some other things, and any time that happened, he would start singing songs to me . . . We're going to do two of the songs he always sang: 'Please Send Me Someone to Love,' and the other by Stick McGhee, called 'Drinkin' Wine Spo-Dee-O-Dee.'"

There were also tributes from Doctor John, New York City mayor Michael Bloomberg, Henry Kissinger, Bette Midler, Ben E. King, Kid Rock, and Jerry Wexler, and more performances, from Phil Collins; Crosby, Stills & Nash; and a stunning version of "Mr. Soul" by Neil Young and Stephen Stills on acoustic guitars. Toward the end of the evening, Mick Jagger delivered the most engaging speech of the night; he was in a good mood. "Oh, he was a father figure, it's true," Jagger said, "but to me, he was more like the wicked uncle with the wicked chuckle." He marveled that Ahmet was the kind of unique animal who could discuss politics and Islamic history in one breath, and then select the next Vanilla Fudge single with the following breath. Ahmet had hired strippers for one of the Stones' after-parties, and Mick described them as "rotund women of a certain age who stripped for free on the weekends."

"I could never keep up with him," Jagger said.

I was in awe of Ahmet. Most of us were.

Jann said, "He was our arbiter, and 'What does Ahmet think?' was our constant refrain in moments of doubt and decision."

Later that year, Ed Kosinski connected me with the Wall Street titan Martin Zweig—I was familiar with his name as somebody who collected high-end sports memorabilia. Zweig was from Cleveland and had become interested in the stock market when he was in high school. In addition to being an investor, he appeared on television as a pundit and had predicted the 1987 stock market crash. Up to this point, people in finance had not donated anything significant to the museum, but Zweig told me that he wanted to make a substantial gift to the Hall of Fame and asked me to meet him at his apartment.

"I live in the Pierre Hotel," he'd said, "so just ask for me when you get to the concierge desk."

I arrived at the appointed time and place, and a few minutes later, Zweig appeared and said, "Let's go upstairs."

"I'll give you a tour," he said in the elevator, with a smirk.

We rode to the forty-second-floor penthouse of the building and entered an enormous commercial kitchen, where Zweig introduced me to his chef and her staff. Zweig and his family occupied the top three floors of the Pierre—which included the hotel's grand ballroom with 360-degree views of the city, along with Long Island and New Jersey—which he purchased a few years earlier for $21.5

million—"the most important sale in the twentieth century," as Elizabeth Lee Sample, one of the real estate agents involved, put it to the *New York Times*. "It is a chateau in the sky." (When the hotel first opened in 1930, Zweig's apartment was known as Club Pierrot, a supper club for high society with members including William Vanderbilt and Walter Chrysler—and an extraordinary display of wealth during the Depression.)

I could also tell that nobody was living there at the time. The only thing left in the space was his memorabilia collection, which included several of Muhammad Ali's Golden Gloves and heavyweight champion belts, one of John Lennon's pianos from the late 1970s, one of Babe Ruth's Yankee uniforms, and arguably the most famous dress of the twentieth century: the beaded gown that Marilyn Monroe wore to sing happy birthday to President Kennedy at Madison Square Garden, now the centerpiece of the four-hundred-capacity ballroom, with a custom mannequin to Monroe's exact proportions. (It was strange to read, years later, that Kim Kardashian wore the dress to the Met Gala, and that beads from the gown fell off while she walked around—but it certainly wasn't the first time somebody had worn a historic garment years after it had been made famous: In the 1970s, George Harrison modeled many of his most famous Beatle outfits, including his *Sgt. Pepper's* uniform, in a video shoot.)

I was in Zweig's penthouse for less than an hour, and somehow, I knew I would never be back. The entire experience was a spectacular reminder of all the amazing—and often secret—spaces that people occupy in New York City, whether for a lifetime or a mere moment or two. Zweig ended up donating a vast collection to us, including that John Lennon piano, Jimi Hendrix's Marshall amplifier and one of his effects pedals, and some wardrobe from Madonna, and the top hat worn by Elton John on the cover of his album *A Single Man*, among others.

This year's induction ceremony would be the fifteenth one that I attended. Each one seemed to come around really quickly, and each one unfolded differently. I never had a set place that I'd be sitting for the evening; sometimes I was on the floor, sometimes I was at the writers' table, which was reserved for everyone who had contributed to the program. This year I was seated upstairs, in the second balcony, at a random table. I mingled and made small talk with the group.

This year, Black Sabbath, Blondie, Miles Davis, Lynyrd Skynyrd, and the Sex Pistols were among those inducted. When the votes came in and it was announced that the Pistols would be inducted, punk rock fans around the world were thrilled. I had seen them on one of their reunion tours at Roseland—an astonishing show; pure, jaw-dropping joy for everyone lucky enough to get a ticket. Their induction, I thought, would be an ecstatic moment. But a few weeks before the ceremony, Johnny Rotten faxed a handwritten note to Jann Wenner. I recognized his distinctive handwriting:

"Next to the Sex Pistols," the note began, "rock 'n' roll and that Hall of fame is a piss stain. Your museum. Urine in wine. We're not coming. We're not your monkeys. If you voted for us, hope you noted your reasons. Your anonymous as judges but your still music industry people. We're not coming. You're not paying attention. Outside the shit-stream is a real Sex Pistol."

And while there was always a certain amount of drama at the ceremony, this year was particularly extreme. Black Sabbath refused to perform—they weren't speaking to each other at the time—but Metallica stepped in for a tremendous tribute. The volume coming from the stage had never been so loud; production staff handed out earplugs to people in the first few rows. When Miles Davis was being inducted, his extended family of nieces and nephews—they controlled his publishing and managed the estate—were on hand to receive the award, but Davis's son Miles Davis IV, who was estranged from the rest of the family, snuck onto the stage, grabbed the award, and left the ballroom. And when the members of Blondie were accepting their awards, guitarist Frank Infante pleaded with Debbie Harry in front of the entire audience, asking if he could play with the band that night. She refused.

When the evening's MC announced that there would be a short break while they reset the stage for the next honoree, Lynyrd Skynyrd, two of the women seated at my table stood up and made their exit.

"We'll be back in a little while," one of them said. "We're playing with the band."

After the members of Skynyrd received their awards, the band played a short set of hits, and it dawned on me: The women from my table were Leslie Hawkins and JoJo Billingsley of the Honkettes, the band's backup singers. When they came back to the table, I congratulated them, and we spoke about their performance and their time in the band. Leslie had survived the 1977 plane crash that had killed Skynyrd founder Ronnie Van Zant—at the Waldorf, she pulled down the side of her dress, revealing burn scars from the accident. (The third member of the Honkettes, Cassie Gaines, died in the crash, along with her younger brother Steve Gaines, Skynyrd's guitarist and vocalist, and several others).

Earlier in the evening, Jann had read the Sex Pistols' profane note from the podium and then said: "So for Johnny Rotten and the rest of them, these [awards] will be in Cleveland at the Hall of Fame. Should they come and want them, they can have them—or come and smash them to bits; they can do that, too. Welcome to the Hall of Fame, Sex Pistols." It was a hilarious moment. While I was disappointed at the time that the band didn't show up, in retrospect, Johnny Rotten demonstrated that he was still a true punk rocker.

(Other members of the group had apparently wanted to attend the ceremony, but when Rotten said no, everyone else fell in line.)

The following week I saw Jann at the office, and we briefly compared notes about the ceremony. Jann instructed me that the Sex Pistols' awards should not be shipped to them under any circumstances: The only way a band member could get their award was if they personally made the trip to Cleveland—no exceptions.

CHAPTER EIGHTEEN

THE TWENTY-FIFTH AT MSG, AND HIP-HOP IS HERE

By 2007, seismic changes within the nominating committee were affecting who would be inducted and who would be playing the epic twenty-fifth anniversary concerts at Madison Square Garden. That year, Jon Landau dismissed a big chunk of the nominating committee—he simply felt it was time to clean house and bring in some new blood. Jon wrote eloquent letters to each committee member who was being removed—so glowing that it wasn't until the end of the letter when the recipient actually learned they were being pushed out.

Some of Landau's decisions, I felt, were short-sighted. He jettisoned Jeff Jones, who had recently been made head of Apple Corps, the Beatles' company, replacing the legendary Neil Aspinall. I saw Jeff in the lobby of *Rolling Stone*, and he was angry about the decision. It certainly made my job harder: Jeff was now the face of the Beatles, and the Hall of Fame had showed him no goodwill. It was a prime example of that disconnect between the New York board and the museum in Cleveland.

The nominating committee had become Jon Landau's fiefdom—a fact that everyone on the new committee acknowledged and was clearly onboard with. Landau was universally admired: He was classy, erudite, and a true believer in rock 'n' roll. Everyone happily served at his pleasure and felt privileged to be there.

The 2007 induction ceremony, though, felt different in other ways. It wasn't only that Suzan Evans was gone. The biggest outward-facing change was that rap and hip-hop were entering the Hall of Fame, with Grandmaster Flash and the Furious Five inducted. They were a groundbreaking group, just as influential and impactful as some of the most important rock 'n' roll artists in the Hall of Fame—but they weren't rock 'n' roll. There was a lot of grumbling and some outright disgust among some artists and fans, who felt hip-hop shouldn't have a place in the Rock Hall. But the board and the nominating committee felt pressure to be more musically inclusive—something which would also help assure the continuing financial support of the music business.

There were other, more subtle, changes to the ceremony. More and more of the induction speeches were now being transcribed and put on a teleprompter, making them less personal and spontaneous. By this point, the Wall Street philistines had also been allowed to run amok, occupying a big chunk of the tables up front, while a lot of A-list artists were now seated in the second and third rows of tables—which, of course, quickly became the hot place to sit.

Earlier that year, I had gone to see Patti Smith, who would be inducted into the Hall of Fame in a few months, at her Greenwich Village townhouse. She and I already had a connection of sorts, as she had introduced me to her mother fifteen years earlier. As she reminded me, "My mother is my biggest fan." Patti proceeded to show me the archive that her mom had created with the kind of love and dedication you only saw from a parent, and we soon acquired a fantastic collection, including several items which Patti had lent years earlier, like her iconic clarinet. She was most proud, though, to show me one of her late husband, Fred "Sonic" Smith's, guitars. The next few months could have been a grind, flying back and forth to Cleveland, but artists like Patti made it more than worthwhile.

The summertime was the one point in the year where everyone was able to relax just a bit. We usually ran at a pretty furious pace, but in July and August, we often worked under a self-imposed slow-down. Joan and I spent a lot of time out at our beach house in East Hampton with our two young daughters, and we often had friends out for the weekends. I would bump into Jann occasionally in the morning at the Springs General Store, which was down the road from the house that he was renting with his partner, Matt Nye. The general store was a super casual place with a legendary history: When Jackson Pollock couldn't afford to pay his tab there, he gave the owner one of his paintings instead. A few decades later, the painting sold at Sotheby's for several million dollars.

One late Saturday afternoon in August, Joan and I and two friends were walking along the side of the road near our beach house on Louse Point in East Hampton. We were down toward the end of the point, hoping to catch the sunset, when we saw a black Audi convertible pass by. Joan and I immediately recognized that it was Lou Reed, whom we often saw driving down to the point. But then, he turned the car around and drove toward us at a very high speed—and swerved directly toward Joan, who had to dive off the road into the dunes to avoid being run over. She could easily have been killed.

As Reed zoomed by, I screamed, "Fuck off, Lou!"

He clearly heard me: He slammed on the brakes, did a quick 180, and started barreling toward us again. We all scattered as he drove by. I still wonder to this day why he acted so recklessly. I guess he was just having a bad day and decided to take it out on us. I'd only met Lou once before, a decade or so earlier. Before arriving at his office to discuss creating an exhibit, his assistant called me to ask me whether or not I smoked, as Lou was trying to quit and couldn't be around anyone who did. Arriving at Lou's office on lower Broadway, I found him sitting behind a large desk—and smoking a cigarette. Lou wasn't the friendliest that day either. I thought to myself: *Wow—the former angry young man still had some serious demons.*

Early in 2008, Joel Peresman was approached by some of his former colleagues at Madison Square Garden with the idea of opening a New York outpost of the Hall of Fame, to be called the Annex. It seemed like a glorious idea—one which would bring more visibility to the museum and provide us with a built-in venue to send our traveling exhibits. Not everyone on staff in Cleveland was enthusiastic about bringing the Rock Hall brand to New York, but Peresman realized it was a great opportunity and made it happen.

The Annex—a twenty-thousand-square-foot-space on Mercer Street in posh Soho, opened in November to great fanfare and critical acclaim. Its exhibits mostly focused on New York. Among others, I created an exhibit about the legendary recently shuttered bar and performance space CBGB that included the venue's iconic awning, along with a great deal of the furniture, chairs, posters, and one of the urinals from the men's bathroom—certainly one of the most notorious restrooms in New York history, a veritable ground zero of nefariousness and debauchery for decades. We sent my Clash exhibition from Cleveland to the Annex, which was fitting considering the band's fondness for New York and the many shows they played there including their iconic residence at Bonds.

The Annex's crowning achievement was an exhibit entitled *Lennon in New York*, which was just that: a focus on John's ten years living in the city after the Beatles broke up. I'd been gathering material for it for some time, making more trips up to the Dakota—one to pick up the black Yamaha piano that Lennon had used to write and record the songs on his final album with Yoko, *Double Fantasy.* I met one of the archivists in the front of the building, but when we went up together to the apartment to meet the piano movers—I got a quick glimpse of the famous white room this time—a member of the house staff informed us that the piano mover had arrived early and had already taken the piano, sending us rushing downstairs in a panic—only to find the piano, indeed, still being loaded onto the truck. The whole experience was kind of comical, but less than an hour later, the piano was safely set in place for our new exhibit, which included the clothing Lennon was wearing when he was assassinated, along with that evidence bag Yoko Ono retrieved from the hospital that I had previously transported to Cleveland.

It was a powerful exhibit, beautifully designed by Ralph Appelbaum, the famed exhibit designer who would later design the exhibits at the Smithsonian's National Museum of African American History and Culture. The entire exhibit was white, evoking Lennon's white room and piano at the Dakota. Yoko even donated one of her iconic wall-mounted telephones—and would randomly call the phone and speak to whomever picked up while the museum was open.

As for the Annex itself: While it received tremendous critical praise and publicity, due to the financial crisis of the moment and its location, which was not in one of Manhattan's densely populated tourist centers, it wasn't a financial success. The Annex would close in January of 2010. It had been a great experiment, however.

I always wondered, though, what happened to that urinal.

More changes were afoot. In 2009, for the first time, the general public would be allowed access to the induction ceremony—a change that the board felt was long overdue. This was an opportunity to inject more energy into the show, with a real live audience, not just a bunch of suits in tuxedos—and ticket sales, of course, brought in more revenue for the nonprofit.

In the end, we decided to have the induction ceremony in Cleveland—a decision that changed the event in many ways, many of them good: For one thing, most rock stars didn't know anyone in Cleveland, so they had more time on their hands—and, often, more time to visit the Hall of Fame or to meet with us to discuss lending pieces, or working with us in other ways. New York or Los Angeles, of course, held many, many more distractions.

The ceremony was held at Public Hall, a grand old theater with a long musical history: Duke Ellington, Elvis Presley, Jimi Hendrix, the Grateful Dead, the Beatles, the Stones, and Janis Joplin all appeared there. Public Hall is also less than five minutes from the museum, and many of the attendees came to visit.

When older artists toured the museum, there was one very common question I received: "Is Swingos still in business?" When I responded that it had closed in the early '80s, the general reaction was a long sigh. Swingos Celebrity Hotel featured a bar attached to the hotel, both of them infamously frequented by bands on tour; it quickly became *the* place to stay in Cleveland, with Lynyrd Skynyrd and Led Zeppelin just two bands who stayed there whenever they were in town. Groupies congregated in the bar and hotel lobby.

"I loved Led Zeppelin," owner Jim Swingos remembered, "because they always traveled with their accountant. Whatever damage they did to their rooms, the accountant always took out his checkbook and paid for everything, down to the penny. I didn't mind, because I always got new stuff for whatever rooms they stayed in after they left."

This was back in the days when musicians would write girls' names and phone numbers on dressing room walls at Richfield

Coliseum and the Agora so that when other bands were traveling through, they would know who was in town. Cameron Crowe filmed a scene at Swingos for his film *Almost Famous*, and Elvis Presley made the place his base of operations when he was doing a tour of the Midwest. The hotel typically was very tolerant about noise and the ensuing mayhem that would occur when rock 'n' roll checked into its rooms.

"Keith Moon once arrived dressed as a policeman," recalled Swingos. "He walked up to a female patron at the bar, slapped a pair of handcuffs on her, and casually walked away."

The location of each induction ceremony, of course, really affected the overall experience for both the artists and the audience. In the early days of the Waldorf, it was all industry people and artists; when the ceremony was held at Public Hall, while there was still a black-tie dress code, the fact that the general public was allowed to attend injected some palpable enthusiasm and energy.

As a middle-aged white guy, I had almost never cried at a rock concert, but at the rehearsals for the 2009 Inductions at Public Hall, there was an aberration. I was watching Jimmy Page and Jeff Beck rehearse the iconic instrumental "Beck's Bolero," which they would perform later that evening at Jeff Beck's induction. Page had traveled from London for the occasion, bringing his original Fender XII electric twelve-string guitar—the very one that he had used on "Stairway to Heaven" and on the original recording session for "Beck's Bolero," which had also featured Beck, John Paul Jones, Keith Moon, and Nicky Hopkins. At the rehearsal, Page played massive, tectonic riffs while Beck played a gliding slide guitar and single notes. As the song concluded, I had tears rolling down my face, and I turned to my colleague Howard Kramer, who was weeping, too. We acknowledged each other. That performance was one of the most powerful performances I had ever seen, and to think it was an instrumental. I hate how the word *genius* is thrown around describing rock musicians—but there are those times when it's justified.

Production-wise, Public Hall was a big improvement: The stage was expanded beyond what the Waldorf could handle, and there was an actual backstage with dressing rooms. (Since the ceremony's inception, the artists and producers had been forced to use the Waldorf's catering kitchen as an ad hoc backstage space.)

The audience in Cleveland was treated to a fantastic show that included performances by Jimmy Page and Jeff Beck, Metallica, Little Anthony and the Imperials, and Bobby Womack. Having real fans present was a game changer.

In 2009, I curated a major photography exhibition focused on George Kalinsky, who had been the principal photographer at Madison Square Garden since the mid 1960s. Kalinsky's most iconic images were of Frank Sinatra and Muhammad Ali, but since he was the staff photographer at the Garden, he captured virtually every major show at the venue for decades.

He was there when the modern concert experience was created. His photographs captured the first time that the Rolling Stones, Janis Joplin, and Jimi Hendrix appeared onstage in '68 and '69; when crystal-clear high sound systems began to deliver high volume concerts that you could actually hear. And perhaps what was most unusual was his access as a staff employee of the venue. He was the only photographer who was allowed onstage, and, consequently, his photographs came from unique perspectives, even from behind the drum riser with views of the audience from the band's point of view.

Later that same year, the Hall of Fame celebrated its twenty-fifth anniversary with two nights of music at Madison Square Garden. (Though, admittedly, the math on that twenty-five years is a little fuzzy: While the hall was founded in 1983, the space itself didn't open until 1995.) Robbie Robertson, CAA's Rob Light—Bruce Springsteen's agent—Joel Peresman, and Jann had conceived a two-day concert, with artists curating their own sections of the show and inviting musical guests. Springsteen, Metallica, U2, and others played sets of their own, and then brought in their own guests (with Bono and U2 inviting both Mick Jagger and Patti Smith to play). On both nights, Jerry Lee Lewis opened the show, kicking over his piano stool. All in all, it was an extraordinary eight hours of music, with Simon & Garfunkel delivering the most emotional and powerful performance over the two days—they brought down the house.

After the anniversary concerts, Jann felt that the board should consider revising the artist eligibility rules. Amidst the many changes on the nominating committee over the years, the so-called twenty-five-year rule had been sacrosanct, but now Wenner and Landau were considering the unthinkable: lowering the eligibility to twenty years—or even holding the ceremony only every two years. (They quickly abandoned the idea.) Landau, who periodically changed the makeup of the committee, invited Rob Light to join, in part to usher in a more popular mainstream voice to the proceedings.

Meanwhile, I was still hard at work on the new library and archives. Since libraries couldn't accept loans, and we couldn't afford to purchase collections, donations were our only real option, and it was a very tall order to land the most world-class collections—we're talking about John Lennon's estate, Bob Dylan's archive, and others. Jann, of course, possessed more than five hundred boxes of some of the most startling papers from the twentieth century, including personal correspondence with Dylan, Lennon, Paul McCartney, Bono, and Hunter S. Thompson, among hundreds of others; his correspondence back and forth with Mick Jagger about Rolling Stones' press coverage of the Altamont concert was meaty enough for an entire book of its own.

The New York board had wanted to name the new library and archives after Jann, but once Wenner saw the building's hard-to-access location, Cuyahoga Community College, he demurred, and his jaw-dropping archive of letters and documents and drawings remained safely tucked away in a New York vault—the big white whale that I never landed. There were, of course, many other white whales, but this one I had my hooks in.

It was a pattern that was unfortunately developing: Many board members were unwilling to gift their collections to the museum, like Jon Landau and Bob Krasnow for instance—which, of course, made it that much harder to receive big donations from important artists. If the library and archives had somehow landed at NYU, or Lincoln Center, I have no doubt that this wouldn't have been the case. I did manage to get Mo Ostin's extraordinary archive from Warner Bros., and also Seymour and Clive Davis came through.

Mica Ertegun, Ahmet's widow, though, had an enormous archive related to her late husband's life and career that she wanted to donate to the Hall of Fame—something I was rather surprised to hear, given that virtually every time I had met with Ahmet, going all the way back to the early '90s, he'd insisted that he didn't have anything for us. I clearly recall asking Ahmet, and more than once: "How is it that someone of your stature and accomplishments could have nothing? It just doesn't seem possible."

Ahmet had been gone for almost two years by this point, and I had almost given up hope that we would be able to build a collection. Jann assured me something would happen. Then Mica called and asked me to come see her for lunch at her townhouse on the Upper East Side.

Mica was very formal and always elegantly dressed, and we sat in her garden room, where we were waited on by her staff. I was amazed to hear that she had a vast collection of material that spanned Ahmet's entire life, from his childhood to his years living at the Turkish embassy in Washington, DC, all the way through the formation of Atlantic Records and his late correspondence into the 2000s. For many years, Mica had an extraordinarily successful interior design business, with its own large staff—her work was meticulous, and so while I was pleasantly taken aback to find out that this material existed, it came as no surprise that it had already been expertly archived.

It took me a month to sift through the entire collection, which was kept in more than fifty bankers boxes. There were great photos of the family back in Turkey, and from Ahmet's days living in DC when he started to build his record collection of jazz and early blues. There was an enormous amount of correspondence beginning in the late 1940s between Ahmet and his brother, Nesuhi, who would eventually join him at Atlantic. (In one letter from Ahmet, he scolds his brother for not repaying a loan of $50.) Also in these boxes was the letter from Ahmet informing Nesuhi that he would be forming a record company. For the museum, this kind of material was solid gold.

Ahmet and Mica had a house on the water in Turkey where they would spend their summers, and I saw lots of correspondence and thank-you notes from people like Mick Jagger and Jerry Hall, Robert Plant, and Phil Collins. The collection also included elaborate seating diagrams that Ahmet had sketched out on paper for the hundreds of dinner parties they had given since the 1960s. It was fascinating to see who attended the parties—from Richard Nixon and Henry Kissinger to Michael Bloomberg—and who they were seated alongside.

After I had looked through the entire collection, I went back to see Mica at her house. I thanked her for her generosity—she had made the decision to donate virtually everything she had relating to her husband—and then placed a box which I had brought with me on the table next to where we were sitting. I then told Mica that I had pulled out a bunch of letters and photographs that I felt were not appropriate for the donation. That I found this kind of stuff wasn't surprising—it was fairly well-known that Ahmet and Mica had always had a certain understanding—and a bunch of letters from random women added no value to the collection from an institutional perspective. I said, diplomatically, "There's some letters and photographs here that I don't think anyone needs to see—if you look at them, you'll know what I mean." Mica simply smiled and said, "Craig, you know that Ahmet was no angel." I insisted that she keep the box, and she was appreciative.

Of course, collecting manuscripts isn't always such a stately affair: Sometimes, it came down to me literally walking up to an artist and asking them to empty their pockets, like when Elton John was on hand at an induction ceremony a year or two later to induct Leon Russell. Elton's speech was scribbled on a small pad of stationery from the Ritz-Carlton—he had composed it the night before—and I wanted that speech for the museum and archives, so I simply followed him back to his table, tapped him on the shoulder gently, explained who I was, and asked if he'd be willing to donate the speech. He grinned and reached into his pocket and handed it to me, and I made a quick getaway. At the end of the night, I scoured the stage for anything that might had been discarded and came up with a few more speeches. In archiving speak, the provenance for material like this is called a "field collection."

A few months later, Mica invited me, along with a contingent of people from Atlantic Records and some family members, to attend an event at the Turkish embassy in DC honoring Ahmet. I was fascinated to see the embassy where Ahmet grew up, and on display were photographs of him and Nesuhi in the house, placed in the same rooms that we were now standing in. The two brothers had staged many jazz concerts when their father was ambassador, and seeing and thinking about their life in this setting, I suggested to Mica that there should be a museum about Ahmet's life. Mica told me she had already been thinking about it, and that the museum should be in Turkey. We got together back in New York the following week to discuss the idea, and she arranged for me to visit Ahmet's childhood home in Istanbul in hopes of getting the ball rolling.

She also asked me to go see the site where Ahmet was interred. Joan and I flew to Turkey and received a guided tour by one of Mica's close friends. He was buried high above the city of Istanbul in a Sufi house of worship called a *tekke* on the other side of the Bosphorus. Ahmet had lived nearby as a child with his family, and Mica's idea was that the museum should be in this elaborate home. The only problem was that there was already a family living there—and with a recent change of government, there was going to be a lot of bureaucratic finessing to get the project off the ground. But as Ahmet had arguably been the most famous Turk living in the United States in the last fifty years, I was confident that the museum could be a success. In the end, the project never moved forward.

One of the most gratifying things about being a curator is developing meaningful relationships with people. In the early 2000s, I met Otis Redding's widow, Zelma, who welcomed me into her sprawling ranch that she and Otis purchased in 1965 with generosity and warmth that I wasn't always used to. The house and grounds, in a rural part of Georgia, were beautiful. Otis was buried on the property. Zelma brought me over to see the headstone.

Over the years, I went to Macon many times to see Zelma and later The Allman Brothers. Part of the fuselage from Redding's aircraft has been on exhibit since the museum opened. To many, it's morbid, but somehow having it on display works. Redding had such a short career but had made such an impact. Zelma lent to the museum the black leather coat he was wearing when the plane went down into Lake Monona in Wisconsin. At a memorial in Madison, I met Ben Cauley from the Bar-Kays, the sole survivor of the crash. Years later, Zelma donated manuscripts and important papers, and one artifact really hit home: Otis Redding's credit card receipt for the fuel purchased for the plane's doomed final flight, the gasoline having been purchased at Hopkins airport in Cleveland. It was a sad reminder of the many musicians who had perished on airplanes while they were working.

In March of 2008, Jann called and asked me to bid on his behalf at an upcoming Christie's rock 'n' roll auction in London. The request was slightly odd: Jann did not typically purchase rock memorabilia. But Christie's was selling the drum head that appeared on the cover of the Beatles album *Sgt. Pepper's Lonely Hearts Club Band*. The entire album cover was one of the most iconic in rock history, and the individual artifacts that had been part of the Michael Cooper photo shoot were widely collected. Aside from the Fab Four's marching band uniforms, though, the drumhead was arguably the most significant piece.

Jann authorized me to bid up to the equivalent of $600,000. And while there were initially five bidders, two dropped out quickly, leaving me bidding over the phone along with two others who were also not in the sales room. The price went up and up, until I reached Jann's limit of $600,000—at which point a competing bidder raised us another $50,000. I made the decision to keep going—I didn't want to tell Jann that I lost out because of $50,000—and then I kept on going and going. We were now at $750,000, and the other bidders showing no signs of slowing down. My heart was racing, but I figured if I went any further, I'd *really* get myself into trouble.

In the end, the drum head sold for the British pounds sterling equivalent of $1,070,000—nearly four times the estimated price. When I called up Jann to inform him of the result, I told him that I had taken it upon myself to bid an extra $150,000. He seemed a bit amused that I had been so cavalier.

A few days later, I heard that I had been bidding against Paul McCartney.

A short time after that, we opened another new exhibit: *Women Who Rock: Vision, Passion, and Power*. Female artists have historically been underrepresented in rock 'n' roll, and this exhibit was long overdue. Cyndi Lauper, Aretha Franklin, Tina Turner, Britney Spears, Madonna, Yoko Ono, Joni Mitchell, and Alicia Keys were among the seventy artists showcased in the exhibit, and to coincide with its opening, the Hall of Fame staged a concert featuring Wanda Jackson, Darlene Love, and Mavis Staples. It was a triumph.

In April 2012, the library and archives opened. Though it wasn't what I had envisioned, it was still a fantastic facility with a talented and dedicated staff. Later that year, Terry Stewart stepped down from his position as president and CEO of the museum. His successor was Greg Harris, who had joined the Hall of Fame in 2008, heading up the development department. Harris had previously worked at the National Baseball Hall of Fame, and he'd cofounded a beloved independent record store in his native Philadelphia.

Around this time, a few of the newly inducted artists started sending guitars and other instruments that they claimed were used to record songs from the '70s and '80s. That was great. Except when I opened up the guitar cases, I would sometimes find a brand spanking new guitar with the tags and shrink wrap still attached and a serial number from the early 2000s.

Some managers must have thought that we were idiots. I promptly shipped them back.

CHAPTER NINETEEN

HIJINKS WITH KEITH RICHARDS AND TOM MORELLO, THE TROJAN HORSE

In 2014, we carved out some new exhibit space on the main exhibit floor in Cleveland, snatching square footage from some open spaces, and made a new gallery. We curated three shows in succession: Paul Simon, Graham Nash, and John Mellencamp. I interviewed all three on camera and produced short-form films that could be viewed while walking through the gallery. (Among the revelations: Graham Nash lightheartedly confided that he was a closet kleptomaniac and had stolen a piece of the fence from the grassy knoll across the street from where JFK was assassinated in Dallas.)

That same year, a reconstituted Nirvana were inducted to the Hall of Fame, fronted by a rotating cast of women. These were transcendent performances, with Kim Gordon from Sonic Youth embodying Kurt Cobain's artistry and rage, screaming like a banshee but fully in control—proof that the Hall of Fame could still conjure up magic. People in the audience were stunned.

In that same class, after years of being snubbed, KISS was finally inducted—thanks, in no small part, to the passionate advocacy of

Tom Morello, the guitarist from Rage Against the Machine—a brilliant musician and an eloquent speaker who had attended Harvard University. This turned out to be the Trojan horse that opened the doors of the Rock Hall to Bon Jovi, Yes, Chicago, Journey, and the Moody Blues, among others—all artists intentionally kept off the ballot for many years, as they didn't seemingly fit into the preferences of old-school rock criticism. The fact is the committee had never been truly "consistent" with their criteria and standards over the years. And how could they? This is not baseball—there no "walks," "errors," or "strike-outs." No stats to go by—no guardrails except perhaps the artists who were already inducted. This is art.

I would occasionally hear somebody say that one or two artists had been inducted that didn't make the grade; but the examples brought up weren't all the same. It was one big moving target. The nominating committee always had their hearts in the right place and did their best.

As it turned out, KISS was the payload that instantaneously transformed the trajectory of the nominating committee—forever.

Jon Landau was no KISS fan—he and many others on the committee felt their music was derivative and not worthy of consideration for induction. He didn't care that KISS had launched a thousand bands and kids to buy millions of guitars. And Landau's opinions were taken very seriously: This is the man, after all, who wrote a highly critical review about a Cream concert in 1969 that upset Eric Clapton so much he broke up the band. Of course, virtually nobody's opinions have that kind of sway in the music business anymore. Landau had fought tooth and nail to keep Miles Davis off the ballot—certainly not because he questioned Davis's musical integrity; quite the opposite: Landau loved Davis's music and considered him one of the giants of the twentieth century. He just felt that jazz musicians should not be inducted as performing artists.

With Tom Morello pressing the case for KISS, though—it certainly didn't hurt that Morello was a kind of adjunct member of Bruce Springsteen's band—Landau was sold on the idea of putting the band on the ballot. I was there to witness Tom's utterly compelling speech, and I knew instantly that anyone still on the fence was going to be swayed. In the end, everyone was sold, including Landau, and with his stamp of approval, others on the committee felt comfortable supporting the nomination. Morello, of course, presented the honors to the band at the induction ceremony. He gave the KISS Army permission to stage a coup: "Tonight, it's not the Rock & Roll Hall of Fame. Tonight, it's the Rock and Roll All Night and Party Every Day Hall of Fame."

Since the mid 2000s, several members of the committee had been working to reorient and expand the kinds of artists that should be placed on the ballot, with John Sykes, Rob Light, and Rick Krim in particular seeking to introduce more commercial acts that would have never been considered years earlier. With Phil Spector in prison and Jerry Wexler no longer alive, their seats went to those with more commercial tastes. Slowly, and then quickly, the makeup of the committee had changed, and by 2017, it was fully embracing artists whose commercial success was immense. There was a lot of grumbling all around that the committee's new direction was being determined by concert ticket receipts.

Landau would purge the nominating committee again, removing some sixteen members, many of whom had focused mainly on roots-oriented music. The fact that Landau had invited Morello to join the nominating committee was somewhat ironic, given that it was Morello who had essentially secured the nomination for KISS and open the floodgates.

Either way: The wind had changed direction.

In 2017, I curated an exhibit about the history of *Rolling Stone*—the first time the museum had created a major exhibition about a publication. *Rolling Stone* had, of course, been part of the cultural zeitgeist for so long, and Jann was such a pivotal figure—not only in rock history, but in the museum's history as well.

Working on the exhibit, I interviewed on camera three key figures in the magazine's history: Mick Jagger, Lenny Kravitz, and Taylor Swift.

Jann also gave me unfettered access to his vast archive. I had now known him for a quarter-century, and he trusted me implicitly.

I interviewed Jagger in Beverly Hills for the exhibition and he added great insight.

On Halloween that year, I was returning a historic Jimi Hendrix guitar to a lender in Greenwich Village and was minding my own business when I heard a voice from shout from across the street, "Hey, I know you!"

I looked over to see Patti Smith sitting on her stoop with her friend, the photographer Lynn Goldsmith. I went over and we talked for a long while. I told Patti that Joan had just finished reading her autobiography, *Just Friends*, and couldn't stop talking about it. Patti went into the house for a moment and came back with a couple of her poetry books and a tote bag, inscribing all of them to Joan.

That same year, Keith Richards decided that he wanted to donate one of his cars—a Jaguar XJ6 from the late '70s—to the Hall of Fame. The car itself wasn't particularly interesting—it didn't have a psychedelic paint job, and it hadn't been driven during some historic event—but the museum was thrilled to receive such a substantial gift from someone like Keith. Still, it's always the stories behind the object—whether it's a car, a stage costume, or a musical instrument—that really brings the object to life for a museum visitor, and so I proposed to Keith's manager Jane Rose that I bring a film crew to Richards's estate in Weston, Connecticut, to film him driving the car on his grounds and sit for an interview.

As a non-journalist, I have always approached the interviews that I do with a curator's eye. My main rule of thumb when first doing this was to avoid all the bombastic questions that had been asked before—but I realized early on that this was sometimes the only way to get an artist's attention. More rote questions often produced rote answers, with nothing new gleaned.

Up in Connecticut, Keith's chauffeur had gotten the Jaguar started and pulled it into the driveway so that Keith could drive it around while we trailed him with our film crew. By the time everyone was set, though, the Jag had stalled and couldn't be restarted, so we decided to start the interview first and do the driving later. Then, just as we were getting set for the interview, Keith's chauffeur rushed in to inform us that the car was now running and ready to go—only to promptly stall again before Keith could get behind the wheel.

Improbably, this scenario repeated itself again. Finally, we all burst out laughing.

"Okay," I said to Keith. "Since we're not able to get the car started, why don't we film you *trying* to start the motor, and then you can tell us that this is why you decided to give it to the Rock & Roll Hall of Fame?"

Keith laughed. "It was perfect this morning!" he said—and told us a little about the car. "I think I bought in '75 or '76 in London. It was Jaguar's latest model at the time, and I knew that I was gonna be in London for several months recording and I wanted a really good, reliable car—I bought it for the engine, quite honestly! I thought it was a fantastic engine, and it never let me down—I had it in London for eighteen months or two years. But now the engine's not working, man, so I decided: We're gonna give it to the Rock & Roll Hall of Fame, that's what we're gonna do."

When we finally sat down for a proper interview, Keith told some stories about driving, starting with a trip up north to Newcastle with Mick in 1963—but he really seemed to come to life when discussing his famous road trip with Ron Wood during the Stones' 1975 tour, when they were arrested in Fordyce, Arkansas:

"I can't tell you why we decided to drive from Memphis to Dallas," he said. "We had a perfectly good jet plane—comfy, with air stewardesses—that could have got us there in less than three hours, but for some reason . . . this is what happens to you on the road, you know: There are times when you just say, 'Oh, I'm sick to death of just sitting here and going in and then being dropped out of the sky somewhere else, and we had a lot of friends in the area, so we start driving, and the first thing we hit is bootleggers—we loaded the cars up; nobody could drink that much, but we liked to look at these interesting brown paper labels with these great illustrations. But by the time we got to Arkansas, we got pulled over there—looking fairly suspicious, I suppose. I mean, I suppose anything looks suspicious in Fordyce, but suddenly the cars pulled us over and asked us how and why we ended up there. They searched the car and they found nothing, and they did nothing, but it was the most hilarious sort of farce going on, with judges falling over, and people coming in to gawk at us, like the Beverly Hillbillies. It was just an amazing trip—the judge is fighting the police, and there's nothing else you can do except watch all of this going on."

We never did get that damn car started.

How much of a Keith Richards fan am I? My friend—and guitar collector extraordinaire—Perry Margouleff promised me years ago that he would arrange for me to meet Keith's guitar tech Pierre de Beauport for a lesson on Keith's open tuning style, and a year or so before our Connecticut meeting, he made it happen: One late afternoon, Perry called to tell me that Pierre was out at his recording studio in Glen Cove, Long Island, and that if I came by right now, I could get that guitar lesson. I hung up the phone and went straight to Penn Station to catch the first train out east. Pierre showed me so much and was so generous—and then he wrote out for me a road map on how to play the songs in the exact tunings and exactly what gauge of strings Keith used:

> Set guitar strap at 54 inches
> For five string open G tuning:
> Low G 38 gauge
> D 28
> G 18
> B 15
> High D 11

I was also fortunate enough to interview Ringo Starr at the London Hotel in Los Angeles in April of 2015, ahead of his solo induction later that year. Here is an excerpt:

> Being a drummer—or wanting to be a drummer, I should say—started when I was thirteen. I was in hospital, and I was in there a long time, so to keep us entertained, all the kids there had things brought in for them—percussive cowbells, maracas, triangles, and little drums. This lady gave me a drum, and I loved the drums from that time on. When I came out, I would go around shops in Liverpool just looking at drums—I wasn't looking at anything else. When I was fifteen, I made my first kit out of biscuit tins and pieces of firewood for the sticks. I would lay it on the floor and bang that. The first kit I heard cost twenty bucks, and it was great—an old Slingerland—but as a teenager, I wanted a new shiny kit, and my first kit was Ajax.

[Legendary session drummer] Jim Keltner is my hero, and I read a thing where Jim Keltner said that Charlie Watts was the best rock drummer. So I called Jim [and said], "What do you mean, Charlie Watts is the best?" He said, "Ring, you swing!" So I tend to swing. Whatever I do—even if it's straight rock—it's got some sort of shuffle swing in there. It's just how it comes out. Charlie plays great straight rock. You know he used to put jazz bands together. He had a boogie band—I saw him in Monte Carlo a couple years ago. He had a couple of boogie players, and he's playing drums, and an old school chum of his was playing bass. So you know, we're still doing it. But I don't compare anybody to anybody really. I play like this—it's just how it happens.

In 2015, the Hall of Fame had decided to collaborate on a new exhibition, entitled *Louder Than Words*. It was about the connections between rock 'n' roll and politics, and the collaborator was the Newseum, a fantastic new museum about journalism that had recently opened in Washington, DC, to great fanfare. (Sadly, the Newseum closed in 2019.) The exhibition made sense: The country was gearing up for the presidential election between Hillary Clinton and Donald Trump, and it gave the Hall of Fame an opportunity to weigh in on how music had long been a potent theme in politics, and vice versa.

Music, of course, had been part of political campaigns in the United States since the days of our Founding Fathers. Big stars were often actively involved in the campaigns of later generations—perhaps most notably when Frank Sinatra actively worked for John F. Kennedy's election, retooling some of his songs for the campaign trail. Having said that, it wasn't until Senator George McGovern ran for the Democratic nomination in 1972 that rock musicians began to support political campaigns.

By the time Jimmy Carter ran for the Democratic nomination in 1976, he knew rock music would play a big role in his campaign. Carter loved American music—especially the blues, country, gospel, and folk; he was friendly with Bob Dylan, and had famously coaxed the Allman Brothers Band into performing a benefit concert for his fledgling campaign. I set my sights on interviewing both the former president and Gregg Allman about just how this came about. Six months later, I had secured a date to interview both men on the very same day.

On January 14, 2016, I traveled to the Carter Center in Atlanta, where I interviewed the former president about his musical tastes, his relationship with Gregg, and the impact the Allman Brothers Band had on the campaign. When I arrived in his office, President Carter told me that he already knew I would be interviewing Gregg later that day down in Macon—Carter's son Chip had spoken to Gregg the night before our meeting. He and Gregg had been in regular touch since the mid-'70s and had become close friends.

My extensive on-camera interviews with both of them reveal an extraordinary story about how Carter was elected president with the help of rock 'n' roll. The Allman Brothers helped him not just with fundraising, but with relating and reaching out to a whole new generation of voters:

> They would give me all the proceeds [from their fundraising concerts]—they only charged like fifteen dollars, or twenty dollars at the most, but then I could take that fifteen dollars or twenty dollars that the Allman Brothers raised for me and I could double that with matching funds from the federal government. He also brought a sign onstage a couple of times, and so people really started knowing who I was. Duane said, "Y'all

brought us into the life" but it was all of their fans who voted, and they were very tangibly helpful to me getting elected.

And so there I was, President, in the White House. We invited Duane to spend some time with us there—I had dinner with him in the White House, and I kept refusing to let him talk about how "I" did this: "We" did it.

I think the political establishment envied that I had this built-in advantage over them in relating so easily with these young people.

From Atlanta, I headed eighty miles south to Macon—the home of Little Richard, the Allman Brothers, Otis Redding, and so many other greats. I met Gregg at the Big House—originally the band's headquarters in the 1970s, but since 2009, the Allman Brothers Band Museum.

I loved Macon and had been there many times over the years, most memorably to see Otis Redding's widow, Zelma, who had generously donated a fantastic collection to the museum.

When I sat down with Gregg, he told me about first meeting then-Governor Carter:

> I was in a studio here, Capricorn, cutting a record. We had been invited to this party Governor Carter was throwing for Bob Dylan, who had come through Atlanta—he was a real Bob Dylan fan, so he threw a party, and they sent me an invitation. [In the studio] we kept saying, "Right after this one, we'll go; I'm gonna try one more take." We had a limo waiting outside. Finally, I said, "Shut it down—let's go, guys; we're gonna miss the damn party if we don't leave now." We got there just as the last guest was leaving, and I said to someone, "Just please go tell Carter I'm sorry—we were in the studio and we just ran late." But then we saw this guy walking back to the limo, and

he said, "Wait a minute, buddy—Governor Carter wants to see you on the porch now." I could see down there—it's still a ways away, but I could see this guy down on the porch—no shirt, no shoes—hanging out at the Governor's Mansion looking like he'd been partying pretty heavy all night, but I walked up there, and Carter opens the door and says, "Come on in—how you doing?" I sit down, and there's a full bottle of J&B Scotch, which we proceeded to drink just about all of. He says, "You know I'm gonna be our next President, and I need you to raise me some money—you and your band." So we started talking—we told each other our life stories, you know, and I guess I must have been there about three hours by now; everybody else had gone to bed—and I left there thinking, *Man—what a hell of a guy*. I just really, really gained all kinds of respect for this guy in those three hours.

I can definitely feel in my heart that we helped him become president—I mean, a lot of other people did, too, you know, but we had a hand in it. That's a good feeling.

Musicians, of course, have been parting with their instruments for as long as music has existed. Celebrated Renaissance court players occasionally had to sell their prized violins—even the occasional Stradivarius—to fund a daughter's dowry or pay off debts. It's simply a natural occurrence of commerce that went on for centuries with little or no fallout—but with the advent of photography and moving images, musical instruments became more than just tools to make music; they became inextricably linked to the person. By the 1930s, a certain iconography in the popular music world was established with indelible images of men wearing natty suits and holding their instruments—think Rudy Vallée, Louis Armstrong, Duke Ellington.

Jazz and pop stars from the first half of the twentieth century led the way for rock 'n' roll stars like Elvis Presley and the Beatles to pose with their guitars—images that cemented the place of rock 'n' roll atop the iconography of popular culture.

So when Eric Clapton decided to auction off fifty-eight of his guitars in 2004 to fund Crossroads, a rehab center he built in Antigua, many fans were mystified: How could Eric possibly part with Blackie, his beloved black Fender Strat—or the Gibson ES-335 he used in Cream, the Yardbirds, John Mayall's Bluesbreakers, and Blind Faith, along with his solo work? Would he still be E. C. without those guitars? The catchphrase "Clapton is God," which had been scrawled on buildings all over London, still resonated in 1995. Many fans felt the sale was crass: Even if the funds were going to a good cause, how could their hero sell to cretinous Wall Street collectors?

Long before celebrity auctions benefitting private charities, musicians had more practical reasons to sell their wares. In 1992, Hendrix drummer Mitch Mitchell sold the white Fender Stratocaster that Jimi played at Woodstock: He needed the money. So did Dave Davies from the Kinks when he sold his Gibson Flying V—a guitar which is now likely worth nearly a half million dollars.

In fact, it was Yoko Ono who jump-started the entire high-end business of selling rock 'n' roll memorabilia at auction. Three years after the assassination of her husband, Ono sold a modest collection of musical instruments, recording gear, paintings, and furniture that had belonged to her and Lennon—and why not? It was, after all, her property, and she could do with it whatever she saw fit.

Some artists feel like they have a cultural duty to hold on to their archives—perhaps for their family; perhaps for their egos; and possibly, just possibly, for a museum. Paul McCartney, Pete Townshend, and Jimmy Page all have extraordinary and meticulously documented and researched collections, but none of them have sold even a guitar pick. It's worth noting, of course, that they're all extraordinarily wealthy and have no need to sell anything.

So when Bob Dylan and his manager Jeff Rosen began holding videoconference calls with dealers and collectors exploring the possible sale of some of Dylan's most important lyric manuscripts, it was quite a surprise. Ed Kosinski, my old client and friend from Sotheby's who had procured Springsteen's *Born to Run* notebook, was having meetings with Rosen and Dylan via Zoom, where he and others were buying handwritten manuscripts directly from Bob himself—including some incredible early manuscripts for songs like "Masters of War," "Maggie's Farm," and "Like a Rolling Stone" which was scribbled on an envelope from a Washington, DC, hotel. It was revealing that Dylan was willing to part with some of the most extraordinary artifacts of the twentieth century.

The value of rock manuscripts had gone through the roof decades earlier, and for whatever reason, Dylan wanted in. He began cranking out pristine, "final" versions of some of his most important songs in very limited quantities—high-end Franklin Mint–style mementos for well-to-do collectors. Halcyon Gallery in London staged a massive show of these brand-new manuscripts, which were handsomely framed and on exhibition at their gallery on New Bond Street.

In a 2016 masterstroke, Dylan then sold his massive archive of papers, artifacts, and master tapes to the Kaiser Family Foundation, which opened the Bob Dylan Center in Tulsa, Oklahoma, adjacent to the Woody Guthrie Center. The archive was for more than \$15–\$20 million. Dylan, of course, didn't need the money. It helped ensure a permanent legacy for him, and provided a central repository where scholars, music journalists, and fans could go to study and learn about his work—a win-win for everyone, Dylan and Guthrie together forever.

Dylan had also been painting and sketching since he was a teenager. In fact, many musical artists from the '60s were talented visual artists as well, including John Lennon and Keith Richards, whose charcoal sketches are stunning: simple, elegant—and rarely seen by anyone. Dylan, on the other hand, has had gallery shows of his paintings, and during the '90s, even took up metalworking. He now has a thriving business crafting custom-made iron gates, which adorn the entryways of estates both in California and elsewhere. Other collections are also getting the institutional treatment: Laurie Anderson sold Lou Reed's archive to the New York Public Library. Tom Wolfe's collection went there too. And Monmouth University is building a center and archive dedicated to native son Bruce Springsteen.

Meanwhile, my colleague Shelby Morrison had been nurturing a friendship with Jerry Lee Lewis and his seventh wife, Judith, for many years. Shelby was from Lubbock, Texas, and just seemed to have a certain way about her that connected with artists, especially those from the South—she had a kind of magic touch. One morning in early 2017, out of the blue, she called me to say that Jerry Lee was planning to donate one of his important pianos and that we needed to get down to Tennessee as soon as possible to secure it. The two of us flew down to Memphis, checked into the Peabody, rented a car, and drove out to Jerry Lee's estate in Nesbit, Mississippi, about fifteen miles south of the city, where we were greeted by Jerry Lee's son Jerry Lee Lewis III. The property was on a lake and had a swimming pool shaped like a grand piano, and the inside of the house was filled with gold records and awards dating back to the late '60s. The piano, though, was the big enchilada: a petite grand built by George Steck & Company around 1955 and given to Jerry Lee by his third wife, Myra Gale Brown, as a wedding gift in 1957. (Not only was Myra just thirteen years old when the couple married, but she was also Jerry's second cousin, and the combination of those two revelations caused a shitstorm that the Killer hadn't anticipated, and his career never completely recovered from the scandal.)

Jerry Lee repainted the piano in the 1980s in gold leaf, which is how it remained. This was the piano that Jerry Lee, one of the original rebels of rock 'n' roll, kept at home—it never traveled on the road. It easily could have gone to the Smithsonian or have been sold to a collector. The instrument was representative of his raw talent and his outrageous behavior and could be used as a vehicle to tell many stories about rock 'n' roll's influence on youth culture, music, and cultural mores—and acquiring it for the museum was a major coup. Afterward, we went to Jerry and Judith's townhouse, and he told us some fascinating stories and showed us his upright piano that he played when he was a kid. It was battered and unplayable but at least it still existed.

In 2017, Tupac Shakur, Pearl Jam, ELO, Joan Baez, Nile Rodgers, Yes, and Journey—those last two bands previously despised by the nominating committee—made it into the hall. With the nominating committee embracing more mainstream acts, record sales and whoever could put large amounts of butts in seats began to matter. Going forward, each inductee class had a mix of commercial acts and critical darlings, along with unabashed pop stars and hip-hop artists—a rather motley crew.

The year 2018 marked a new apotheosis for the Hall of Fame. For the board, pop now equaled rock, and in 2018, the hall welcomed in Whitney Houston. Madonna, after all, was inducted a decade earlier, beginning the trend. And while expanding the umbrella to include hip-hop was transformative (recall 2007's induction of Grandmaster Flash and the Furious Five), arguably the most significant change was including real rock bands that would have never passed muster twenty-five or thirty years ago—groups whose main contribution to the art form is popularity through huge record sales. With most of the snobs on the nominating committee either dead or kicked off, elders like Landau had thrown their hands up, but at big ceremonies, financial fat cats could still show up and pay hundreds of thousands of dollars to sit up front wearing black ties and gowns.

After it was announced that Bon Jovi—one of Rob Light's clients—would be inducted in 2018, Jon invited me out to his house in Red Bank, New Jersey. I had been there a few years previously, overseeing the return of his collection after Bon Jovi had made it onto the ballot but failed to be inducted. This time, I met his whole family, who were all gracious and charming. He showed me several paintings from his art collection including a stunning portrait of Benjamin Franklin painted by the eighteenth-century artist Joseph Siffred Duplessis. Jon was understandably proud, as he said, "This is the portrait of Franklin that's on the one-hundred-dollar bill."

Jon took me down to the lower level of his house, where he stored his collection of stage clothing and memorabilia, along with some of his guitars. Everything was meticulously organized. As he pulled out various stage outfits, guitars, and lyric manuscripts, I pressed for a donation (not just a loan), explaining that it would ensure that his music and life would be represented at the museum in perpetuity, but Jon just smiled and said, "Let's see how you guys treat me." It still stung him that his band hadn't been inducted the first time around. But when he arrived in Cleveland, he was on cloud nine. He was really touched by the honor and graciously asked me to be in a photograph with him in the museum's lobby.

The emerging populist criteria for induction, though, didn't seem to apply to big-selling rock bands from the '70s, which still weren't getting a look. You could argue that Grand Funk Railroad and Bachman–Turner Overdrive, two hugely popular acts—solid bands musically akin to Bon Jovi that were also detested by highbrow music critics—should get consideration. But that didn't happen.

The inconsistencies extended beyond which artists were placed on the ballot. Things could get complicated even after some bands were inducted. The committee, of course, did their damnedest to induct the right people from the band, and sometimes that was easy and clear-cut, as it was when Cream, Led Zeppelin, or ZZ Top were inducted. But when it came to groups with various personnel changes throughout the years, judgment calls had to be made. As I mentioned earlier, the committee inducted every member of the Rolling Stones, including Ian Stewart, which I would argue was the right move—but in later years, some full-fledged band members like Fleetwood Mac's Bob Welch (who played on five albums!) were excluded, head scratchers and major blunders. And while there were different approaches and explanations for who got in and who didn't, the simple reality is that the Rock & Roll Hall of Fame does not in any way, shape, or form resemble something like the Baseball Hall of Fame, which largely looks at statistics. The Baseball Hall of Fame occasionally even elects to *not* induct any ballplayers in a given year, judging that absolutely nobody was worthy of the recognition.

All of the machinations about who was or wasn't getting inducted were always secondary to me. As always, my main focus was on curating exhibits. I typically had a year at most to plan and get a show done and installed, and it was never enough time. So I decided once and for all that I would aim for the stars and conceive the big show, knowing it would take many years to deliver.

CHAPTER TWENTY

ROCKING AT THE METROPOLITAN MUSEUM OF ART

Thor, Athena, Zeus, Osiris, Aphrodite: It's not uncommon to see Greek, Roman, and Egyptian gods at the Metropolitan Museum of Art. But to see a living god? Highly unlikely—until the morning of Monday, April 1, 2019, when the living, breathing rock deity Jimmy Page strolled up to the microphone in the museum's famed Petrie Court to give opening remarks about a landmark exhibit that I cocurated with Jayson Dobney from the musical instruments department at the Met. The story of how this happened seems almost fantastical to me now.

A few years earlier, I was sitting at the bar at Keens Steakhouse in Midtown Manhattan when I started sketching out an idea on a coaster: What if I created an exhibition at the Met that would feature four of the world's most influential and distinctive living rock guitarists—Jimmy Page, Keith Richards, Jonny Greenwood, and Eddie Van Halen? The idea, I knew, was ludicrous: I wanted to convince them to hand over their entire recording rigs and their primary instruments, to submit to an interview, and to provide a musical demonstration of how they create their trademark guitar style in their recording studios. A pipe dream—right?

And yet there was Jimmy Page, right in front of me now, speaking at our press conference: "I'd been approached about possibly lending some pieces to this exhibition," Page said, "and Jayson and Craig came to my house to give me some idea of what the exhibits would be. And as they explained to me, you'd walk through the Greco-Roman statues to this particular gallery, and then you'd see Chuck Berry's guitar, standing there, lit up. And I said, 'That's all you're going to see as you approach it?' And they said, 'Yeah.' I said, 'Okay—what do you want? What can I give you to help this along?' It was so magical—this chalice standing there, like the Holy Grail."

Page seemed in awe that we'd pulled it off. "This day is something that I would never have dreamed of in my life," Page said. "You're talking to somebody here who got a guitar when he was about eleven, twelve years old—I'd take my guitar to school, had it confiscated, and given back at the end of the day. So that's the sort of respect you had for guitars. And I don't know if my teacher is alive anymore, but I'd love her to reflect on this day at the Met."

Other artists who participated in the exhibition spoke, including Steve Miller, Don Felder, and Tina Weymouth, who was similarly awestruck.

"When I was a young student of art history, I used to come to the Met to sketch the Greek statues, all the marbles. I did not dream then that I would one day loan three of my favorite guitars to be displayed not far from my old haunts—your weapons of the Middle Ages and the sarcophagi of ancient Egypt. I kid you not, this turnaround is very surprising to me."

Weymouth quoted from theologian and civil rights leader Howard Thurman's address at Spelman College entitled "The Sound of the Genuine." The assembled crowd was riveted.

It was back in 2014 when I first approached the Metropolitan Museum of Art with the idea of a collaborative exhibit, working with their musical instruments department. I knew that the synergy of the Met and the Rock & Roll Hall of Fame working together could produce extraordinary results. This was my second collaboration with the Met; the two institutions had worked together back in 1999 on *Rock Style*, a fashion exhibit in collaboration with the museum's Costume Institute. This new exhibit would be far more ambitious and complicated. Twenty years on, the Hall of Fame was an accomplished institution with an extraordinary collection to draw from for the show.

Not only did Jimmy Page agree to participate; so did Keith Richards and Eddie Van Halen. Jonny Greenwood passed, but we were very fortunate to receive the participation of Rage Against the Machine's brilliant guitarist Tom Morello. It was a dream team.

The exhibition was presented in seven galleries and featured 130 instruments on display, many of which had been used to create the soundtrack visitors heard as they toured the galleries, each with a distinct theme. That crazy concept I had dreamed up at Keens occupied one of the galleries and was the nerve center of the show—a self-contained exhibit entitled *Creating a Sound.*

The opening section, *Setting the Stage*, explored the origins of rock 'n' roll, from Chuck Berry's guitar to that piano my colleague and I picked up at Jerry Lee Lewis's house in Tennessee. We had unprecedented cooperation: There were guitars in the exhibit that were being played onstage just days prior to being delivered to the museum.

The exhibit included guitars and basses from rock goddesses who helped define the genre, from Sister Rosetta Tharpe and Wanda Jackson to Joni Mitchell, Tina Weymouth, Kim Gordon, and St. Vincent. And there were, of course, instruments from the guitar gods—not just instruments to represent them as artists but, in most cases, their primary axes: Eric Clapton's Blackie, Eddie Van Halen's Frankenstein, Stevie Ray Vaughn's Number One, Prince's "symbol" guitar, Bruce Springsteen's iconic Fender Esquire, Jimi Hendrix's painted Flying V, and Keith Richards's 1957 Les Paul, which he'd painted in a colorful psychedelic pattern while tripping on LSD—just an embarrassment of riches that went on and on.

Other sections of the exhibit included the rhythm section, where drum kits and basses were displayed, and included examples from Sonic Youth's Kim Gordon, Paul McCartney, Sheryl Crow, and John Entwistle. Another gallery featured the eclecticism of rock with instruments you wouldn't normally associate with the genre like Patti Smith's clarinet, Ravi Shankar's sitar, and the Rolling Stones' Mellotron and Brian Jones's dulcimer that I had scooped up back in the '90s.

There was a small but extraordinary selection of concert posters that included the only known poster from the Quarrymen, the earliest incarnation of the Beatles; one of the only posters from the Altamont concert in '69; and some of the most rare Elvis Presley posters—Elvis Presley at the Mississippi-Alabama Fair & Dairy Show from Tupelo, Mississippi, in 1956. And Jimi Hendrix at Sick's Stadium in Seattle—his last hometown appearance before his death in 1970.

Having an exhibit at the Met was a different experience from the usual shows I'd curated. As Joel Peresman stated at the press conference, "[The Met] raised the bar for us." Artists were coming to *me* for a change, asking to be involved, and some were angry or disappointed they weren't included. While there were lots of twists and turns along the way, the preposterous wish list that we had created years ago had become a reality. The most important instruments were all there—from Muddy Waters, Jimi Hendrix, Wanda Jackson, Neil Young, George Harrison, John Lennon, Ringo Starr, Jerry Garcia, Prince, Joan Jett, Joe Strummer, Joni Mitchell, Bruce Springsteen, and on and on.

I was immensely proud of the gallery I'd specifically willed into being, based on that old coaster scrawl: *Creating a Sound*. Each of the four guitar players in the exhibit had a distinctive and instantaneously recognizable sound. There was the nuanced simplicity of Keith Richards, the perfectionism and virtuosity of Jimmy Page, the ceaseless invention of Eddie Van Halen, and the out-of-the-box innovation of Tom Morello. I interviewed Page, Richards, and Morello in their go-to recording studios, while Eddie Van Halen provided his rig and extensive written notes, which we buttressed with existing archival film footage.

The exhibit—built like an anechoic chamber to contain sound, similar to a mid-twentieth-century recording studio—provided visitors with an expert tutorial on how these four legendary guitarists created their sounds in four complete stage setups, including guitars, effects pedals, amps, and mics, with accompanying videos of the artists talking about both their craft and the geeky specifics of what they do and how they do it.

In the world we live in, most people encounter and hear music. Period. Whether it is their choice or not—a car with the windows rolled down blasts heavy metal as an elderly lady crosses the street; college students gleefully enter a loud, pulsing fraternity house; an unlucky fellow reclines to smooth jazz in a dentist's chair; and a group of schoolchildren attend their first Broadway musical. Music is simply coming at us like never before, and unless you are fitted with the best earplugs, music will be processed by your eardrums and sent to your brain at a blisteringly fast speed. Often you just catch a snippet, a guitar chord or two—or even a single note—and you can instantaneously identify who is playing. When this happens, you are likely hearing rock 'n' roll. We can say this because rock 'n' roll is intrinsically different from other musical forms, in a profound way. Yes, there's the stereotypical rebellious attitude and the kind of preening archetypes that don't exist in, say, classical music, or folk, or many other musical genres—but here we are talking about a tonal distinction powered by electricity: *That's* what makes rock 'n' roll different.

Without electricity, there is no rock 'n' roll, because electricity makes amplification—and the numerous options and variables that come with it—possible. How else could rock 'n' roll artists play to large audiences? To create the equivalent volume with acoustic instruments, you would need a full orchestra.

The best rock musicians—most of them guitarists—can be immediately distinguished by their unique sound. The creation of that sound is an essential part of the aural aesthetics of rock music and is a product of everything from the choice of instrument to how it is paired with amplifiers and electronic effects. It is the combination of these limitless variables that give an individual musician their sound—combined, of course, with their creative style and virtuosity.

In effect, a rock guitarist's selection of instrument, amplifier, effects, and technique becomes their palette. Relative to the mind-numbing amount of effects available in today's digital world, guitar players beginning in the 1950s had far fewer options, but that didn't prevent the most important and talented rock pioneers from creating their own distinctive sound. Even with limited technology, guitar players had numerous paths to explore.

I was very proud that my napkin-scrawl had become this conduit for people to better understand what's behind the sound of rock.

On November 15, 2018, Abbey Road Studios was brimming with activity. Thank God, the greatest recording studio in the world had not been converted into a museum. It was still doing what it had always done. That morning, we arrived as the staff cafeteria was churning out proper English breakfasts: eggs, sausages, grilled tomatoes, beans, and mushrooms. It was heartwarming to see Jimmy Page on a first-name basis with cooks and servers. He had, of course, been working at Abbey Road since the early 1960s, when he began his professional career as a studio musician.

Page's amplifiers, guitars, effects, and other primary instruments had been delivered to Studio Two earlier, and his guitar tech Lionel Ward and my good friend and consultant extraordinaire Perry Margouleff had set up the gear in the exact configuration that Jimmy had employed during Led Zeppelin's many tours. After everything was arranged, I was able to walk around and look at the guitars, violin bow, theremin, and various effects pedals; glancing behind it all, you could see all the vacuum-tube amps. Together, it was an amalgam of incredible analog technology and industrial design.

It's worth noting again that no such exhibit as this had ever been attempted before. In museums, musical instruments were customarily displayed with a short description about the maker, the date, and some more background information. The idea here, though, was to drill down—to explain each player's creative methods, unpack how different technologies are utilized, and how each artist's playing styles created their unique, trademark sounds.

Inside Abbey Road, history emanated from every corner—and not just the Beatles and Pink Floyd, both of whom made landmark albums here. Fela Kuti, Amy Winehouse, Radiohead, Lady Gaga, Adele, Oasis, and countless film scores were recorded here. I was milling about, ogling Page's guitars, which were sitting on a rack, including the Number One Gibson sunburst, the Danelectro, the iconic Gibson double-neck, the newly repainted dragon Telecaster from the Yardbirds, and the Harmony acoustic guitar, which was his main writing instrument and used to record the acoustic parts of "Stairway to Heaven" and other songs.

Soon, the video crew arrived and began unpacking their gear and doing blocking. Typical of such shoots, there was a lot of sitting around that morning; Jayson Dobney and I were killing time, sitting on metal folding chairs and staring at the iconic sound panels on the walls. I walked up the long staircase to the tiny control room where the Beatles listened to their playbacks with George Martin. Still waiting to begin filming, I skulked around the studio and came upon the famous Mrs. Mills Steinway piano, which was intentionally out of tune and was used by the Beatles to record "Lady Madonna" and other songs. I played it for a few minutes and then moved on to the celeste keyboard that John Williams used to record the main *Harry Potter* theme and Pink Floyd used on *The Dark Side of the Moon*.

Sitting back down on my folding chair, I saw Page from out of the corner of my eye picking up that iconic Gibson double-neck and sitting down on a folding chair right behind me, maybe two feet away, and checking to see if the guitar was in tune. He played a couple chords on each neck, and though the guitar was unplugged, I could nevertheless hear it perfectly. When Page started playing the intro to "Stairway to Heaven," Jayson and I quickly made eye contact—and then sat quietly for the next five minutes as Jimmy went through a slightly sped up, truncated version of the first two sections of the song, consisting of chord progressions and arpeggios, before playing the famous first rhythm section (which starts with an A minor 7) and finishing up with the fanfare section. The entire situation was hard to process: Page had just delivered one of the most extraordinary low-volume performances in rock history—for a two-person audience! Hearing this in Studio Two at Abbey Road made the experience even more ridiculous. Page, of course, knew exactly what he was doing: He was messing with us—with no ceremony or comment. He hadn't even acknowledged we were there.

I had selected Page as a subject for *Creating a Sound*, one of the subsections of the exhibit because of Led Zeppelin's thunderous power and immortal riffs, which paved the way for heavy metal, but their music defies classification, drawing on blues, folk, funk, Eastern raga, North African, Baroque, and classical music in traditional, modern, and avant-garde styles. Augmenting his playing with reverb, echo, wah-wah, and distortion, Page had an uncanny ability to create sonic portraits, from the elegance of "Thank You" to the iconic power chords of "Whole Lotta Love." I was so happy and so relieved—not only that Jimmy was cooperating on such a project, but that he knew exactly what we wanted and why. A perfectionist to the core, Page was one of the people who revolutionized recording production, capturing precise sound in the studio. He was obsessed with microphone placement.

At Abbey Road, in addition to his Marshall stack, which was now set up, Page had brought the original Supro amplifier he had used to record Led Zeppelin's debut album. I was shocked that the amp was still working—and beyond excited that I would be able to hear him play through it.

I asked Jimmy if he could demonstrate how he had created the sound for several specific Led Zeppelin songs, starting with "Communication Breakdown." "In the early '60s, [the Telecaster] was with me all the way through, to the point that I used it as a writing tool," he said. "[It] is the vehicle whereby the first album of Led Zeppelin is written, the second album is written, the third album is written, and the fourth album is written."

Page demonstrated how he created the harmonic sounds in "Dazed and Confused" with the Telecaster and his wah-wah pedal. It was fascinating to see him bend the neck of the guitar to achieve the sound, instead of merely bending a string. He also employed his Danelectro, playing the cascading riff from "Kashmir" in DADGAD tuning. And then he strapped on the Gibson double-neck to play "Stairway to Heaven"—at full concert volume—up until just before the solo. As a kind of coda, Page then played the theremin, followed by the iconic "Whole Lotta Love" riff with his Number One Les Paul.

Page's answers to the interview questions I asked him on July 31, 2018, are fascinating:

The guitar chose me before I was a teenager. We had an acoustic campfire guitar in our house, and once somebody had shown me how to tune it, I played it at every opportunity. I managed to teach myself from records, and my ability and interest grew in time from acoustic to electric—I was attracted to all forms of six-string guitar playing.

Once I started to play the solid-body electric guitar as a teenager, my influences were the Johnny Burnette trio, Grady Martin, Scotty Moore on the early Sun recordings by Elvis, James Burton on the Ricky Nelson records, and Buddy Holly, Gene Vincent and the Blue Caps, and Les Paul, to name a few. This was before I got to hear the acoustic blues players and then the electric Chicago blues movement of the '50s—B. B. King, Freddie King, Albert King: The vocabulary in their playing had a massive effect on me. Of course, in those early days, the music of Chuck Berry was the complete package.

Starting out, I had a Grazioso Futurama, which was made in Eastern Europe and was clearly a copy of the Fender Stratocaster, which at the time wasn't readily available in the UK. I have some early recordings of myself live, and you can hear I was trying to emulate the rock 'n' roll and rockabilly players of the '50s, but I hoped to make my guitar sound and technique—or lack of technique—instantly identifiable. That would still hold true for me today. Especially with the work of Led Zeppelin, I was changing my overall sound and approach to apply a character to playing so that no matter what, the guitarist would be recognizable.

During my studio session days, I originally had a Les Paul Custom, but friends like Eric Clapton and Jeff Beck were playing the Les Paul Standard, and I realized that Les Paul Custom did not have the facility to enable a mix of the bridge and neck pickups, and this was clearly a setting that should be required during my time with the Yardbirds and the recording of Led Zeppelin's first albums. I played my Telecaster until Joe Walsh offered to sell me a Les Paul Standard in San Francisco in 1969. I had an immediate connection with that guitar, and pretty much made a swap from the Telecaster to the Les Paul from that point in live situations and recording. It is the principal guitar on *Led Zeppelin II*.

With the recording of 'Stairway to Heaven,' I wanted to employ the texture of an acoustic six-string and an electric twelve-string, along with the six-string electric lead for solo during the process of recording. I wasn't actually thinking of how I was going to perform it live, but when the song was completed and ready to go out on the fourth album, I came to the conclusion that a double-neck guitar with both six-string and twelve-string would allow me to approach the song successfully in the live situation. They were not readily available, so I had a special order commissioned from Gibson—the song dictated the guitar.

I personally prefer to have the guitar connected straight into the amplifier to ensure that the guitar and amplifier are interacting satisfactorily. Effects units like foot pedals and tape echo units are okay with me and can be added accordingly, but not rack-mount units, because I would want to start from my good, basic sound with the amp and guitar. I wouldn't want much to get in the way of that—only to augment it.

Play It Loud also featured an absolute deluge of instruments from other artists: There was Keith Moon's most visual drum kit, the "Pictures of Lily" kit, which had been assembled from collections all over the world. We had acquired Bob Dylan's Fender Stratocaster that he played when he went electric at Newport and Jimi Hendrix's white Fender Stratocaster from Woodstock on which he famously played "The Star-Spangled Banner." It was head-spinning for the visitors; many people cried, and I saw visitors come back sometimes three or four times.

A few months after my trip to Abbey Road to talk with Page, I met Keith Richards at Germano Studios in Lower Manhattan.

Keith creates his signature sound—something that has influenced generations of rock 'n' roll musicians—by utilizing open tunings. He began playing this way with the lowest E string removed and the other five strings tuned to a major chord. Richards's open tuning creates what he describes as a "beautiful resonance" and a long sustain, because the vibrations of the notes in different octaves reinforce one another through sympathetic resonance. Because of this, his rig has always been fairly modest, reliant on basic equipment.

Below is an excerpt from my interview with Keith on December 12, 2018:

> I went to art school to learn art and came out having become a guitar player. It chose me—I had no say in this. The guitar was accessible, and it was fascinating—not a difficult thing like a piano, this enormous structure. You could get your hands on one fairly easily. The guitar seemed to me to be in the long tradition of minstrels: It's handy, you could go from town to town. The compactness and mobility really turned me on.
>
> Leo Fender made the most workable electric guitar in the world. This is [Micawber], my workman: I wear him when I go to work. He's pretty beat-up—like me. Incredibly well-made, beautiful necks, tough as nails: Tougher than these [pointing to his psychedelic Gibson Les Paul]. Fenders are a bit lighter than the Gibsons, but also I wanted to try that dryer sound of

the Fender, and I realized it's in these pickups. This is just a plank of wood, and somehow it's become this iconic thing and the most beautiful instrument in the world.

There's something about the electric guitar, about the pickup; there's some vibration set up by electromagnetics. In fact, *we* are electromagnetic—that's what makes us think. So I realized I was very close to the source—the whole mystery of life right here. If you love these instruments, and the love that's gone into making them, the love that's gone into playing them, I hope you come up with a little love in your heart.

I didn't really work on [drawing], but art school was great because of this atmosphere—you're at that age where you're ready for anything. I suppose I did learn things at art school, but to me, I was just happy to be there because I'd just been expelled from high school. There was nowhere else to go; art school to me was a sense of freedom.

If you want to know what kind of paint [I used on the psychedelic Les Paul], I believe these were very early acrylic pens. I was just playing it half the time, and then I'd stop—maybe there was a song here, maybe the moon is up and the sun is down. This is definitely acid, man—this is great inspiration. The idea that it's gonna be in the Metropolitan . . . ? Jesus Christ.

I've never been one of those floor pedal guys. The idea of dancing around and poking buttons gets in the way of what I'm doing. Just give me the good sound; I'll work with that. Probably because I'm lazy!

On the Stones, very first tour, the Everly Brothers are headlining the show, and I'm watching Don Everly, and I realized that he's not moving his fingers. It's all going on down here [gesturing with his right strumming hand]. That was the first time I realized that different tunings were an intriguing part of music—and an open tuning means that you're actually tuning the strings to one chord. I wouldn't think I was innovating anything, because everything I've learned, I've learned from somebody else. I've developed things . . .

A five-string rhythm guitar, on a good night, can move heaven and earth. I always try and keep it simple. I just want to lay down something solid that touches the heart. That's basically what I do.

Tom Morello was the first guitarist we filmed for *Creating a Sound.* I was fascinated with his guitar style: For starters, Morello operated a toggle switch on the guitar's face, like a hip-hop DJ operates a turntable. When I first saw this, it seemed a truly head-scratching concept—something completely different from other guitarists. That, in combination with the large pedal board that he utilized—and his amazing virtuosity—led him to create his own unique signature sound. Tom, like many other players of his era, was also influenced by Eddie Van Halen, the final piece of the exhibit.

Below is an excerpt from my interview with Tom at his home studio, Veritas, in Los Angeles on February 7, 2018:

I was a failed French horn player at nine years old—I exclaimed confidently to my mother that music was not for me. Then I discovered rock 'n' roll. I wanted to be the Black Robert Plant. Before my voice changed, I could hit those "baby baby babies" pretty well, but then when the rich baritone that you hear now set in, that also went out the window. So I decided to play guitar.

I started playing guitar very late, at seventeen years old. I loved guitar players like Randy Rhoads, Eddie Van Halen, and

Jimmy Page, but it was so foreign from my experience. It felt like these were magical people on magic pedestals with castles on Scottish lochs; a basement in the suburbs of Illinois was my domain, so it was punk rock music that was my bridge: the Sex Pistols' *Never Mind the Bollocks*. I was in a band within twenty-four hours of buying the cassette. I didn't even know how to play a single chord on the guitar, but I was compelled by this music. It was as powerful as any I'd ever heard, but soon it was in my technical grasp to be able to play it. A lot of punk rockers sort of gave up the classic rock and hard rock stuff, but I always kept one foot firmly in each world.

The first guitar I had was a fifty-dollar Kay guitar—it was the only guitar I could afford—but then I bumped up to a Gibson Explorer. It was the guitar the Scorpions used at the time, which was one of my favorite bands. This was also when Eddie Van Halen was ascendant. He was the greatest guitar player, and the minimalism of his rig was appealing. He had one knob—volume—which is awesome. My guitar was saddled with four knobs and a toggle switch and a bunch of crap on it. It was very, very unhip and very uncool. However, it did lead to my first breakthrough moment of individual creativity, which was that I had this toggle switch on the guitar, and one day I was playing around in my room and set one of the volumes to zero and the other to ten and kind of beeped back and forth between the pickup selector switches, and it sounded like a synthesizer. . . .

The amp was a fifty-watt Marshall half stack, which, in a small dorm, makes an awful lot of noise. I never really aspired to have the wall of Marshall stacks. A guy at a music store told me—there was a revelatory moment: "Really, no matter what size amp you have, if you put a microphone up to it, you can make it as loud as you want." I thought, *Well, that would be a lot less expensive, wouldn't it?* That combination of a JCM800 head and that amp is what I've played at every show and on every recording ever since that day.

I began playing because of punk rock, but the goal was to be a shredding ripper like my favorite guitar players. I was practicing scales for countless hours a day, but I had another crossroads moment in the earliest days of Rage Against the Machine. We were opening for two cover bands, and between them, there were three guitar players who were phenomenal technicians. I watched them at soundcheck, and the light bulb went off: *If there's three really gifted and adept guitar players at one lousy cover band gig, there doesn't need to be a fourth one.* So I began concentrating on the eccentricities in my playing. It was a new way of looking at the instrument.

The electric guitar is not sacred; it's just a piece of wood, wires, and electronics, and there's no bible that says it needs to be played the way Chuck Berry played it or Keith Richards or Eddie Van Halen or Jimmy Page. Who knows what sounds it can make and how those sounds can be crafted into songs? It's like the blinders fell off, and I was completely uninhibited in my playing: any noise, any piece of feedback or chirp or twerp—what if I played that a hundred times in a row and we put a beat to it? Well, it doesn't sound like "Sweet Little Sixteen," but I might be onto something.

There are probably four main components to my palette. One is riff-riding and my love of Tony Iommi, Led Zeppelin, Deep Purple: huge riffs that have a deep and mighty groove to them is one part of it. Another part is the craft of songwriting, and a third component is technique—if I imagine an idea, to not have technical limitations so that I'm able to play it. And then the signature component is, for the lack of a better term, the barnyard animal noises—the off-road guitar playing where the influences are as much the lawn mower outside or the elephant at the zoo as they are any traditional guitar player.

In Rage Against the Machine, I was the DJ, and I was listening to electronic music and hip-hop—everything from the Dust Brothers to Public Enemy's Bomb Squad—and in sound collages, I would try to approximate that digital music on an analog instrument. I wasn't able to replicate it, but it certainly took my playing to a much different place than if I was just stuck within the traditions of rock guitar playing.

People often mistakenly think that I use a lot of guitar effects pedals, but the guitar itself can create noise—and not necessarily by playing notes on frets—and then those noises can be manipulated with this small number of pedals to make sounds you've never heard come out of a guitar before.

Eddie Van Halen, meanwhile, came to the guitar via a circuitous route. As a young child, he started playing classical piano but then fell in love with the British Invasion sound. "I loved the Dave Clark Five," he recalled later, "and with the money from my paper route, I bought a cheap St. George drum kit. Little did I know that while I was out throwing papers, my brother, Alex, was playing my drums, and he just flat-out got better than me." So Eddie grabbed Alex's guitar—they essentially swapped instruments.

In the early 1970s, Eddie began building his own guitars—most famously, the one now known as the "Frankenstein," so-called because it came from various parts from various guitars. He later recalled: "It's a very basic guitar: one pickup, one knob, and I'm off to the races. I figured out what I needed and built it myself, because nothing like that existed."

Van Halen had one main influence that he always cited: Eric Clapton's time in Cream. (It made sense, now, that Eddie was at that

Cream soundcheck back in 1993.) Even Van Halen's lack of funds influenced his sound. "I couldn't afford a fuzz box or a wah-wah or whatever Hendrix had in his rig," Van Halen said. "I just plugged into an amp and turned it up to eleven. In order to get different or unique sounds, I had to learn to squeeze it out of the strings with just my fingers.

"From day one, when I tried to copy other players, it just never sounded the same—no matter what I did, it sounded like me when we started playing clubs or discos. Songs like [KC and the Sunshine Band's] 'Get Down Tonight' would sound like Black Sabbath! And it was always my fault that we wouldn't get hired—I used to hear everything from 'You're too psychedelic' to 'You're too loud'—it just never sounded like the records. It was a blessing and a curse, but a blessing in the end."

Van Halen's astonishing bag of tricks—the harmonics, the pull-offs, and fretboard tapping—left other guitar players slack-jawed, frightened, and jealous. Another early inspiration was Jimmy Page—Eddie and his brother were at the LA Forum watching Led Zeppelin, and he saw Page play a short fill with his left hand while his right hand was high in the air. That led to Van Halen's use of his trademark pull-off and hammer-on style. Other guitarists eventually copied his technique, but compared to Eddie, it often sounded generic and soulless.

Van Halen's epiphanic first album showed the guitarist's sound fully formed. "Eruption," the album's one instrumental, displayed everything: Eddie's tone, the mind-numbing velocity of his finger-tapping techniques, and the entire rest of his bag of tricks—all delivered with his virtuoso style. "I've always relied on the basics—a guitar, a cable, an amp—to achieve distinctive sounds," Van Halen said, "but I will do and use anything available to get an interesting sound—everything from sliding a beer can down the strings on 'Intruder' to using a power drill on 'Poundcake.' If I can get a sound out of it, I'm going to get a sound out of it."

Due to space constraints at the Met, the musical instruments department and the Hall of Fame were informed that all the instruments and gear for *Play It Loud* would need to arrive at the museum only a few weeks before the show opened. There were, of course, an enormous amount of road cases for such an exhibition, and there was simply no place to store them all if they had arrived too early. Those last few weeks of March were a mad rush: Jimmy Page's entire rig and his guitars arrived at JFK in crates custom-built expressly for the exhibition. Massive shipments of precious cargo were coming in from around the world—some of the most important musical instruments of the twentieth century. Many instruments from the West Coast arrived by truck, while some of the most valuable and fragile instruments were hand-carried by the musicians' own guitar techs—with some guitars getting their own seat in first class alongside the guitar techs.

Still, we're talking about rock 'n' roll—and so of course not *every* instrument arrived in a custom-built, climate-controlled environment. Several of the most important guitars in the exhibit traveled up to the Met via subway and were carried from the Eighty-Sixth Street station to the loading dock of the museum.

One guitar tech made me promise that no one would have access to the instrument while it was out of his control—and that I would be there when the guitar was put back in the case. Another artist's representative insisted that nobody could touch the strings of his client's guitar or remove any debris from them—there was a serious concern that if the wrong person got hold of any samples of dried blood on the instrument, it could trigger a paternity lawsuit. I guess that's rock 'n' roll, too.

On April 1, 2019, *Play It Loud* opened at the Met. I secured the Roots to play at the opening, with the band set up on the south side of the Great Hall. Several contributors to the show attended the party, including Jimmy Page, Don Felder, Steve Miller, Tina Weymouth, and Kate Pierson. Anna Wintour, cochairman of the Costume Institute, made sure that there was a signature cocktail for the evening. That fantastic press conference held earlier that day was attended by more than one hundred reporters and editors and a dozen television crews. While I was elated, I had mixed feelings: The amount of press clippings that I collected for that show filled three binders. But Cleveland could just never draw that kind of attention. And while we had all accepted this fact long ago, I still couldn't help whining about it like a petulant child.

The exhibit demonstrated just how far the Rock & Roll Hall of Fame had come. This was a far cry from my early days of being ghosted by managers as I tried to fill our fledgling collection. What was once a rag-tag team of industry vets trying to honor the artists who had created rock 'n' roll was now an internationally known institution—one still run by a rag-tag group of music nerds, but now with a more modern, commercial, and streamlined approach.

Jann Wenner stepped down as chairman and was succeeded by John Sykes, a founder of MTV and a longtime member of the board. Sykes was a fantastic and logical choice. Whereas Jann was a print media guy, Sykes was in the television and radio world.

Six months later, *Play It Loud* closed at the Met. I was heading to London that evening for meetings, but I needed to be there for that last day to say goodbye to the exhibit. Professionally, it was my greatest achievement to date, and knowing that the exhibit would soon be dismantled was heartbreaking. At the same time, I knew that it would be traveling to Cleveland, where it would begin its second life.

I had been determined to use *Play It Loud*'s visibility and prestige to the Hall of Fame's advantage; and I had leveraged the exhibit as much as possible over the past six months. At the top of my list of networking and acquisitions, of course, was the Beatles. I had now had half a dozen meetings with Apple Corps staff over a ten-year period, and finally, at least, we had made it to the finish line, lining up a major exhibition to complement Peter Jackson's monumental docuseries *The Beatles: Get Back*, which was based on the fifty-two hours of footage that had been shot by Michael Lindsay-Hogg in 1969 for the original *Let It Be* documentary.

That exhibition was my best show in Cleveland, a powerful and immersive experience that marked a highlight of the museum's history. The Metropolitan Museum of Art's brilliant designer Daniel Kershaw designed the show, and an all-star crew—Paul McCartney, Ringo Starr, Yoko Ono, Olivia Harrison, and Glyn Johns—delivered a jaw-dropping collection of artifacts, including guitars, drums, wardrobe, and manuscripts from the rooftop concert and recording sessions. It was the only time in history that all four Beatles principals collaborated with the Rock & Roll Hall of Fame. For me, it was a glorious capstone.

CHAPTER TWENTY-ONE

ROCK 'N' ROLL CAN NEVER DIE

In 1965, the Lovin' Spoonful asked the world, in a song, "Do You Believe in Magic?" But John Sebastian, who wrote and sang the tune, wasn't really asking a question: He was making a declaration. Sebastian was singing about the power of music—what it can do to you, how it can make you feel, how it can change your mind, free your body, and yes, maybe even make the world a better place. It's the "magic of a young girl's soul," "the magic of rock 'n' roll," and ultimately "the magic that can set you free."

The power of rock music and those who created it is what led Ahmet Ertegun to assemble the group he dubbed "The Funky Nine"—himself, Jann Wenner, Suzan Evans, Allen Grubman, Seymour Stein, Bob Krasnow, Noreen Woods, Jon Landau, and Ahmet's brother, Nesuhi—to honor and preserve the legacies of the artists who created the music. Ahmet and his crew knew that rock 'n' roll had historically been underappreciated and that the artists hadn't been given nearly enough respect for the art they had created, the music that would change the world. The Rock and Roll Hall of Fame Foundation was formed for the very purpose of fixing that problem.

Eight years later, I was very lucky and privileged to join the team to help fulfill their mission, and for more than thirty years, our team was powered together by camaraderie and esprit de corps. I have been fortunate to witness history up close while getting to know many of the artists who created this cultural force. There were some wild rides—I especially enjoyed working with the incorrigible, brilliant, and unstoppable Jann Wenner, and Suzan Evans, the unsung hero of the Rock Hall. Along the way, I became one of the driving forces who created the Hall of Fame's collections and archives from scratch—curating exhibitions, preserving history, relics, instruments, and papers that might have otherwise be lost, sold, stolen, or tossed into a landfill.

I'd like to think I did a bang-up job for the artists and rock 'n' roll in general, but there were nevertheless the ones that got away. Amy Winehouse comes most readily to mind. In July 2011, when I saw her face on the front page of an Italian newspaper while on vacation in Rome, I knew she was gone and it crushed me. She was a true great—and I had repeatedly tried to get to her to no avail.

You could say it all started with the induction ceremonies. At the beginning, of course, it wasn't even a given that the artists would show up—but Ahmet made that happen. He was the most respected and beloved record man of all time, and he had the Midas touch to get everything going in those early days. Such a great deal of thought went into selecting the presenters—artists revered in their own right who were there to honor their mentors and heroes and peers. In the earliest days, speeches weren't even written down on paper—almost everything was delivered right off the cuff, right from the heart, but everybody who attended quickly marked their calendars for the following year.

It wasn't a given, either, that the artists would participate in the early jam sessions, but they did—and they loved it. Having Bill Graham there to wrangle the performers quickly established the induction ceremonies as a joyous, no-pressure place to jam and hang with friends and idols. The fact that the ceremony wasn't televised made all the difference: It was essentially a private event for the artists, their families, and the music business, and that closeness and conviviality encouraged détente (some band members, after all, were barely on speaking terms with each other; sometimes the situation was far worse than that). In fact, it was the artists who eventually asked for the ceremonies to be aired on television, realizing that the events were so special that they needed to be shared with the public. They also understood the gravitas of the event, which encouraged everyone to get along. As Suzan Evans said, "This wasn't like the Grammys, where you voted for the best album of one year: This is a lifetime award."

There are now music museums throughout the country—including in Los Angeles, Seattle, Memphis, and Nashville—and in Europe, with more coming. Thirty years ago, though, there was just the Rock & Roll Hall of Fame in Cleveland. We established the template for everything that would follow.

The Hall of Fame is, without a doubt, the jewel of Cleveland, delivering $200 million in tourism revenue annually to Northeast Ohio. The decision to locate a museum right on the Lake Erie shoreline seems like a no-brainer now, but back in the early 1990s, Cleveland, like many Rust Belt cities, had let their waterfronts languish, putting industry first and people last. Even today, you can count on one hand how many waterfront restaurants are operating in Cleveland. Unquestionably, the museum's major new expansion—more on that in a bit—will further develop the city's waterfront, but further development is still desperately needed to invigorate the city, to make it a true, people destination. A falling population, lower property values, and a shrinking tax base need to be reversed—a tall order.

For twenty years, there have been discussions and studies examining the feasibility and impact of closing Burke Lakefront Airport, which is sited adjacent to the Hall of Fame. Converting that three-hundred-acre parcel into a cultural destination with hotels, restaurants, and shops would be the game-changer the city needs to avert a doom loop that has crushed once vital cities.

One of my greatest pleasures, when walking through the museum, isn't to marvel at everything I collected, or reminisce about the stories involved. Or to remind myself I was guilty of hagiography. What I love the most is giving a museum tour to an inductee. Most often, they aren't particularly interested in seeing their own exhibit—they usually make a beeline to see the work of another artist; someone who moved them. Often it was Muddy Waters's red Fender Telecaster, or Lead Belly's twelve-string Stella, or engineer Bob Heil's electronic inventions. Their wonder and excitement were contagious. A few hours visiting the Rock Hall, soaking up all that music, can transport you to another place. The vehicle for that isn't necessarily a sweet, 1960s pop tune by the Lovin' Spoonful—maybe the payload is delivered by heavy metal titans Judas Priest or Black Sabbath. "War Pigs" will most certainly open your eyes and ears. Or perhaps it's seeing artifacts from Aretha Franklin, Elton John, Kraftwerk, Hank Williams, Tina Turner, KISS, or the Cramps.

Since the 1970s, musicians, fans and critics have posed the question: Is rock dead? Is it on its way down—or maybe it's already done and dusted? Could rock 'n' roll possibly meet the same fate as jazz? It's ironic that bebop, one of the artistic high points for the genre—something which made the music more intellectual, more complicated, and more challenging—marked the beginning of the end. But jazz's mainstream demise didn't come down to one thing. Yes, the sophisticated rhythms of modern jazz made dancing almost impossible. But undoubtedly, rock 'n' roll helped shove jazz aside—and folk, too. In the end, jazz lost its mainstream popularity.

My parents witnessed jazz's waning firsthand. It was 1959, before they were married, and my father's jazz band was playing a gig in Brooklyn when the audience began to pelt them with beer bottles, demanding they cede the stage to the rock 'n' roll act that was next on the bill. Fleeing the venue, my mother recalled that "the band had to carry me over a cyclone fence, along with all of the band's instruments." Jazz was still supreme, but cracks were forming. Can you imagine if rock 'n' roll had ceased to be the vibrant and popular art form it was in the 1970s—or the 1980s or '90s, for that matter?

I would argue that rock 'n' roll's popularity and cultural force hit its final apex somewhere in the mid 1990s. West Coast bands like Nirvana and Pearl Jam had the wind at their backs, and in England, there was Oasis, Blur, and Radiohead, among others. *Rock was still a thing:* It had cultural currency, and it provided fodder for water-cooler moments and those widely shared experiences that no longer exist.

Despite this trend, some of the greatest rock 'n' roll ever recorded arrived in the new millennium. In 2000, Radiohead released their masterpiece *Kid A,* a revolutionary and radical album that turned rock on its head. Tellingly, the band was intent on breaking free from the rock star paradigm. Despite this fact, the album topped the US and UK charts. But rock 'n' roll as a movement was waning. So it wasn't a complete surprise when hip-hop helped push rock off the center stage. U2's brilliant song "Kite" summed it up, lamenting "the last of the rock stars" and pointing out that hip-hop artists "drove the big cars." And now we are entering a new era of pop goddesses, including Olivia Rodrigo, Gracie Abrams, and Chappell Roan, who have commandeered what it means to be a rock superstar.

When I first saw Oasis, back in 1995 in New York, I witnessed my ultimate rock payload. The opening act, Velvet Crush, was giving it their all, but the Brit-heavy crowd was having none of it. Impatient to see their new heroes, they booed them into oblivion.

Velvet Crush walked off the stage mid-set, defeated. Moments later, the Gallagher brothers, Liam and Noel, and the rest of the band swarmed the stage like hooligans; Liam, out front with his arms swinging and swaggering gait. Their opener: "Rock 'N' Roll Star" had an intro that sort of resembled a car revving up like the engine and then it was off to the races.

Oasis's song was a declaration that rock 'n' rock could still create magic. I imagined what it must have been like to see the Rolling Stones on their first US tour in 1964. Oasis was the closest equivalent I witnessed. They were like the Stones—louche, reeking testosterone, and had that hair too; they couldn't give a toss what you thought. The swagger, the melodies, the beat, the danger—it was all there with a '90s sheen, and Liam Gallagher's voice that could cut glass. Oasis may be the last rock band to write a standard—"Wonderwall"—which is now performed at weddings and sung in bars around the world. The juggernaut reunion tour is on now, as of this writing.

Rock is, of course, a different animal than it was when the Rock & Hall of Fame was established. Back then, the music business still resembled its old self. Record shops abounded, selling CDs in long boxes; this was years before Napster, file-sharing, and iTunes would put an end to the entire business model. Back then, Ahmet Ertegun and Jann Wenner launched the Hall of Fame with the ethos of a temple, and the institution was both erudite and idealistic in its formative years. Gradually, though, the vision of the Hall of Fame became more corporate, polished, commercial, and eventually hard-boiled. Somewhat reluctantly, the board expanded the umbrella of what constituted rock 'n' roll to suit the institution's financial and political needs. Now it's more like a megachurch—with all the advantages and shortcomings.

In 2019, the Rock Hall opened a six-thousand-square-foot interactive space called the Garage, where visitors can come and jam. Chock-full of electric guitars, basses, keyboards, drums, and other instruments, it was a game-changer for the institution and instantly became the museum's nerve center. It's still heartening to see who uses it these days: Sometimes it's balding, gray-haired men jamming to the Grateful Dead while looking like they're auditioning for an AARP commercial; other times it's a goth band on tour that's visiting the museum for the afternoon. During spring break in 2021, I witnessed a quartet of teenage girls cranking out Soundgarden's "Black Hole Sun."

That same year, I worked on an exhibit about the Super Bowl halftime shows titled *The Biggest Show on Turf*. The timing was perfect: The NFL draft was held in Cleveland from April 29 to May 1. We had never done a sports-themed exhibit, but since this one focused on the music during the halftime shows, it made sense. I created three short films for the show, which ran in succession as you walked through the galleries. The NFL executives who descended on Cleveland loved the exhibit, and so did the public. As a curator, it was exciting to try something new.

In 2022, the museum broke ground on a fifty-thousand-square-foot expansion. It draws roughly 600,000 visitors every year and has built an extraordinary collection with grit and verve and without any acquisition budget or endowment to speak of. John Sykes, Joel Peresman, and Greg Harris, and the Rock Hall's board and staff, are relentlessly determined to move forward in preserving rock 'n' roll—one of America's most cherished contributions to culture, art, and society. Later that year, Rick Krim, who spent his career in television and music publishing, ascended to head of the nominating committee.

Admittedly, the ceremony no longer has that Old World gravitas, or the intimacy it once possessed. Now, though, with fans along for the ride, there's more energy, more passion, and more love. And, thankfully, the makeup of the nominating committee is no longer an antediluvian boys' club.

At the same time, the induction ceremonies are now akin to most standard awards shows—heavily reliant on young pop stars. Gone are the rambling speeches, the profanity, the shambolic jam sessions. The production values have never been higher—but, thankfully, there's sometimes still room for heartfelt moments and old-fashioned brilliance. When Jimmy Page walked onstage in 2023 and strapped on his iconic Gibson double-neck guitar to play "Rumble," he was paying tribute to the Native American rock pioneer Link Wray, who in the 1950s invented the power chord. In 2024, the hall made room to posthumously honor British blues pioneers John Mayall and Alexis Korner, with Korner one of the true unsung heroes of rock 'n' roll—the man who created the London blues scene that nurtured and helped birth the Rolling Stones, the Animals, the Pretty Things, and the Yardbirds.

But when I recently rewatched the epic jam session from 1988, when the massed assemblage of legends played "Like a Rolling Stone," "Satisfaction," and "I Saw Her Standing There," it reminded me how that type of event almost certainly couldn't happen again. As rock 'n' roll has grown older and more diverse, and the catalog of songs has expanded, it's also become less feasible for all artists to know the same type of material. It's hard to imagine, for instance, Mary J. Blige, Nine Inch Nails, Taylor Swift, and Dave Matthews Band playing an impromptu version of "Mr. Soul" or "Pennyroyal Tea" on the fly.

I was born on March 1, 1964, in Brooklyn, and on that day, the Rolling Stones played two shows—a matinee and an evening concert at the Liverpool Empire Theatre. The Stones existed before I was born, and they're still, miraculously, around to this day, as I type these words. In 2023, the preternaturally preserved Mick Jagger and the exquisitely beat-up Keith Richards seemed to crack the code, releasing the Rolling Stones' twenty-fourth album, *Hackney Diamonds*, an extraordinary work with brilliant songwriting and musicianship that nearly everyone doubted they could pull off again.

The band managed to record an utterly brilliant album about staying young while getting old. And you can dance to it.

"Sweet Sounds of Heaven," their gospel-inspired collaboration with Lady Gaga, says it all, letting us all know that they're "not going down in the dirt" and asking us to "Let the old still believe that they're young."

People are still craving rock 'n' roll—music that means something to millions of people, a unifier that brings them together. Vinyl sales have come back strong, with pressing plants operating around the clock. The world would be different—a worse place, I would argue—if it weren't for rock 'n' roll, and there's no better place to celebrate that legacy than the Rock & Roll Hall of Fame. I'm grateful to have played a part in building it.

The king is gone, but he's not forgotten.

APPENDIX A

More on the Instruments Pictured in the Book

I would be remiss if I didn't include some extra tasty content here for all the gearheads out there. My job is akin to rock 'n' roll archaeology, after all, and every archaeologist needs to provide the provenance and measurable traits of an artifact. So let's dig into some of the killer gear/ instruments I wrote about in Chapter 20: "Rocking at the Metropolitan Museum of Art."

Here, we start with Jimmy Page's rig: his full Led Zeppelin setup that, in various combinations, he used onstage since 1969 and was presented in the "Play It Loud: Instruments of Rock & Roll" exhibition. This version features the symbol of Saturn, which Page first presented as his signature glyph on *Led Zeppelin IV* in 1971. Below is an astounding array of analog gear that would set the standard for a generation of guitarists.

- Danelectro 3021 electric guitar
- Harmony Sovereign acoustic guitar
- Marshall 4x12-inch speaker cabinets
- Orange 1x15-inch straight speaker cabinets
- Echoplex EP-3 tape echo units
- Sonic Wave Theremin
- Conn Strobotuner
- Vox Clyde McCoy Wah
- Sola Sound Tone Bender Fuzz Professional MKII

Without question, one of the most important musical instruments in rock history is Jimmy Page's "Number One" Les Paul Standard. Joe Walsh was in the James Gang in 1969 when he sold the instrument to Page, and it already had its neck shaved down to a thinner profile. Page used it as his main guitar in every Led Zeppelin performance and recording from 1969 to the 2007 reunion tour, even playing it in his post-Zeppelin work with the Firm and others. He still uses it today as his primary guitar, as of this writing. Want some specs? Here you go:

- Mahogany body and neck, carved maple top, rosewood fingerboard
- Circa 1959–60
- 24.75-inch scale
- Sunburst finish
- Two PAF humbucking pickups
- Three-way selector switch
- Two volume controls and two tone controls
- Neck shaved to thinner profile
- Push-pull pickup phase switch

And then there is his Gibson EDS-1275 double-neck, which he custom-ordered from Gibson. Page used it to play the acoustic and electric parts of 1971's "Stairway to Heaven" live without needing to change instruments. He also played it on "The Rain Song," "Celebration Day," and "The Song Remains the Same."

- Mahogany body and neck, rosewood fingerboards
- 1971
- 24.75-inch scale length
- Cherry red finish
- Set twelve- and six-string necks
- Two humbucking pickups per neck
- Three-way pickup and neck selector switches
- Two master volume controls and two master tone controls
- Inlaid mother-of-pearl Gibson logos on headstocks

How about something pre-Zeppelin? Perhaps pre-Yardbirds? Check out Page's 1961 Danelectro Model 3021, which he acquired in 1963 for his session-recording work. Purchased from London's Selmer shop, he finally played it live in 1967 with the Yardbirds on the instrumental "White Summer." With the strings tuned to DADGAD ("Celtic tuning"), he played it with Zeppelin on "When the Levee Breaks," "In My Time of Dying," "Kashmir," and "Black Mountain Side."

- Semi-hollow body

- 1961
- Tempered Masonite top and back; poplar neck, core, and sides; rosewood fingerboard
- 25-inch scale
- Black finish
- Two single-coil pickups
- Three-way selector switch
- Two concentric volume/tone controls

And last but not least, for Page, we have his 1959 Fender "Dragon" Telecaster (serial no. 50062), given to him by Jeff Beck. You can hear it in his 1967 work with the Yardbirds and on experimental live versions of "Dazed and Confused" being played with a violin bow. This same guitar was used by Page to record all of *Led Zeppelin* (1969). There was once a dragon design hand-painted by Page on the body and a transparent acrylic over silver-gray diffraction film that replaced the white pickguard. A well-meaning friend later stripped the finish while Page was on tour, but in 2018, Page restored his original design. Fender released an impeccable, limited-edition version of the guitar in 2019.

- Ash body, maple neck, rosewood fingerboard
- 25.5-inch scale
- Natural finish with dragon design
- Two single-coil pickups
- Three-way selector switch
- Psychedelic dragon design hand-painted on body and clear-coated.

Let's move on to a Keith Moon drum set: his "Pictures of Lily" setup from Premier Music Intl. Ltd. that Moon received at the beginning of the Who's 1967 US tour. Talk about custom artwork! There are nude photos of Lillie Langtry, the subject of the Who's '67 single "Pictures of Lily," a Union Jack, and, in reference to Moon's packing his drum shells with flash powder and detonating them onstage, the text "Keith Moon Patent British Exploding Drummer." When I saw the kit (described below), two original bass drums were lost, possibly destroyed by Moon's pyrotechnics. To create a complete kit for the exhibit, it was assembled from various owners.

- Birch ply shells
- Nine-piece kit with custom artwork and non-original cymbals
- Three 9x15-inch mounted toms
- Two 14x22-inch bass drums (not original)
- 5.5x14-inch snare
- Two cymbals
- Two 18x16-inch floor toms
- One 16x16-inch floor tom

When Bob Dylan went electric, the folk world went apoplectic. Let's look at the electric guitar at the center of all the anger. It was the 1964 Stratocaster that he played when he debuted his electric band at the Newport Folk Festival on July 25, 1965—a turning point in popular music. The politics and intellectual sophistication of folk music collided with the youthful revolutionism of rock. Enter the folk-rock movement. (The guitar was lost for many years and then resurfaced at an auction in 2013.)

- Contoured alder body, maple neck, rosewood fingerboard
- 25.5-inch scale
- Sunburst finish
- Bolt-on neck with clay dot inlays
- Gold "spaghetti" Fender logo decal on headstock
- Three single-coil pickups
- Three-way pickup selector
- One volume control and two tone controls
- Chrome "synchronized tremolo" vibrato bridge
- "Ashtray" cover
- Recessed input jack
- Nickel tuners
- White plastic knobs
- Three-ply white and black plastic pickguard

Like the song "All Along the Watchtower," let's move on from Dylan to Jimi Hendrix and the 1968 Fender Stratocaster he played at Woodstock. The Strat's popularity waned in the late 1960s until Hendrix's use of the guitar at the legendary 1969 music festival and in his radical reinterpretation of "The Star-Spangled Banner," which helped reestablish the instrument in the rock world. Hendrix bought the guitar in New York in '68, and as he did with other right-handed guitars, he played upside-down, using it until about 1970.

- Contoured alder body, two-piece maple neck
- 25.5-inch scale
- Olympic white finish
- Bolt-on neck with black dot inlays
- Black Fender logo decal on headstock
- Three single-coil pickups,
- Three-way selector switch
- One volume control and two tone controls
- Chrome "synchronized tremolo" vibrato bridge and recessed input jack
- Nickel tuners
- White plastic knobs
- Three-ply white and black plastic pickguard
- Nut-and-strap buttons modified for left-handed string

"Micawber." That's the name Keith Richards applied to the Fender Telecaster he received from Eric Clapton on his twenty-seventh birthday in December 1970. All you Charles Dickens fans out there would recognize the name—it's a character in *David Copperfield.* Richards removed the low E string and tuned the five-string guitar to an open G chord (GGDGBD) to record *Exile on Main St.* in 1971, and that open tuning became an essential part of his signature sound.

- Ash body, one-piece maple neck with walnut "skunk stripe"
- 25.5-inch scale length
- Yellowed butterscotch finish
- Bolt-on neck with black dot inlays (one missing at seventeenth fret)
- Silver "spaghetti" Fender logo decal on headstock
- Pedal steel-style single-coil pickup at bridge
- Gibson PAF humbucking pickup at neck
- Three-way selector switch
- Volume and tone controls
- Schecter brass bridge with five saddles

- Chrome barrel knobs and control surface
- Chrome Sperzel tuners
- Pickups, tuners, and bridge replaced

Another Keith Richards special to discuss here is his 1957 Gibson Les Paul Custom (serial no. 7 7277). He decorated the instrument using paint pens, giving it a colorful abstract design on the body and silver stars on the controls. This was after the Stones' February 1967 drug arrest while they were on break from performing. You can see the guitar in Jean-Luc Godard's film *Sympathy for the Devil* (1968), which covered the *Beggars Banquet* sessions during which "Sympathy for the Devil" was written and recorded. Check out *The Rolling Stones Rock and Roll Circus* (1968, released on film in 1996) to catch another cinematic turn for this guitar.

- Carved mahogany body and neck, ebony fingerboard
- 24.75-inch scale
- Black finish with hand-painted design, seven-ply white and black binding
- Set neck with mother-of-pearl block inlays and white binding
- Truss rod cover inscribed "Les Paul CUSTOM," inlaid mother-of-pearl Gibson logo
- Split diamond design on headstock with five-ply white and black binding
- Three PAF humbucking pickups
- Three-way selector switch
- Two volume controls and two tone controls
- Gold-plated ABR-1 Tune-O-Matic bridge
- Kluson tuners, and pickup covers
- Clear and black plastic knobs
- Black and white plastic three-ply pickguard
- Colorful abstract design on body
- Silver stars on knobs drawn with paint pens

To finish out a Keith Richards trifecta, let's examine his 1959 Gibson Les Paul Standard, which he played during the Rolling Stones' first appearance on *The Ed Sullivan Show* in 1964. Richards and Eric Clapton were among the influential guitarists to use the Les Paul Standard after its 1961 discontinuation, and they revived interest in the model to such a degree that Gibson produced the Les Paul Deluxe in 1968. Richards's use has helped establish the 1958–60 sunburst-finish Les Paul Standard as one of the most sought-after electric guitars in the world, though he later switched to Fender Telecasters for the majority of his playing. (Years before the exhibition, I got to play the guitar one glorious afternoon.)

- Mahogany body and neck, carved maple top, rosewood fingerboard
- 1959
- 24.75-inch scale
- Sunburst finish
- Inlaid mother-of-pearl Gibson logo on headstock
- Two PAF humbucking pickups
- Three-way selector switch
- Two volume controls and two tone controls
- Patent-numbered Bigsby B7 vibrato
- Tuners replaced
- Bigsby vibrato installed

Rage Against the Machine and Audioslave guitarist Tom Morello expanded the electric guitar's expressive range playing in the bands, using digital effects like the DigiTech Whammy pitch shifter and analog guitar modifications, like the kill switch, to toggle his signal on and off. Think: DJ scratches and synthesizer-like effects. From 2000 to 2007, Morello used his ca. 2000 Fender "Soul Power" Aerodyne Stratocaster on songs such as Audioslave's "Cochise," "Like a Stone," "Be Yourself," and "Your Time Has Come."

- Contoured alder body, maple neck, rosewood fingerboard
- 25.5-inch scale
- Black finish with white binding
- Bolt-on neck with dot inlay
- Matching black headstock with silver Fender logo decal
- Two single-coil pickups and one humbucking pickup
- Five-way selector switch
- Volume control and two tone controls
- Kill switch added
- Ibanez Edge locking tremolo and nut
- Nickel tuners
- Chrome barrel knobs and recessed input jack

- Mirrored plastic pickguard
- "SOUL POWER" written on body
- Seymour Duncan Hot Rails humbucking pickup in bridge

Going back in time with Tom Morello, we have his ca. 1979–83 Gibson Explorer II, his main instrument during his teenage and college years. To produce extreme "dive bomb" effects, where the vibrato bar is used to rapidly lower the pitch of a note, creating a sound similar to a bomb dropping, he modified the instrument with a Kahler locking tremolo. Eddie Van Halen and others originated the effect, and it was vital to the sound of hard rock and heavy metal in the 1980s.

- Maple and walnut body and neck, ebony fingerboard
- 24.75-inch scale
- Flat gold finish
- Set neck with dot inlays
- "Scimitar" headstock with truss rod cover inscribed "E/2" and inlaid mother-of-pearl Gibson logo
- Two humbucking pickups with coils exposed
- Three-way selector switch
- Two volume controls and one tone control
- Gold Kahler locking vibrato bridge and nut
- Gold tuners
- Clear and black plastic barrel knobs
- Three-ply black and white plastic pickguard
- Stock bridge replaced

How could we explore the tools of Morello's trade without looking at his rig? He's used this rig and pedalboard throughout his career to achieve his signature mix of DJ-style scratches, sound effects, wild pitch-shifting bends, and classic rock tones. Morello is known for his extensive use of effects and his techniques such as using the kill switch on his guitar—which turns the signal on and off to create a stutter effect—and scratching the strings with an Allen wrench. I saw his whole rig, which consists of a basic amplifier setup along with a customized pedalboard, in addition to some of his most-used guitars. Below is a version of the rig as exhibited in "Play It Loud."

- Gibson Explorer II
- James Trussart Steelcaster

- Marshall JCM 800 50-watt tube amplifier head
- Marshall 412 speaker cabinet
- Custom pedalboard: Digitech Whammy WH-1, Dunlop Cry Baby Wah, DOD FX40B EQ, two Boss DD-3 Digital Delays, MXR Phase 90, and a Voodoo Labs Pedal Power II Plus

It's impossible to write about guitars and gear without covering Eddie Van Halen's 1975 composite electric guitar, "Frankenstein." Pieced together by Eddie from modified factory seconds and mismatched odd-lot parts, then spray-painted, it combined some of the most desirable elements of Gibson and Fender guitars into a single instrument. This unique guitar—a symbol of Van Halen's ultimate goal for tone, playability, dependability, and functionality—embodies the legend's groundbreaking and unorthodox playing style, as well as his ingenuity in design and engineering. Frankenstein spawned legions of copies from other manufacturers and inspired generations of fans to design their own instruments.

- Contoured ash Strat-style body and two-piece maple neck
- 25.5-inch scale
- Spray-painted red finish with black and white stripes
- Bolt-on neck with rosewood dot inlays
- Unmarked headstock
- Modified Gibson PAF humbucking pickup from a Gibson ES-335
- Dummy neck pickup
- Heavily modified pickup cavity routing
- Single volume control knob labeled "Tone"
- Chrome Floyd Rose locking vibrato bridge and nut
- Recessed input jack
- Nickel Schaller tuners
- Hand-cut plastic pickguard
- Eye bolt strap hooks
- Rolled duct tape on lower horn for attaching picks
- Plastic reflectors attached to back
- 1971 quarter to shim and level bridge
- Fender neck plate with serial number 61071

The Eddie Van Halen Rig—a guitar gearhead's Promised Land. I saw a reconstruction of it as it looked onstage in 1978 to the specifications of the self-taught guitarist, who created a new vocabulary on his instrument through an array of jaw-dropping techniques and electronic effects. The man did two-handed tapping, using both hands to sound the strings from the fingerboard to produce fluid phrases at dizzying speeds. He perfected "dive bombing," depressing and releasing the vibrato bar to create dramatic descents and ascents in pitch, which drove innovations in guitar design, like the locking vibrato system. The entire rig we exhibited included amplifier speaker cabinets and tube-powered amplifiers (heads), effects units, and a reconstructed pedalboard featuring effect pedals identical to the originals, alongside a replica of the 1978 version of the Frankenstein guitar. To top it off, there was the casing of a World War II–era practice bomb repurposed as a rack for housing Van Halen's Univox tape echo units.

- EVH "Super 78 Eruption" guitar replica, white with black stripes
- Two Marshall 412 Slanted cabinets, late 1960s
- Two Marshall 412 Straight cabinets, late 1960s
- Marshall 412 Slanted cabinet, 1978
- Marshall 412 Straight cabinet, 1978
- Two Marshall 1959 SLP Super Lead 100W heads, late 1960s
- Two Univox EC-80A Echo effect units, Mid 1970s
- US Air Force MK 22 Practice Bomb rack (replica)
- Ohmite Variable Voltage Controller
- Pedalboard: 1970s MXR Flanger & MXR Phase 90, two remote footswitches for EC-80A tape echo units

APPENDIX B

Inductees to the Rock & Roll Hall of Fame

1986 Inductees

Chuck Berry
James Brown
Ray Charles
Sam Cooke
Fats Domino
Everly Brothers
Buddy Holly
Jerry Lee Lewis
Little Richard
Elvis Presley
Robert Johnson [early influence]
Jimmie Rodgers [early influence]
Jimmy Yancey [early influence]
Sam Phillips [Ahmet Ertegun Award]
Alan Freed [Ahmet Ertegun Award]
John Hammond [Ahmet Ertegun Award]

1987 Inductees

The Coasters
Eddie Cochran
Bo Diddley
Aretha Franklin
Marvin Gaye
Bill Haley
BB King
Clyde McPhatter
Ricky Nelson
Roy Orbison
Carl Perkins
Smokey Robinson
Big Joe Turner
Muddy Waters
Jackie Wilson
Louis Jordan [early influence]
T-Bone Walker [early influence]
Hank Williams [early influence]
Leonard Chess [Ahmet Ertegun Award]
Ahmet Ertegun [Ahmet Ertegun Award]
Jerry Leiber & Mike Stoller [Ahmet Ertegun Award]
Jerry Wexler [Ahmet Ertegun Award]

1988 Inductees

The Beach Boys
The Beatles
The Drifters
Bob Dylan
The Supremes
Woody Guthrie [early influence]
Lead Belly [early influence]
Les Paul [early influence]
Berry Gordy, Jr. [Ahmet Ertegun Award]

1989 Inductees
Dion
Otis Redding
The Rolling Stones
The Temptations
Steve Wonder
Ink Spots [early influence]
Bessie Smith [early influence]
Soul Stirrers [early influence]
Phil Spector [Ahmet Ertegun Award]

1990 Inductees
Hank Ballard
Bobby Darin
The Four Seasons
Four Tops
The Kinks
The Platters
Simon & Garfunkel
The Who
Louis Armstrong [early influence]
Charlie Christian [early influence]
Ma Rainey [early influence]
Gerry Goffin & Carole King [Ahmet Ertegun Award]
Holland-Dozier-Holland [Ahmet Ertegun Award]

1991 Inductees
LaVern Baker
The Byrds
John Lee Hooker
The Impressions
Wilson Pickett
Jimmy Reed
Ike and Tina Turner
Howlin' Wolf [early influence]
Dave Bartholomew [Ahmet Ertegun Award]
Ralph Bass [Ahmet Ertegun Award]
Neshi Ertegun [Ahmet Ertegun Award]

1992 Inductees
Bobby "Blue" Bland
Booker T & the M.G.'s
Johnny Cash
The Isley Brothers
Jimi Hendrix Experience
Sam & Dave
The Yardbirds
Elmore James [early influence]
Professor Longhair [early influence]
Leo Fender [Ahmet Ertegun Award]
Bill Graham [Ahmet Ertegun Award]
Doc Pomus [Ahmet Ertegun Award]

1993 Inductees
Ruth Brown
Cream
Creedence Clearwater Revival
The Doors
Etta James
Frankie Lymon & the Teenagers
Van Morrison
Sly & the Family Stone
Dinah Washington [early influ-

ence]
Dick Clark [Ahmet Ertegun Award]
Milt Gabler [Ahmet Ertegun Award]

1994 Inductees

The Animals
The Band
Duane Eddy
The Grateful Dead
Elton John
John Lennon
Bob Marley
Rod Stewart
Willie Dixon [early influence]
Johnny Otis [Ahmet Ertegun Award]

1995 Inductees

The Allman Brothers Band
Al Green
Janis Joplin
Led Zeppelin
Martha & the Vandellas
Neil Young
Frank Zappa
The Orioles [early influence]
Paul Ackerman [Ahmet Ertegun Award]

1996 Inductees

David Bowie
Gladys Knight & the Pips
Jefferson Airplane
Little Willie John
Pink Floyd
The Shirelles
The Velvet Underground
Pete Seeger [early influence]
Tom Donahue [Ahmet Ertegun Award]

1997 Inductees

The Bee Gees
Buffalo Springfield
Crosby, Stills & Nash
The Jackson 5
Joni Mitchell
Parliament-Funkadelic
The Rascals / Young Rascals
Mahalia Jackson [early influence]
Bill Monroe [early influence]
Syd Nathan [Ahmet Ertegun Award]

1998 Inductees

The Eagles
Fleetwood Mac
The Mamas & the Papas
Lloyd Price
Santana
Gene Vincent
Jelly Roll Morton [early influence]
Allen Toussaint [Ahmet Ertegun Award]

1999 Inductees

Billy Joel
Curtis Mayfield
Paul McCartney
Del Shannon
Dusty Springfield
Bruce Springsteen

The Staple Singers
Charles Brown [early influence]
Bob Wills & His Texas Playboys [early influence]
George Martin [Ahmet Ertegun Award]

2000 Inductees

Eric Clapton
Earth, Wind & Fire
Lovin' Spoonful
The Moonglows
Bonnie Raitt
James Taylor
Nat King Cole [early influence]
Billie Holiday [early influence]
Hal Blaine [musical excellence]
King Curtis [musical excellence]
James Jamerson [musical excellence]
Scotty Moore [musical excellence]
Earl Palmer [musical excellence]
Clive Davis [Ahmet Ertegun Award]

2001 Inductees

Aerosmith
Solomon Burke
The Flamingos
Michael Jackson
Queen
Paul Simon
Steely Dan
Ritchie Valens
James Burton [musical excellence]
Johnnie Johnson [musical excellence]
Chris Blackwell [Ahmet Ertegun Award]

2002 Inductees

Isaac Hayes
Brenda Lee
Tom Petty & the Heartbreakers
Gene Pitney
Ramones
Talking Heads
Chet Atkins [musical excellence]
Jim Stewart [Ahmet Ertegun Award]

2003 Inductees

AC/DC
The Clash
Elvis Costello & the Attractions
The Police
Righteous Brothers
Benny Benjamin [musical excellence]
Floyd Cramer [musical excellence]
Steve Douglas [musical excellence]
Mo Ostin [Ahmet Ertegun Award]

2004 Inductees

Jackson Browne
The Dells
George Harrison
Prince
Bob Seger
Traffic
ZZ Top

Jann Wenner [Ahmet Ertegun Award]

2005 Inductees
Buddy Guy
The O'Jays
The Pretenders
Percy Sledge
U2
Frank Barsalona [Ahmet Ertegun Award]
Seymour Stein [Ahmet Ertegun Award]

2006 Inductees
Black Sabbath
Blondie
Miles Davis
Lynyrd Skynyrd
Sex Pistols
Herb Alpert & Jerry Moss [Ahmet Ertegun Award]

2007 Inductees
Grandmaster Flash & the Furious Five
R.E.M.
The Ronettes
Patti Smith
Van Halen

2008 Inductees
The Dave Clark Five
Leonard Cohen
Madonna
John Mellencamp
The Ventures
Little Walter [musical excellence]
Kenneth Gamble & Leon Huff [Ahmet Ertegun Award]

2009 Inductees
Jeff Beck
Little Anthony & the Imperials
Metallica
Run-DMC
Bobby Womack
Wanda Jackson [early influence]
Bill Black [musical excellence]
DJ Fontana [musical excellence]
Spooner Oldham [musical excellence]

2010 Inductees
ABBA
Jimmy Cliff
Genesis
The Hollies
Iggy Pop & the Stooges
Jeff Barry & Ellie Greenwich [Ahmet Ertegun Award]
Otis Blackwell [Ahmet Ertegun Award]
David Geffen [Ahmet Ertegun Award]
Barry Mann & Cynthia Weil [Ahmet Ertegun Award]
Mort Shuman [Ahmet Ertegun Award]
Jesse Stone [Ahmet Ertegun Award]

2011 Inductees
Alice Cooper
Neil Diamond
Dr. John
Darlene Love
Tom Waits
Leon Russell [musical excellence]
Jac Holzman [Ahmet Ertegun Award]
Art Rupe [Ahmet Ertegun Award]

2012 Inductees
Beastie Boys
Blue Caps
The Comets
The Crickets
Donovan
The Famous Flames
Guns N Roses
The Midnighters
The Miracles
Laura Nyro
Red Hot Chili Peppers
The Small Faces / The Faces
Freddie King [early influence]
Cosimo Matassa [musical excellence]
Tom Dowd [musical excellence]
Glyn Johns [musical excellence]
Don Kirshner [Ahmet Ertegun Award]

2013 Inductees
Heart
Albert King
Randy Newman
Public Enemy
Rush
Donna Summer
Lou Adler [Ahmet Ertegun Award]
Quincy Jones [Ahmet Ertegun Award]

2014 Inductees
Peter Gabriel
Hall & Oates
Kiss
Nirvana
Linda Ronstadt
Cat Stevens
E Street Band [musical excellence]
Brian Epstein [Ahmet Ertegun Award]
Andrew Loog Oldham [Ahmet Ertegun Award]

2015 Inductees
Paul Butterfield Blues Band
Joan Jett & the Blackhearts
Green Day
Lou Reed
Stevie Ray Vaughan & Double Trouble
Bill Withers
Ringo Starr [musical excellence]
The "5" Royales [early influence]

2016 Inductees
Cheap Trick
Chicago
Deep Purple
N.W.A.
Steve Miller

Bert Berns [Ahmet Ertegun Award]

2017 Inductees

Joan Baez
Electric Light Orchestra
Journey
Pearl Jam
Tupac Shakur
Yes
Nile Rodgers [musical excellence]

2018 Inductees

Bon Jovi
The Cars
Dire Straits
Moody Blues
Nina Simone
Sister Rosetta Tharpe [early influence]

2019 Inductees

The Cure
Def Leppard
Janet Jackson
Stevie Nicks
Radiohead
Roxy Music
The Zombies

2020 Inductees

Depeche Mode
The Doobie Brothers
Whitney Houston
Nine Inch Nails
Notorious B.I.G.
T. Rex
Irving Azoff [Ahmet Ertegun Award]
Jon Landau [Ahmet Ertegun Award]

2021 Inductees

Foo Fighters
The Go-Go's
Jay-Z
Carole King
Todd Rundgren
Tina Turner
Kraftwerk [early influence]
Charley Patton [early influence]
Gil-Scott Heron [early influence]
LL Cool J [musical excellence]
Billy Preston [musical excellence]
Randy Rhoads [musical excellence]
Clarence Avant [Ahmet Ertegun Award]

2022 Inductees

Pat Benatar & Neil Giraldo
Duran Duran
Eminem
Eurythmics
Dolly Parton
Lionel Richie
Carly Simon
Harry Belafonte [early influence]
Elizabeth Cotton [early influence]
Jimmy Jam & Terry Lewis [musical excellence]
Judas Priest [musical excellence]
Allen Grubman [Ahmet Ertegun

Award]
Jimmy Iovine [Ahmet Ertegun Award]
Sylvia Robinson [Ahmet Ertegun Award]

2023 Inductees

Kate Bush
Sheryl Crow
Missy Elliott
George Michael
Willie Nelson
Rage Against the Machine
The Spinners
DJ Kool Herc [musical influence]
Link Wray [musical influence]
Chaka Khan [musical excellence]
Al Kooper [musical ex cellence]
Bernie Taupin [musical excellence]
Don Cornelius [Ahmet Ertegun Award]

2024 Inductees

Mary J. Blige
Cher
Foreigner
Peter Frampton
Kool & the Gang
Dave Matthews Band
Ozzy Osbourne
A Tribe Called Quest
Alexis Korner [musical influence]
John Mayall [musical influence]
Big Mama Thornton [musical influence]
Jimmy Buffett [musical excellence]
MC5 [musical excellence]
Dionne Warwick [musical excellence]
Norman Whitfield [musical excellence]
Suzanne de Passe [Ahmet Ertegun Award]

2025 Inductees

Bad Company
Chubby Checker
Joe Cocker
Cyndi Lauper
Outkast
Soundgarden
The White Stripes
Salt-n-Peppa [musical influence]
Warren Zevon [musical influence]
Thom Bell [musical excellence]
Nicky Hopkins [musical excellence]
Carol Kaye [musical excellence]
Lenny Waronker [Ahmet Ertegun Award]

ACKNOWLEDGMENTS

After I finished college and was in the working world for a few years, I began to accumulate experiences that I thought might be worthy of a book. But I wasn't certain the trend would continue. After all, I had no idea how my career would unfold. Things turned out pretty good, and my rollicking ride is documented herein.

Writing this book was a labor of love. Getting up in the morning, knowing I had a whole day of writing ahead of me, was a gift; dusting off distant memories, going down assorted rabbit holes, and obsessing about minutia that nobody besides me would likely care about. The whole experience was immeasurably enjoyable, and there was no drudgery that I can recall as I stitched it all together.

I received a great deal of help and support along the way. My wife, Joan, our daughters, Ana and Alex, and my mother, Anne, were hugely supportive, as were other family members and close friends. I am immensely grateful to Suzan Evans Hochberg, an amazing colleague and friend who read the manuscript, provided keen insight and edits, and sat with me for two interviews. I'd like to thank my brilliant editor at Diversion Books, Keith Wallman, publisher Scott Waxman, and project editor Noah Perkins. Many thanks to my amazing agent, Rick Richter, at Aevitas Creative Management and his colleague Caroline Marsiglia, who did heavy lifting. And great appreciation to my friend Andy Greene for his advice and my friend Corey Seymour for tightening the manuscript.

I will be forever grateful to Jann Wenner, who hired me and whom I worked with for twenty-eight years. I learned a lot from him. I am very fortunate to have known Ahmet Ertegun and Seymour Stein, both legendary record men and great raconteurs whose love of music and mirth was infectious. A huge shoutout to Tom Morello, Jimmy Page, Keith Richards, and Eddie Van Halen. Their warmth, cooperation, and generosity enabled me to do some of my best work.

And in no particular order, I would like to thank these individuals who supported me along the way: Dana Hawkes, Jane Rose, Perry Margouleff, Dan Kershaw, Alan Dunn, Jon Savage, Joel Peresman, David Fricke, Terry Stewart, Shelby Morrison, Jayson Dobney, Michelle Wheeler, Karen Herman, Mish Tworkowski, Bob Santelli, Holly George-Warren, John Corcoran, and Lisa Testa.

SOURCES

7 "Inadvertence, accident, happenstance, and serendipity.": Rock & Roll Hall of Fame and Museum Grand Opening program. 1995.

13 "According to Krasnow, Ross said, 'I'm not getting involved.' Krasnow signed Metallica.": Greenfield, Robert. *The Last Sultan: The Life and Times of Ahmet Ertegun*. New York: Simon and Schuster, 2011.

14 ". . . Alan Freed, the DJ who coined the phrase *rock 'n' roll* loved it, played it, and brought it to the world.": Wenner, Jann S. *Like a Rolling Stone: A Memoir*. New York: Little, Brown and Company, 2022.

17 "'. . . catching on fire from its industrial waste,' said Wenner.": Wenner, *Like a Rolling Stone*.

17 ". . . cost $100 million, which it did.": Wenner, *Like a Rolling Stone*.

19 ". . . honored for their way of life.": Wenner, *Like a Rolling Stone*.

24 ". . . Ringo Starr, who ran upstairs to collect everyone.": Loder, Kurt. *Rolling Stone*. Issue 521. March 10, 1988.

27 "Brandwen called it a 'beautifully crafted stall.'": Hagan, Joe. *Sticky Fingers: The Life and Times of Jann Wenner and* Rolling Stone *Magazine*. New York: Knopf, 2017.

52 ". . . I took it back to the Iroquois Hotel and wrote 'Heaven Knows I'm Miserable Now' and 'Girl Afraid,' immediately.": Leonard, Michael. "Guitar Legends: Johnny Marr—a unique guitar hero with a chameleonic talent." Guitar.com. November 19, 2020.

67 ". . . but how sloppy the show was." Wenner, *Like a Rolling Stone*. p282.

86 ". . . The love and the grooves will never be taken out by the hate in his heart.": *Rolling Stone*. Issue 649. February 4, 1993.

91 "'Jann told me I had the job,' Barrie recalled, 'and told me that I had fifty-one percent of the vote.' He laughed. 'That's classic Jann.' The reality was that Wenner wanted to run the museum from his corner office at *Rolling Stone* in midtown Manhattan—and, to an extent, that is what he did for decades to come": Nite, *The House That Rock Built*.

106 "Well, the limits of the building, the way it goes up, precludes you from doing certain things.": Nite, Norm N. *The House That Rock Built: How It Took Time, Money, Music Moguls, Corporate Types, Politicians, Media, Artists, and Fans to Bring the Rock Hall to Cleveland*. The Kent State University Press, 2020. p114.

107 "violate the spirit of rock 'n' roll.": *Rolling Stone*. Special Issue. Issue 1092. November 26, 2009.

SOURCES

114 "... they rehearsed for just six minutes.": Greenfield, *The Last Sultan.*

122 "... gets in his car, and drives away: Now *that's* rock 'n' roll.": Lofgren, Nils. From an oral history interview conducted by the Hall of Fame for its library.

146 "I knew exactly what those dynamics were all about.": Washington Post Live. "Transcript: 'Unrequited Infatuations' with Stevie Van Zandt." *Washington Post.* September 28, 2021.

168 "... only fair and polite to inquire of the others.": Crandall, Bill. Interview with Joe Strummer. *Rolling Stone.* Issue 914. January 23, 2003.

192 "... refrain in moments of doubt and decision.": From Ahmet Ertegun's memorial at Rose Theater at Lincoln Center.

202 "... new stuff for whatever rooms they stayed in after they left.": Roy, Chris. "Swingos Keg & Quarter: Chaos and Class in Downtown Cleveland." *Cleveland Historical.* April 21, 2020.

236 "... guitar players had numerous paths to explore.": Inciardi, Craig J. and Jayson Kerr Dobney. *Play it Loud: Instruments of Rock & Roll.* New York: Metropolitan Museum of Art, 2019.

239 "... from the elegance of 'Thank You' to the iconic power chords of 'Whole Lotta Love.'": Inciardi and Dobney, *Play it Loud.*

239–40 "Page's answers to the interview questions I asked him on July 31, 2018, are fascinating": Inciardi and Dobney, *Play it Loud.*

237 "... Alex, was playing my drums, and he just flat-out got better than me.": Inciardi and Dobney, *Play it Loud.*

247 "... I figured out what I needed and built it myself, because nothing like that existed.": Inciardi and Dobney, *Play it Loud.*

248 "... I had to learn to squeeze it out of the strings with just my fingers.": Garbarini, Vic. "The Well Tempered Guitarist." *Guitar World.* October 1999.

248 "... blessing and a curse, but a blessing in the end.": Inciardi and Dobney, *Play it Loud.*

248 "... I'm going to get a sound out of it.": Inciardi and Dobney, *Play it Loud.*

INDEX

INDEX

INDEX

INDEX

INDEX

INDEX

INDEX

INDEX

AUTHOR PHOTO CREDIT:
Alessandra Inciardi

ABOUT THE AUTHOR

CRAIG INCIARDI is the founding curator of the Rock & Roll Hall of Fame and began working for the museum in 1991. Inciardi was instrumental in launching the museum and built the institution's collection from the ground up. He has curated numerous award-winning exhibitions including *Rock Style*, a collaboration with the Costume Institute at the Metropolitan Museum of Art in 1999. He also curated major exhibitions on the Rolling Stones, the Who's *Tommy*, John Lennon, the Clash, *Rolling Stone* magazine, and *Louder Than Words*, an exhibition about rock 'n' roll and politics in collaboration with the Newseum in Washington, DC. He was also in charge of building the collection to open the Rock & Roll Hall of Fame's Library and Archive.

In 2019, Inciardi cocurated *Play It Loud: The Instruments of Rock & Roll* with the Metropolitan Museum of Art. He has conducted numerous on-camera interviews with artists, including Mick Jagger, Keith Richards, Jimmy Page, Tom Morello, Taylor Swift, Bono, Ringo Starr, Paul Simon, and former President Jimmy Carter. He is the coauthor of *Play It Loud: Instruments of Rock & Roll*, which was published by the Metropolitan Museum of Art. He is a contributor to the documentary *Jimmy Carter: Rock & Roll President*, which was released in 2020. Previously, he worked at Sotheby's auction house in New York, where he developed specialized sales of rock 'n' roll memorabilia and pop culture materials. He graduated from Fairfield University in 1986, where he studied communications and English.